[illegible] Rebecca
[illegible] of the Welsh
[illegible] ts 1839-1844

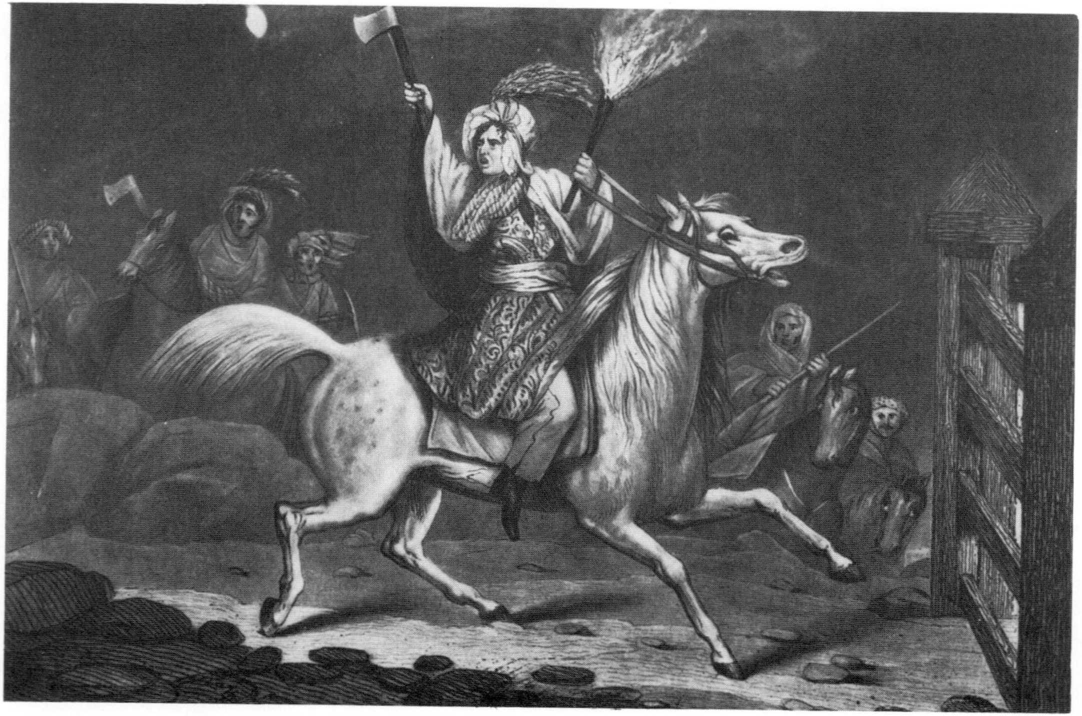

A legend called Rebecca

(*Nat. Library of Wales*)

And they blessed Rebecca

An account of the Welsh Toll-gate Riots 1839-1844

Pat Molloy

Gomer Press
1983

First Impression — December 1983

British Library Cataloguing in Publication Data

Molloy, Pat
And they blessed Rebecca
1. Toll roads — Dyfed 2. Rebecca Riots, 1839—1844
I. Title
942.9'6'081 DA722

ISBN 0 86383 031 5

Printed by
J. D. Lewis and Sons Ltd., Gomer Press, Llandysul

To the man *The Times* forgot:

Thomas Campbell Foster

ACKNOWLEDGEMENTS

When it was suggested that I should write a history of the Rebecca Riots my reply was that it had been done before. It was then suggested that I should look again. I did, and it soon became evident that while academic historians have delved into the sociological and historical background of the period in sufficient detail to satisfy the most demanding and pedantic of readers (and, incidentally, to relieve this author of the burden of covering the same ground again), there *was* something missing. There was room not only for a different view of the affair, but also for a more detailed and animated account of the two hundred and fifty or so incidents which make up the story of the Rebecca Riots and for a closer look at those involved. And so this book is aimed at the reader who wishes to savour the action and excitement of the Rebecca Riots, the trials and tribulations of those who took part, and the dilemmas and difficulties of those responsible for tackling them, while acquiring sufficient knowledge of the whys and wherefores to understand the reasons behind them. If the reader concludes that I have filled a gap in the literature of the Rebecca Riots, then I shall be more than satisfied.

In acknowledging the help I have received in the preparation of this book I must begin by acknowledging the invaluable contribution provided by the wealth of source references in the fourteen hundred-odd footnotes of David Williams' *The Rebecca Riots: A Study in Agrarian Discontent* (University of Wales Press, 1955). His book is and always will be the indispensable starting point for any serious study of this fascinating episode of Welsh history. My two and a half years of research have also led me to many museums and other institutions in Wales and England, to many amateur local historians, many locations relevant to the story and many people whose ancestors took part. I thank all concerned for their unfailing courtesy and help, and would mention in particular the staffs of the National Library of Wales, the University College of Swansea, the Welsh Folk Museum at St. Fagan's, the Carmarthen, Haverfordwest, Rhayader and Aberystwyth (Ceredigion) Museums, the Carmarthen, Haverfordwest and Aberystwyth (Ceredigion) Libraries, the Dyfed County Record Offices at Carmarthen and Haverfordwest, the British Library Newspaper Library at Hendon, the Public Record Office, the National Army Museum, the Crown Estates Commissioners, the Liverpool Walker Art Gallery, the Regimental Museums of the Black Watch (for the 73rd Regt.), the Queen's Own Royal Irish Hussars (for the 4th Light Dragoons), the Duke of Wellington's Regiment (for the 76th Regt.), the Royal Greenjackets (for the 52nd Regt.), the Gordon Highlanders (for the 75th Regt.) and the Royal Marines; the Army Museums Ogilby Trust, the Société Jersiase (St. Helier, Jersey), the Police Museums at Bridgend and Carmarthen and the Archivist of *The Times*.

My thanks are also due to Mrs. Eilyr Thomas, Headmistress of the village school, Mr. Lloyd Davies of Capel Farm, and other residents of Mynachlog-ddu for their help in connection with Twm Carnabwth, with whom their ancestors rode to Efail-wen. Mr. A. D. G. Williams and other members of the Gwendraeth Valley Historical Society are thanked for their help in connection with the Rebeccaites of south-east Carmarthenshire, as is Mrs. Lettie Richards of Tŷ Isha Road, Tumble, for hers in regard to her ancestor, Jac Tŷ Isha, the most notable of them. It is due largely to the efforts of local historical societies such as the Carmarthenshire Antiquarian Society and the Gwendraeth Valley Historical Society and to individual amateur historians such as Mr. Donald Davies and Mr. Tony Bowen of Cardigan and St. Dogmael's that so much of local history is preserved, and they and others like them are thanked for making their knowledge, records and picture collections available to me.

Pat Molloy

FOREWORD

by
Wynford Vaughan Thomas

A distinguished Welsh historian once noted—no doubt with a quiet chuckle—that all writers on the history of Wales are naturally anti-Establishment. In Wales our heroes are always the rebels: the Owain Glyndŵrs and the Lloyd Georges, the men who are 'Agin the government'. The only well-known Welshman in our history who comes to mind as the supporter of law and order is Judge Jeffreys, and he is hardly a shining light! As Welshmen we find ourselves automatically cheering on the protestors, for the very existence of Wales is a protest against all the odds; a gesture of defiance against acknowledged Authority. And, generally, the point of view of Authority goes by default.

It is therefore all the more refreshing to find Pat Molloy, who has already made an important contribution to local history in his *A Shilling for Carmarthen* (a fascinating account of the taming of that once unruly town), now turning his attention to a wider theme—the Rebecca Riots, which have passed into popular folk-lore as a classic example of the Welsh Art of Rebellion.

Professor David Williams' book will always remain the standard work on the wider aspects of the disturbances that shook rural south-west Wales in the years after 1839, but there is room for a new look at the evidence; a view, as it were, not from the dock but from the policeman in the witness box. As Detective Chief Superintendent of the Dyfed-Powys police force, Pat Molloy brings special qualifications to the sifting of the evidence: 'Will the facts stand up in court?', and I approached his account of the destruction of the Bolgoed Gate at Pontardulais with some trepidation, for my own grandfather was the local Rebecca and was sent for trial at Cardiff. Luckily he escaped transportation, with satisfactory consequences for our family.

Pat Molloy's story of the riots is firmly based on hard facts, but he does not neglect the human side of the story. He tells it with impartiality but, above all, with sympathy.

CONTENTS

LIST OF MAPS

LIST OF PHOTOGRAPHS

Chapter One

DISTANT THUNDER

The warning sounds would soon become familiar to himself and other toll gate keepers, but they were not recognised by the keeper of the turnpike gate at Efail-wen on the west Wales border of Pembrokeshire and Carmarthenshire when he heard them for the first time in the late evening of Monday 13 May, 1839. As dusk blurred the outlines of road and hedge and stilled the familiar sounds of the countryside, the call of horns floated across the evening air and then what sounded like the beat of a drum, with voices too, growing louder, as of the approach of a large group of revellers down the Cardigan road. A wedding party perhaps, or revellers returning from the drunken aftermath of a farmer's funeral. Whoever they were they seemed to be enjoying themselves and if, as was likely, they were on foot they would pass toll-free, with no more exchange than a few insults to a gatekeeper grown thick-skinned to such occupational hazards.

Suddenly they had arrived at the gate, with horns, drums and a few blasts of gunfire. Still nothing unusual. But then a loud voice shouted a command which could not be ignored, and the toll collector opened his door . . . to see a sight he would remember for the rest of his life.

The leader of the black-faced mob outside was a huge and frightening figure seated upon a large white horse, bundled up in what seemed like several layers of women's nightgowns or petticoats, his black-smeared face topped by a nightmarish wig hung with ringlets. He waved a sword in the air and his followers responded by shouting 'Hurrah for free laws! Toll gates free to coal pits and lime kilns!' to a cacophony of horns, bugles, flutes and drums, while a hundred arms stabbed the air with a profusion of axes, sledgehammers, crowbars, scythes and sticks, and while the flashes and sparks of several shotgun blasts added spectacular lighting effects to what might have been some ghastly Victorian melodrama.

The terrified toll collector and his family fled as the gate was attacked with felling axes and their house was sledge-hammered and put to the torch. It was over in minutes and the jubilant crowd, responding instantly to their leader's command, went back the way they had come and disappeared into the gathering darkness, leaving only the echoes of their discordant music, their shouts for 'free laws' and the crackling flames of the gatehouse ruins to mark their visit.

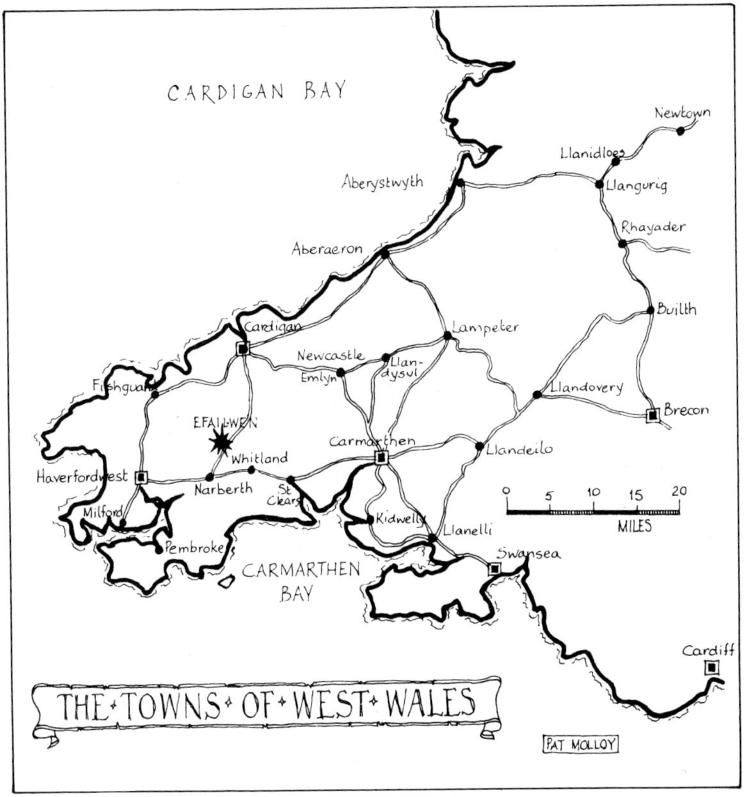

The days that followed in that remote and hitherto tranquil corner of west Wales saw the spread of fearsome stories of the attack at Efail-wen and even more fearsome rumours of outrages to come and, there being nothing resembling a regular police force in that part of the world in the 1830s, the magistrates swore in special constables right and left. But they seemed to have no idea what they should be doing with them, and their sense of helplessness increased with the discovery of notices pinned to chapel doors announcing a further meeting 'for the purpose of considering the necessity of a toll gate at Efail-wen', an ominous reference to the new gate quickly placed across the road alongside the ruined gate house.

The magistrates took precautions and on Thursday 6 June seven special constables were guarding the Efail-wen gate when, at about half past ten, the sounds that had pressaged the first attack came louder and clearer across the fields from the east. And the sight of that large mounted leader and the crowd of three or four hundred well-armed, black-faced rioters following him around the bend of the road from Login was just too much. But in the instant before they took to their heels the special constables witnessed a little bit of history-making as they heard for the first time the name by which the leader was addressed by those who called themselves 'her' daughters. It was a name that would become known not only to people throughout Wales, but also to those in the furthest parts of England, to Queen Victoria herself, to her Ministers . . . and to history. That name was Rebecca!

And then the constables fled for their lives, pursued by Rebecca and a number of other female-garbed horsemen, who over-ran them as they scattered into fields along the roadside and beat them to the ground with stout sticks, leaving them battered, bleeding and in no mood to risk life and limb again in the service of the Crown.

The toll gate reduced to a pile of matchwood, Rebecca and her followers disappeared in noisy triumph. More notices were posted, more handed out at the chapels and read from the pulpits and, nine days later, as darkness fell, two hundred men, some on horses, most on foot, descended on the Maes Gwynne gate, near Llanboidy, five miles from Efail-wen, and to the roar of gunfire chopped it to pieces. There was not a special constable in sight, for Llanboidy was a lonely place of narrow lanes at night, and Rebecca was already threatening vengeance on those who opposed her. It was the birth of a legend.

All the stuff of legend

The hard truth of history often dulls the edge of legend, but that of Rebecca has survived the publication of much historical fact and thrived in the hands of writers of romantic fiction since she and her daughters shattered the tranquility of rural west Wales nearly a century and a half ago. The Rebecca Riots as they are known have become a powerful and emotive part of Welsh folk lore, conveying to some the spirit of a long and continuing resistance to English domination and exploitation; to others a romantic, if less clear, image of female-garbed horsemen galloping out of the darkness and disappearing as quickly and dramatically as they had come, leaving behind them the burning wreckage of toll gate and toll keeper's house to baffle the hapless forces of law and order.

All the stuff of legend: of Ché Guevara or Robin Hood, depending on the point of view. But as in most cases where fact and folk lore intermingle, both points of view suffer from a degree of over-simplification. On the one hand, attacks on toll gates were only part of the story. The causes of discontent in rural Wales ran far deeper than mere annoyance with having to pay exorbitant road tolls at illegally erected gates, and the expression of that discontent took many different forms. The erratic and uncertain course of the Rebecca Riots, as seen in the diversity of their targets, the intrusion of a vicious criminal element and the venting of personal grudges, was typical of the course of any collective violence in pursuit of social or political change. The initial response by the authorities was also typical of those days when police forces were either non-existent or in a primitive state of development and not yet accepted by the people at large; typical of the time when the army was the real mainstay of law and order and when the musket ball, bayonet, cavalry sabre, convict ship and the rope were often the only answers that suggested themselves to a remote and uncomprehending ruling establishment. Typical, too, was the dismay and disarray of those whose oratory and tacit support had unleashed the violence, when they discovered how little control is exerted over an angry tiger by the mere holding of its tail.

Rather less than typical of the first half of the nineteenth century was the outcome.

On the other hand, the Welsh were far from alone in the 1840s in resorting to violence in the pursuit of justice and social change. The Home Office 'Disturbances' file covering the period of the Rebecca Riots in Wales[1] contains copies of correspondence relating to disturbances in at least fifty districts of England alone. And throughout that period, readers of Welsh newspapers were regaled with a weekly catalogue of riot, military intervention, death and destruction, under the heading 'The State of the Disturbed Manufacturing Districts'. But so far as the peaceful countryside of west Wales was concerned before Rebecca took to the roads, they might have been reports of a war

[1] Public Record Office: Home Office series HO 40.

fought on far-flung foreign battlefields. Violence on that scale was unknown and largely incomprehensible to those who scraped a living in that remote and rural corner of the Kingdom.

Even the use for disguise of blackened faces and female clothing in attacks on toll gates had been known in England for over a hundred years before men in the west of Wales first put on their mop caps and petticoats and mounted their horses on that momentous spring day of 1839.[2] And yet for all that, this mode of attack, this disguise, has become Wales' very own. One reason for this was undoubtedly the total unexpectedness, rapid spread and sheer bravado of such a violent eruption in a part of the country noted for its generally peaceful state, but the real magic, the real stuff of legend, lies in the enigma of the lady Rebecca herself. Who was she? Was she an all-powerful and ubiquitous leader? From what class of society had she come? What were her motives? Did she and her daughters want political power for themselves or was Rebecca really a shadowy figure in the background, manipulating the poor people and exploiting their hardships for her own political ends? Or was 'Rebecca' a name adopted by many leaders, over a wide area, and if so were their activities co-ordinated or did they spread spontaneously?

Of such questions are myths born. The kind of myths that excite the popular imagination. The kind of myths that can, and do become powerful weapons in unscrupulous hands through future generations. The kind of myths that make governments uneasy. The question 'Who was Rebecca?' is one that tantalises to this day; one that makes the Rebecca Riots stand out in high relief from the broad picture of social and political violence of early nineteenth century Britain.

The Great Defender

In the late eighteenth and early nineteenth centuries the fact of an outbreak of rioting in any part of the kingdom, be it city, town or village, was as often as not hardly a matter for remark. It was merely a matter of which company of infantry or which troop of cavalry would be called out to quell the disturbance when the

[2] To cite but four examples, toll gates were demolished by bands of armed men dressed in women's clothing and wigs in Somerset in 1731 and 1749, in Gloucestershire in 1728 and in Herefordshire in 1735 . . . all in the style, but without the name, later adopted by the Rebecca rioters.

A cavalry charge 'in aid of the Civil Power': the Yeomanry attack demonstrators in St. Peter's Fields, Manchester, August 1819, in an incident which became known as the Peterloo Massacre. *(The Mansell Collection)*

authority of the magistrates and the efforts of such parish or 'special' constables as might be available to them had proved useless.[3] It was a fact of British life, and all involved would know what to expect: imprisonment with hard labour or transportation to the penal colonies for anything from seven years to life for the basic crime of riot; death if they were found at the scene of the riot after the expiration of one hour from the moment a magistrate had read the Proclamation from the 1714 Riot Act, which indemnified the magistrates, constables and troops for 'killing, maiming or hurting' the rioters when using necessary force to disperse them. That indemnification was relied upon by many magistrates, constables and troops at many a coroner's inquest, in those troubled years. Indeed, between 1730 and 1840, nearly five hundred rioters died on the spot at the hands of the military

[3] The use of 'Special Constables' was a custom dating back to Saxon times, when every freeman was bound by oath to assist in preserving the peace when called upon. It is a measure of just how unpopular the system had become by the troubled 1830s that it was given statutory form by the Special Constables Act of 1831, which provided penalties for failure or refusal to be sworn.

Infantry in action against Kentish rioters, 1838: note the mounted magistrate behind the tree on the right. *(National Army Museum)*

and civil authorities, while more than a hundred others were hanged after trial by jury.

For a hundred years, Great Britain and Ireland were more prone to civil disturbance than any other part of Europe, a statement which even the violence of the French Revolution does not invalidate. It has been said that Britain had riots while the continent had revolutions, since few British riots were either nationally co-ordinated or inspired by national movements—a singular exception being the Charter movement of the late 1830s and 1840s, a movement which has a particular relevance to this story.

The Charter movement, whose members and followers were known as the Chartists, had for its aims six constitutional changes that to-day seem remarkable only for their reasonableness. In the first half of the nineteenth century, though, they sent shudders throughout the land. They wanted votes for all adult males, electoral districts of equal size and representation, secret ballots, the payment of members of parliament with the removal of the need for them to be possessed of property of a given value, and annual elections—demands put forward in a People's Charter designed to give the masses a voice in government and a share in the national wealth created by their labour. Reasonable enough, perhaps, but a wholely revolutionary concept in the challenge it represented to all the traditional rules of British politics.

As the great movement rolled forward in the manufacturing districts of the north, the midlands and the south Wales valleys, it was soon rent by disagreement as to how best to achieve those aims. Would the ruling establishment be persuaded by a peaceful campaign conducted through lawful constitutional channels, or was the wall of privilege so unyielding that it would succumb only to siege and storm? It was a division summed up neatly by the choice which the Chartists themselves defined: were they *Moral Force* men, which most of their leaders claimed to be, or were they *Physical Force* men, the followers of a mad Irishman from County Cork—Feargus O'Connor—who, conveniently forgetting his land-owning origins, loudly drew blood-curdling parallels between the manpower available to him and that which brought about the French Revolution.[4]

Moral Force or *Physical Force.* Neat labels, but the seeds of civil disorder and the movement's eventual destruction lay in that fundamental choice, which besets all emotionally-charged causes, however laudable. For whenever powerful orators get carried away by their own emotions, their message, non-violent though it may be, is often hardly distinguishable from that of the men of violence. This was particularly so in an age when the uneducated masses were incapable of unravelling the subtleties of high-flown language and grasped at the most literal interpretation of what they heard. Blood was blood; the sword was the sword; and any intention of investing such terms with a figurative sense simply went over their heads. And there were powerful orators on both sides, and their effect on the crowds was great.

Small wonder that revolution seemed to be in the air.

But the more direct relevance of the Charter movement to the

[4] Fergus O'Connor (1794-1855) was a powerful orator, the sight of whom 'was calculated to inspire the masses with a solemn awe'. It was said that, 'There can be little doubt that O'Connor's mind was more or less affected from the beginning and that he inherited tendencies to insanity. He was insanely jealous and egotistical and no one succeeded in working with him for long. The absolute failure of Chartism may indeed be traced very largely to his position in the movement.' He was declared insane in 1852 and was in an insane asylum for two years before his death. (*Dictionary of National Biography*)

Hugh Williams, Carmarthen Attorney *(Nat. Library of Wales)*

Rebecca Riots lies in the fact that its leading figure in west Wales is seen by many people to this day as 'The instigator and undiscovered leader of the Rebecca Movement', a movement which, it was said, 'he had meant from the first to be a preparation for farther political action.'[5] That man was a Carmarthen lawyer named Hugh Williams, 'a man of large business till he lost favour by his defence of poor men',[6] whose reputation as a leader of violent men also owes much to what has been seen by many as a 'most treasonable' speech he made at the massive Chartist torchlight meeting in Carmarthen in January, 1839, at which he was elected its delegate to the London Chartist Convention . . . just four months before Rebecca's first foray against the turnpike gate at Efail-wen.

[5] *Memoirs* by William J. Linton.
[6] Ibid.

In the weeks following Hugh Williams' torchlight meeting and his further endorsement at a most convivial 'hot supper' in Carmarthen's Red Lion Hotel, the poor but peaceable country people of Carmarthenshire and Pembrokeshire received visits from speakers sent by him from the Chartist strongholds of Glamorganshire and Monmouthshire, and at meetings held in market places and inns throughout west Wales they heard the Chartist message. Surely the Chartist cause, which had sprung from the excesses of the industrial revolution and the awakening of political consciousness among its victims, must strike a chord in the hearts of people in an area so depressed as this? Had not all classes of countrypeople already declared their opposition to the new Poor Law, itself one of the prime causes of the rise of Chartism? Should not the political aspirations of the Charter also find support among a people so manifestly oppressed by the kind of government it sought to replace?

That the presence of Chartist orators in west Wales 'must have contributed to the turmoil of opinion in the area which saw the first outbreak of the Rebecca Riots three months later'[7] cannot be doubted, but *opinion* was one thing. The real question was could a predominantly peaceable rural population whose chief preoccupation was scraping a living really be aroused to great political action; the kind of action necessary to achieve such a fundamental shift of power as was envisaged in the Charter?

The answer when it came seemed to be a resounding 'Yes'. But it came from a totally unexpected quarter of rural Wales, a hundred and twenty miles away . . . and a fortnight before Efail-wen.

The answer came from mid Wales, from the little market towns of Rhayader, Llangurig, Llanidloes, Newtown and Welsh-pool. The industrial revolution was making itself felt there for it was the centre of an extensive flannel weaving industry, stretching so far back in the life of mid Wales that the very word flannel has its roots in the Welsh language,[8] an industry now facing ruin under the twin impacts of economic depression and competition from the great steam-driven mills of the north of England. There, as in many other rural districts, a whole way of life was on

[7] *The Rebecca Riots* by David Williams, (University of Wales Press, 1955).
[8] The Welsh *gwlanen*.

Newtown, scene of Chartist Thomas Powell's seditious speech, which sparked off the riot at Llanidloes.

(Mr. Elwyn Jones, Severn Press, Newtown)

the point of extinction, undermined by the rapid mechanisation of processes hitherto carried out in cottage and country workshop. There, too, the accompanying poverty and distress were made worse by a concurrent depression in agriculture, so that the two-pronged influx of Chartist orators brought in by the Welshpool Chartist Thomas Powell, and of hardened militant ironworkers and coal miners from Merthyr Tydfil, proclaiming the message of the coming struggle and providing the means of acquiring and using arms for it, found fertile ground indeed.

On the evening of Monday 29 April, 1839, the men of Llanidloes, enraged by the presence in their town of magistrates and special constables come to arrest their leaders, armed themselves and rose as one to batter their way into the Trewythen Arms Hotel, sack and loot the place, drag out and mercilessly beat the law men and drive them out of town, and declare Llanidloes a Chartist stronghold. And it took a week for Lord Clive, the Lord Lieutenant of Montgomeryshire, to muster enough troops to re-occupy the town and throw forty of the rising's leading lights into the county gaol. Thus it was that Carmarthen lawyer Hugh Williams, newly introduced into the Chartist Convention in London as the Carmarthen delegate, was given the assignment that as much as anything else helped to establish his reputation not only as a fervent Chartist but as 'the instigator and undiscovered leader of the Rebecca Movement'. He was to go to Montgomeryshire to take up the defence of all forty Chartist prisoners, a service he performed entirely free of charge, the first of many such defence assignments stretching over a period of nearly five years and culminating in the trials of two of the most notorious characters in the whole Rebecca saga —'Shoni Sgubor Fawr and Dai'r Cantwr'.

This and his involvement with the monster meetings of Carmarthenshire farmers and the petitions that came out of them in 1843—the great Rebecca year—invested Hugh Williams not only with the mantle of Rebecca's Champion but even, in the eyes of many, of Rebecca herself.

A slender thread

As has been said, the disorders arising from the Charter movement were a singular exception to the general pattern of social violence in Britain. The overwhelming majority of riots were against local grievances, as many as two thirds of the two hundred and seventy five or so riots recorded between 1735 and 1800 being touched off merely by sudden rises in the price of basic foodstuffs. And it is noteworthy that even where petitions were presented for what appeared to the ruling establishment to be changes of revolutionary proportions (as, for example, the Chartist petition), they were almost without exception couched in the most loyal and humble terms. The people had an overriding belief that they had only to penetrate the wall of intransigence surrounding a benevolent monarch for all their grievances to be resolved peacefully, and it was this patriotism and loyalty to the Crown of even the poorest of the poor which guaranteed that fundamental stability that even now is the envy of many of the world's republics. The revolution expected by many in Britain in the early nineteenth century was never more than a spectre, despite all the violent portents.

But love of Queen and Country was about the only thing that the British people as a whole had in common. The readiness of certain of them to riot sprang from a deep and unbridgeable cleft in their society—the fact that, as Benjamin Disraeli wrote, Britain was really 'Two nations, between whom there is no intercourse and no sympathy; who are as ignorant of each other's habits, thoughts and feelings as if they were dwellers in different zones or inhabitants of different planets; who are formed by different manners and are not governed by the same laws.' Those two nations, he went on, were the rich and the poor.[9]

The poor man on his particular planet reacted as a matter of course to such events as sudden increases in food prices, church taxes, rents or road tolls, food shortages, evictions for arrears of rent on cottage or patch of land, or to the introduction of machinery which either made human labour redundant or reduced wages—or both. He rioted. And no other course suggested itself to him. As he saw it there was no other course since those in parliament did not consider themselves as representing him, but only the privileged voting class that had sent them there, so this kind of collective violence was a perfectly natural consequence of any imposition from the other 'Nation'. As natural as was the respect for authority and loyalty to the

[9] *Sybil,* a novel by Benjamin Disraeli, published in 1845.

Crown which characterised the normal day-to-day attitudes to life of the labouring poor.

The slender thread tying the two nations together in the rural areas of mid and west Wales at the close of the eighteenth century was formed by two key strands: the country landowner and the magistrate—in many cases one and the same. It was to the landowner that the labouring class (in which could be included the small farmer) looked for employment or land to rent, and for a paternal understanding and concern for their problems. And in the absence of any kind of democracy so far as the ordinary people were concerned, it was to the magistrates that they looked for the control of food prices, wages, rents and road tolls, and the dispensation of justice tempered by the magistrates' knowledge of local needs and conditions. For so long as the common people had confidence in those institutions, the west Wales countryside was (apart from the occasional eruption) peaceful. It is significant, for instance, that while in the 1830s the countryside of southern England saw much violence between farmers and their labourers over such matters as wages and agricultural mechanisation, west Wales saw none of it. There the small farmers and their labourers were bound together not only by ties of common hardship but also by a tradition of living and working so closely together than no barrier or hostility of class divided them. They stood more or less together in their relationship to the land-owning class.

Above all, though, it was the peaceable and obedient nature of the Welsh countrypeople themselves that ensured tranquility. It took rather more than 'ordinary' hardship or injustice to arouse their wrath. The credit for this must go to the strong hold exerted over them by their chapel ministers and their own devotion to the Bible, by which their lives were ruled in a form of religion rendered all the more powerful and exclusive by its adherence to the Welsh language and its hostility towards the established church. But, as events would show, the countrypeople's acceptance of their own station and duty in life was also bound up with their expectation that those of a higher station would remain aware of their responsibilities, and that right and justice as it was then understood would be done to them.

It was a balance that was becoming increasingly hard to sustain, for in the late 1830s and early 1840s the pressure of over-

A Cardiganshire cottage *(Welsh Folk Museum, St. Fagan's)*

population on ever more scarce and expensively rented land was reducing small farmers to the level of their labourers, whose condition after three disastrous harvests in succession resembled that of the starving wretches of Ireland. A visitor to Wales in 1843 described what he found in north Carmarthenshire, for instance:

> . . . I entered several farm labourers' cottages by the roadside, out of curiosity to see the actual condition of the people, and found them mud hovels, the floors of mud and full of holes, without chairs or tables, generally half filled with peat packed up in every corner. Beds there were none; nothing but loose straw and filthy rags upon them. Peat fires on the floors in a corner filling the cottages with smoke, and three or four children huddled around them. In the most miserable part of St. Giles,[10] in no part of England, did I ever witness such abject poverty.[11]

It was a time and place where the iniquities of turnpike road tolls and church taxes, the harshness of the new Poor Law which seemed to make poverty a crime, the real and imagined wickedness of the absentee (and even the resident) landlord, the

[10] The most notorious slum quarter of London.
[11] Thomas Campbell Foster writing for *The Times,* 7 October, 1843.

exorbitant cost of taking disputes to court, and the apparent failure of the magistrates to dispense justice with an even hand, turned the most God-fearing and law-abiding to the violence of despair. And there was no shortage of agitators in pulpit and market place to spur them on.

All of this lay behind the outbreak of rural unrest in Wales known as the Rebecca Riots.

But they were heady days too, for the 'Rebeccaites', as the rioters and their supporters became known, found that they enjoyed the thrill and excitement of it all. Many of Rebecca's proceedings exhibited a carnival-like atmosphere and seemed to provide an opportunity for happy release from the otherwise predictable, hard and unexciting routine of field or workshop. Which is not to say that the lives of the ordinary people were unrelieved gloom and despair, as modern writers all too often portray them. Seasonal festivals, family events, church and community activities, celebrations for coronations, royal

'Opportunities for happy, communal revelry' *(Nat. Library of Wales)*
(a) A 'Bidding': bringing gifts for the betrothed

(b) A Welsh village wedding

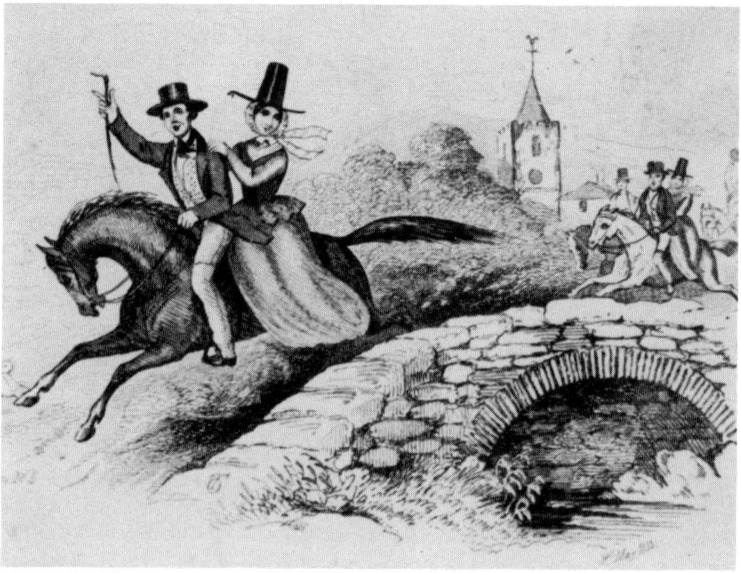

(c) Returning from the wedding

(d) Hymn singing in chapel

weddings and births, and military victories, visits to fairs, markets, friends and relations, all provided opportunities for happy communal revelry—within the context of a lifestyle which to us would be of unimaginable hardship and oppression. But it was the only lifestyle and the only world they knew or could imagine, and what one does not have one does not miss. And did not their Bibles, which provided the justification for their existence, promise a glittering reward for patience and dutiful acceptance of their temporal burdens?

Hindsight is easy, and the actions and feelings of people who lived a century and a half ago are too often judged by the standards of our own times. What is much more difficult is to put oneself into the ideas, attitudes and behaviour of people upon whom, for example, the realisation had begun to dawn that what had always been thought to be ordained—the gulf between the rich and the poor and the existence of a class born to rule and a class born to be ruled—might not necessarily be so. To those who had hitherto accepted their place among those ordained to be ruled as their natural lot in life, without question, that realisation must have been stunning. It was certainly explosive in the thrust it gave to the process of social change. As one observer of the Rebecca Riots declared: 'The people have thus discovered their immense power, without knowing how to use it constitutionally.'[12] On the other hand, to those who saw that they sincerely believed to be the most perfect and benevolent democracy in the world—not to mention their own hitherto impregnable bastions of privilege—coming under the ranging shots of what they were convinced was a revolutionary army, resistance would come more naturally than compromise.

Traditional ideas, attitudes and behaviour would not change overnight, nor even in step with each other, and the Rebecca Riots were just one manifestation—and a very important one for Wales—of the momentous, often violent and yet rather ragged process of change that was taking place in Britain as a whole in the first half of the nineteenth century.

A far country

The Rebecca Riots were a classic example of mass protest against a logjam of inequity which had been allowed to accumulate as a result of the tremendous industrial, economic and social changes of the early nineteenth century, to which the governing class had no coherent answer, and other circumstances peculiar to rural Wales. Not the least of those circumstances was the remoteness of west Wales from all centres of influence and decision-making. At a most critical time, that remoteness placed on the local landowners and magistrates a responsibility for which neither their experience nor their lack of empathy with the countrypeople really fitted them, for they were the lynchpins of a system of peace-keeping which, fashioned in a remote age, was fast crumbling under the impact of the greatest social upheaval in British history. Thus, not only would the Rebecca Riots be looked back upon as the catalyst for righting at least some of the wrongs done to the countrypeople and for the introduction of a hated system of education designed to supplant the Welsh by the English language, but they would bring to rural Wales something that many people of *all* classes regarded with dismay . . . the creation of a paid police force! The Riots were therefore a major landmark in more than one aspect of Welsh history.

[12] Edward Crompton Lloyd Hall, loc.cit.

There were other consequences of the geographical remoteness of the country. At the time of the Rebecca Riots the nearest railheads to west Wales were at Bristol and Birmingham, each a day's travel by stage coach and Bristol an additional steamer trip across the Severn Estuary. It would be a whole year after the ending of the Rebecca disturbances before the extension of the Great Western Railway line from Paddington as far as Gloucester (in 1845) brought west Wales to within less than a day's travel of London. The arrival of the railway as far west as Carmarthen in 1852 accelerated the development of the economically backward west so rapidly and to such a degree that it would unquestionably have opened a safety valve to much if not all of the pressure that had no other outlet but to explode into riot and destruction. If the railway had reached west Wales ten years earlier, the Rebecca Riots might never have occured at all.

Stage coaches made speeds of five to eight miles an hour depending on the terrain, some typical journeys being four

The winter snows, which brought the stage coaches to a standstill.
(Haverfordwest Library)

hours for the thirty miles or so from Carmarthen to Haverfordwest, Tenby or Swansea, and five for the hilly road to Cardigan. The hard pull on the fifty miles to Aberystwyth took eight hours, and the crack long-distance coaches heading eastward for England to connect with services to all other parts of the Kingdom could take six hours to make the fifty miles to Brecon and fourteen to cover the hundred and twenty miles to Cheltenham. But stage coaches were out of reach of all but the well off and the wealthier class of tradesmen and, like the infinitely slower team-drawn wagons, vulnerable to the rains for which the mild and moist climate of west Wales was notorious, and which turned rough and rocky roads into quagmires. Winter snows brought them to a standstill altogether. Such was the cost of road transport in those years that it was cheaper to send agricultural produce from Carmarthenshire to the industrial areas of Glamorganshire—the adjoining county—by ship to Bristol and back across the Severn Estuary to the port of Cardiff, to be hauled up the valleys by road!

Even so, there was a good deal of movement around the countryside by the ordinary people, for whom long journeys on foot over several days were a natural part of life. Men whose holdings were too small to support their families would walk as far as a hundred miles down to the south Wales valleys and spend part of the year working in the coal mines or ironworks, walking back home in time for the harvest. The livestock fairs held in towns and villages throughout Wales attracted people from great distances, one calculation being that the average farmer visited fairs over a radius of thirty miles in search of the best prices for his animals, often taking three or four days to visit the most distant of them.[13] These and the once or twice weekly produce markets in even the smallest towns provided a network for the communication of news, rumour and gossip not to be surpassed until the coming of the telephone.

At the annual hiring fairs, men and women, boys and girls, by the hundred stood in line offering themselves as farm servants and labourers to live in, thereby spreading families over great distances to work and marry, and to contribute to a phenomenon seen nowhere else in the British Isles except, perhaps, in

[13] *Land and People in Nineteenth Century Wales,* by David W. Howell (Routledge and Kegan Paul, London, 1978).

A village cattle fair later in the century: Cilgerran (north Pembrokeshire) before the arrival of the railway. *(Mr. Donald Davies, Cardigan)*

Aberystwyth Market *(Ceredigion Museum, Aberystwyth)*

southern Ireland; a phenomenon which, to this day, strikes the newcomer to Wales most forcibly. Nowhere else does one find people travelling, meeting, knowing and being related to each other over such a wide area.

A Day for the Queen

With this amount of movement, any maladministration or abuse of the turnpike road system, on which travellers had to pay tolls, would inevitably be a constant and pressing irritant to farmers and countrypeople, particularly in times of failed crops or agricultural depression.

Properly managed and supervised, the turnpike trusts would have made a greater contribution than they actually did to the proper maintenance of the Welsh road network. They were intended to replace the system under which roads had been maintained by the parishes, a system which had degenerated to the point where the day per year required of every able-bodied man in the parish to work on the roads accomplished so little that it was regarded as a day off—'A day for the Queen'—an expression used in west Wales to this day. The turnpike trusts were founded (and intended to be regulated) by Act of Parliament, with funds provided by private investment, the incentive for which was the economic advantage of a good road system and the modest profit derived from charges made for passage through the toll gates.

But there was a fundamental weakness in the Welsh turnpike system—a weakness that brought trouble on a scale unknown in England. It lay in the piecemeal way it had developed, which had led to a proliferation of small, almost non-viable, trusts. With so many trusts there were as many boundaries, and wherever those boundaries met, the luckless traveller would find a profusion of gates as he passed from the one to the other. And where several trust boundaries met with a town like Carmarthen or Lampeter at the centre, that town would be surrounded by a veritable wall of gates. When road users protested to the trusts, or to the magistrates whose duty it was to ensure that the turnpike laws were properly observed by trusts and users alike, the response was often such as to raise the suspicion that there was little to choose between them. It was difficult, for example, to persuade a poor and uneducated man whose first language was

Welsh of the fairness of court proceedings conducted entirely in a language he barely understood—if at all. Not only that, but here he was, charged with refusing to pay an exorbitant toll at what many believed to be an unlawfully placed toll gate, being fined by a magistrate whom he well knew had a financial stake in the very trust with which he was in dispute!

Furthermore, the practice of 'farming out' toll gates to men who rented from some of the trusts the right to take the tolls, led not only to widespread abuse, such as the erection of patently unlawful gates and bars and the imposition of prohibitive toll charges, but also to such a neglect of many stretches of road that it fell again to unreliable and amateur 'parish' labour to fight the losing battle to maintain them while those who laboured had still to pay for the privilege of passing through the toll gates! Witness the experience of a newspaper reporter from England travelling along the turnpike road from Swansea to Bryncwmllynfell on horseback:

> As I rode along after passing Pontardawe I travelled over one of the most execrable roads ever seen. Imagine a turnpike road on which a traveller has to pay heavy tolls, worse than any lane leading to a farmhouse in England, full of deep holes at almost every step, covered here and there with large loose stones and so thoroughly bad that a traveller who would venture to go faster than a walk after nightfall would do so with the certainty of either breaking his own neck or his horse's leg, or perhaps both.[14]

Quite clearly the intention of parliament that there should be local investment and therefore a community stake in the state of the roads had to a marked extent been thwarted by the intrusion of the profit motive. The 'toll farmers', as the professional toll renters became known, were responsible for much of the resentment (whether always justified or not) that made the toll gates Rebecca's prime targets. The fact that most of them were English helped not at all. Such a one was Thomas Bullin, whose offer of £800 cash to an almost bankrupt Whitland Turnpike Trust on condition that additional gates should be strategically placed on the roads of the Pembrokeshire/Carmarthenshire border country to enable him to entrap the impoverished farmers as they began carting lime to their fields, led directly to

[14] *The Times,* 28 September, 1843.

the first appearance of the lady Rebecca—outlaw to some, saviour and champion to many—and to the birth of a legend.

There can hardly have been a more unpopular man in north Pembrokeshire in 1839 than Thomas Bullin. If there was he could only have been a workhouse master. Even Church of England vicars and curates did not rate so low as those of Bullin's kind, for all the hatred of the church taxes that kept them—taxes squeezed from an already impoverished and overwhelmingly chapel-going countrypeople. As a toll farmer, Bullin was even lower than a special constable, which was also saying something. His holdings of toll gates stretched right across the south of the country, from the east end of London, along the Hackney and Portsmouth roads, around Bristol, across south Wales to Swansea and into Carmarthenshire and Pembrokeshire, on the roads of the Whitland Trust. But the handicap he already had in being seen as an interloping English-speaking profiteer was to be turned into a veritable millstone around his neck by the sheer clumsiness and insensitivity of himself and the Whitland Trust in the spring of 1839 when they put up additional gates at the very moment farmers began to haul lime to their fields. And wriggle as he might when the time came for counting the cost, Thomas Bullin could not evade his share of responsibility for the storm that followed.

The last gate and house being finished, Thomas Bullin's toll collectors took up their posts—at almost the same time, incidentally, as the troops were being formed up to retake Llanidloes from the Chartists—and the monetary consequences of the trap that had been sprung on them suddenly bore in on the hard-pressed farmers of the Pembrokeshire border country. Inevitably, the timing of the move was seen as a deliberate attempt to squeeze money from the people just when their financial state was at its weakest and equally inevitably there were several rows and arguments at the new gates during the first week of May, 1839. The scandal of Thomas Bullin and the Whitland Trust was second only to the depressed livestock prices as a topic of conversation at that week's fairs in Pembroke, Haverfordwest, Tenby, St. Clears, Eglwyswrw, Fishguard, Laugharne, Newcastle Emlyn, Lampeter and Llandysul, and in all the inns and lodging houses where countrypeople spent the nights on their journeys over the thirty miles of country in between.

Who actually called the meeting of the enraged men of Maenclochog, Llangolman, Mynachlog-ddu and Llandisilio, and who attended it will never be known for certain, but what a rich source of folk lore it would prove to be, that first gathering of Rebeccaites in the barn of Glynsaithmaen farm in the remote heart of Pembrokeshire's Presely hills. And folk lore is never a bad guide when recorded history leaves no signposts. Though its message will have been distorted during its passage down the years it has the great merit of having been sent on its way by those who were there when it happened. Thus there can be no doubt that the man selected by that meeting to lead the attack on the new gate at Efail-wen was Thomas Rees, the larger than life, red-headed character who lived in Carnabwth cottage in the Parish of Mynachlog-ddu.

Twm Carnabwth

Life was hard on thirty-three year old Thomas Rees' tiny holding at the foot of the Presely hills, but he was just the man to lead a night ride and cock a snook at the law. An independent character if ever there was one, he had proved he was his own man by raising his own rough dwelling of stone and sods of earth

Carnabwth, built by Thomas Rees on the site of his Tŷ Unnos. *(Pat Molloy)*

on the marshy land alongside the stream opposite Glynsaithmaen farm. He had raised it on the ancient 'squatter's right' tradition of *Tŷ Unnos* (literally 'a one-night house') by which a dwelling, however primitive, could be erected overnight on common land and gain for its builder the right of occupancy, provided that smoke was seen issuing from the chimney, or even a hole in the roof, by the following morning. He also followed the tradition of claiming the ground around his dwelling for as far as he could throw an axe in any direction.

It did not take long for Thomas Rees to acquire the nickname Tom Stone Cottage—or rather its Welsh form *Twm Carnabwth.* And there, in his tiny cottage, first called *Treial* (the Welsh for homestead) and later *Carnabwth,*[15] he lived with his wife Rachel and their children Elizabeth, Daniel and John, aged thirteen, ten and five—in one room only twenty feet by twelve with its half ceiling for a sleeping space and its nine feet wide hearth, in which the iron *cawl* pot never ceased to simmer.

As well as being independent, Twm Carnabwth was also regarded as something of a tearaway and he lived a life which was remarkable for its blend of devout religious observance and outrageous behaviour. He was the chief reciter of the *Pwnc*—the catechism of the points of the Scriptures—at Bethel Chapel in Mynachlog-ddu where he always did the recitation for the Whitsun Festival—though they had to keep him off the drink for two days beforehand. And he was known across three counties as a prize fighter who would take on and beat all comers at the country fairs and would always be good company in the ale houses afterwards as he stood rounds of drinks on his winnings. Though he lost an eye in the process, he even beat the renowned Carmarthen bruiser Gabriel Davies, son of Benny Het Wen (Benny of the White hat), a hawker and himself a man of no mean knuckles. Gabriel Davies, hard as nails, who had cut off his own trigger finger so that he would be declared medically unfit for army service in the event of his being got drunk—*again* —by a recruiting sergeant.

Twm Carnabwth was game for anything, especially for the excitement and fun of the *Ceffyl Pren* (literally a wooden horse), the old Welsh method of frightening or punishing those who

[15]The Census return of 1841 gives the name as *Treial;* by the Census of 1851 the cottage was known as *Carnabwth.*

offended against the strong rural sense of morality and justice and of righting the wrongs they had done; of carrying in rowdy procession (on the wooden horse), and then burning, the effigy of such offenders as adulterers, harsh landlords, and the fathers of bastard children who, hiding behind the hated provisions of the new Poor Law, which made the mother entirely responsible for her own predicament, failed to face up to their moral obligations. And riotous affairs they were. Frightening and embarrasing—and not infrequently physically painful—to their victims, but great occasions for letting off steam in exciting nocturnal rides in boisterous company. And for coming home at daybreak with that marvellous feeling of self-righteousness born of doing The Lord's work for Him in punishing the wicked.

It was but a short step to extend the *Ceffyl Pren* and all its attendant carnival-like paraphernalia to the destruction of toll gates, especially since the use of women's clothes and blackened faces for disguise was such a well-established part of the *Ceffyl Pren* tradition.

So, we have the leader and we have the tradition behind the disguise and the night-riding. But why the name Rebecca?

One suggestion is that the name was used to commemorate the first attack at Efail-wen, being taken from the name of the gatekeeper's wife, Rebecca Davies.[16] But the gatekeeper at Efail-wen was none other than Benjamin Bullin, brother of the hated toll farmer Thomas Bullin.

Another and almost universally accepted theory is that Twm Carnabwth was of such great stature that only one woman for miles around was large enough to have a petticoat to fit him, and she was a 'tall and stout old maid named Rebecca' who lived in the neighbouring Parish of Llangolman.[17] But the name Rebecca was (perhaps surprisingly when one considers the popularity of the Bible as a source for names in the mid-nineteenth century) extremely rare, in fact almost non-existent, in south Wales at the time.[18] And there was only one Rebecca living in the Parish of Llangolman, in a cottage called Garn—

[16] *Rebecca and Her Daughters,* by H. Tobit Evans, 1910.

[17] Ibid.

[18] Out of nearly 3,000 women's names taken at random by the author from the 1841 Census returns for Pembrokeshire and Carmarthenshire, only two Rebeccas could be found.

Rebecca Thomas, eighty years old, a widow living with her sixty years old son. Certainly not an 'old maid' and hardly, one might think, the kind of 'tall and stout' lady who could provide a petticoat to fit big and muscular Twm Carnabwth. What is more, she lived nearly three miles from the dwelling on Mynydd Bach, across the stream from Twm's cottage, known in local tradition as 'Rebecca's Cottage', where no Rebecca lived when Twm went looking for a good fit in women's clothes.[19]

No. The Biblical connotations of the name Rebecca must provide the answer. Among a people steeped in Bible learning to such a degree as almost to monopolise every thought, idea and instinct but those related to scraping a living, the coincidence is too much to be accidental. The influence of the Bible was too profound not to have played a part if not in initiating what was done, then at least in giving its participants the justification and emotional drive for doing it.

Possess the gates

The influence of the Bible and the use of the Scriptures as almost the only vehicle for learning among the mass of the people in the west Wales countryside thirty years before the coming of education for the masses cannot be overstated. Such secular education as was available in the country areas was provided by public subscription, charity or self-employed teachers of varying, and often dubious, qualifications and ability. There was no education 'system', little regulation and no inspection, and only a tiny minority of children were able to attend day school. The conditions under which such children as did attend them were accommodated in the few-and-far-between and virtually useless rural schoolrooms were appalling, as witness some contemporary observations:[20] 'The room was so dark that the few children whom I heard read were obliged to go to the door and open it, to have sufficient light.'; '. . . a ruinous hovel of the most squalid and miserable character; the floor is of bare earth, full of deep holes; the windows are all broken. Such of the scholars as write kneel . . . on the ground while they write. The Vicar's son informed me that he had seen *eighty* children in this

[19] Census records.

[20] Extracts from *The Reports of the Commissioners of Inquiry into the State of Education in Wales,* 1847.

hut. In summer the heat of it is said to be suffocating—and no wonder.'; 'The floor of this school was of the bare earth, very uneven and rather damp. There was a fire in an iron stove placed in the middle of the room. The steam which arose from it was quite insufferable, so much so that I was obliged to keep both door and window open to enable me to breathe. The master remarked that it was "bad to a stranger but nothing to those who were used to it".'

Clearly, the part played by those dreadful institutions in such little education as did exist in a poverty-stricken countryside was minimal.

It was to the chapels and their Sunday schools—attended by young and old alike—that the people really owed such literacy as they had. Strangers to the country were struck by the immensity of the people's achievements in providing from their own meagre resources the wherewithall for worshipping and educating themselves in their own way and in their own language; and by the extent to which the Scriptures dominated their lives and ideas, and, in fact, the entire learning process of the mass of the countrypeople. As one contemporary record said of the west Wales labouring man:

> . . . his worship, like his life, has grown different from that of the classes over him. Nor has he failed of tangible results in his chosen province of independent exertion. He has raised the buildings and maintains the ministry of his worship over the whole face of his country. The Sunday schools exhibit the most characteristic development of native intellect and the efforts of the mass of a people, utterly unaided, to educate themselves upon their own model.
>
> These schools have been almost the sole and most congenial centres of education. Through their agency the younger portion of the adult labouring classes in Wales can generally read the Scriptures in their mother tongue. A fifth of the entire population is returned as attending these schools; half of this number is returned as able to read the Scriptures.
>
> The Sunday schools effect a great deal in the moral and religious instruction of the people and very few children fail to attend some Sunday school or other. The instruction, however, is inadequate to their wants, being confined to purely religious topics and the art of reading. Each boy looks out for the verse that is coming to him; beyond that verse he concerns himself with nothing, except the cue

of the preceding one. Suddenly break the order either by stopping in the middle of a verse or by missing a boy or two, and the chance is no one can go on.[21]

Since little or nothing was required of children in the way of understanding or imagination—merely of memorising short answers to questions framed around well-known biblical texts—it is not surprising that one contemporary witness could make '. . . a tolerably safe guess that the answer to nine out of ten questions which they are ever asked in connection with their reading lessons will be either God, Jesus Christ, Bethlehem, the Virgin Mary, To Save Sinners, or the Devil.'

'Almost every adult scholar possesses his own Bible' said another observer, 'and I have heard the most minute accounts given of such customs as Expulsion from the Synagogue and the constitution of the Jewish Councils, and a familiar acquaintance with formulae embodying the more abstruse parts of Divinity is far from being uncommon. Maps were seldom in use, but the Rev. David Rees of Llanelli told me that *he believed the generality of Sunday scholars to be better versed in the geography of Palestine than of Wales.*' And all this in a part of the country which can even now boast of villages and hamlets with such biblical names as Hebron, Bethesda, Carmel, Bethlehem and Nazareth.

Given that the Bible was studied and memorised in such minute detail, that any matter of current concern or importance was aired in the religious meeting places and in the sermons there—with appropriate biblical texts to illustrate them—and, even more to the point, given the unquestioning and literal acceptance of biblical quotations by the congregations, the effect of Genesis, chapter 24, verse 60, on a people incensed by the antics of Thomas Bullin and the Whitland Trust must have been electrifying:

> And they blessed Rebecca, and said unto her, 'Thou art our sister; be thou the mother of thousands of millions, and let thy seed possess the gates of those which hate them.

No matter that the expression 'possess the gates' was an ancient term of warfare signifying the taking of a fortified town or city; no matter that the whole story of Rebecca related to tribal

[21] Extracts from *The Reports of the Commissioners of Inquiry into the State of Education in Wales*, 1847.

matters among the Jews. Genesis 24, 60 meant only one thing to those who heard it thundered out in the chapels, or who read it in their own Bibles, at that time and in those circumstances. It meant that the Bible was telling them to possess Bullin's gates and that they were doing the work of The Lord. How else would this normally peaceable and God-fearing people, a people so inured to hardship and injustice, be persuaded to take so violently to the roads?

It is worth remembering that Twm Carnabwth was the chief reciter of the *Pwnc* at Bethel Chapel in Mynachlog-ddu, a man who for all his partiality to the jug knew his Bible back to front. He above all would have been able to recite Genesis 24, 60 by heart.

Whether or not Twm and his followers were persuaded or encouraged by their chapel ministers to attack the gates, would be a subject of fierce controversy, but what is certain is that Twm Carnabwth was renowned for his recitation of the *Pwnc* on Whit Sunday, his big day of the year, the day on which religious fervour reached a peak in Bethel Chapel. And Whit Sunday in 1839 was on 12 May—the day before the attack on Bullin's gate at Efailwen.

So, was Twm Carnabwth, under the name 'Rebecca', the inspirer, prime mover and sole leader of the enterprise? Or was there someone else? Apart from the suspicion surrounding lawyer Hugh Williams, it would be a matter of considerable debate that those who had the most cause to demolish the toll gates were the farmers who paid the tolls and not their labourers, who did not. There would be rumours that the larger farmers were using their labourers and tenants to do their dirty work for them, and some evidence that the men were being paid a 'going rate' to join an attack on such-and-such a gate. All in all, strong indications that the level of command was rather higher than that of labourer or small tenant. And Thomas Rees—Twm Carnabwth of lasting memory—was not a farmer. He was a lowly agricultural labourer, scratching what little food he could from a tiny patch of bogland and hiring out his labour to farmers around him. It is interesting that his nearest farmer-neighbour, his cousin Lloyd Davies, farmed Glynsaithmaen, on the lower slope of Foel Cwmcerwyn . . . the farm in whose barn the Rebeccaites gathered for their first march on the gate at Efail-

Twm Carnabwth's grave by his beloved Bethel Chapel at Mynachlog-ddu, its inscription refurbished by the small children of the village school. And the epitaph for the first Rebecca—'Nid oes neb ond Duw yn gwybod/Beth a ddigwydd mewn diwornod. Wrth gyrchu bresych at fy nginio,/Daeth angau i fy ngardd i'm taro' ('No one but God knows what may happen in one day. While fetching a cabbage for my dinner, death came into my garden and struck me').

(Pat Molloy)

wen. That march led to the first of a series of riots for which the authorities—for all their frantic efforts, including the mobilisation of the Pembroke Yeomanry, the manacling and committal for trial of a frail old man,[22] and the offers of large rewards—never succeeded in getting one conviction nor even in identifying the huge and frightening figure on the white horse who had so exposed the vulnerability of an anachronistic system of law and order to determined popular action. It was an exposure of far-reaching consequence.

But this is where the mystery begins. Twm Carnabwth never rode again after terrorising the local magistrates and the Whitland Trust into submission and the removal of the offending gates in that early summer of 1839, and peace reigned in west Wales for the next three and a half years.

But Rebecca was not dead. She was merely sleeping.

[22] Morris David, the 80 year old Efail-wen blacksmith, who was humiliatingly taken in chains to Haverfordwest gaol to spend eight months awaiting trial at the Assizes. In the event, he was released for lack of evidence.

Chapter Two

THIS VISITATION OF PROVIDENCE

In the closing weeks of 1842, after more than three years without a single attack on a Welsh toll gate, Thomas Bullin did it again. This time it was on the Main Trust, whose turnpike roads ran across fifty miles of Carmarthenshire, from its border with Breconshire in the east and into Pembrokeshire in the west, on the route towards Milford Haven and the ships for Ireland and the Americas.

It had occurred to him that the hundreds of people travelling back and forth through the bottleneck of St. Clears, between Carmarthen and the many fairs and markets of the west, were making detours over the adjoining Whitland Trust roads, to avoid toll gates on several miles of the Main Trust. Putting one at a strategic spot just a couple of hundred yards to the east of St. Clears cross-roads would catch everyone. To the south the way would be blocked by the River Taf, and to the north a long detour through Meidrim would be the only alternative to paying toll at the new gate.

The trustees agreed to Bullin's proposition and a gate was duly erected by the Mermaid Tavern, less than a mile from that at Pwll Trap on the Whitland Trust road to the west of St. Clears . . . forming the very kind of toll trap that would most arouse the people's anger. The new gate was up for only a matter of hours before it was down again, in a noisy re-enactment of Efail-wen complete with a new 'Rebecca' and all her trappings. And for good measure they cleared the roads around St. Clears completely by pulling down the Pwll Trap gate and the side bar on the Taf Bridge as well.

Thomas Bullin had also shown yet again his impeccable sense of timing. Never had the bulk of the population been so desperately short of the means of even the most basic subsistence. Indeed, the depression in the economy of rural Wales and its effect on small farmers and labourers was assuming the proportions of a disaster. James Rogers, a St. Clears corn dealer, described it graphically:

> In the year 1840, which was a very wet summer, nearly all the farmers of the Principality had to purchase corn, either for seed or bread, and, from the general poverty of the farmers, the labouring population as well as the trading community felt the effects of this visitation of providence severely.
>
> This distress has not been the result of one, two or three years, but a series of at least twenty which has been gradually coming upon us, and the late deficient and defective harvests have been also instrumental in hastening this crisis. The capital of the farmer for the last few years has materially diminished in value, while the rates, taxes, tithes, county stock and even rents have been increased.
>
> High rents, heavy taxation, want of trade and the difficulty of obtaining by hard labour the amount necessary to meet the demands laid upon the farmer have been causes mainly instrumental in bringing about the present state of things and have caused many to look on with dismay and almost to despair of a remedy.[1]

Small wonder that the state of rural west Wales was being likened to the dreadful conditions then developing in the west of Ireland, which were destined, with the coming potato famines, to reduce the Irish population by as many as two million. Small wonder, too, that before this campaign was half way through, Rebeccaism broke out so suddenly, simultaneously and at such widely separated places as to show that the whole countryside was up in arms.

Off with it then my dear children

The destruction of the Mermaid gate in St. Clears marked the beginning of Rebecca's four and a half month war on the Main, Whitland and Tavernspite Trusts. Toll gates and side bars across the fourteen miles between St. Clears in Carmarthenshire and Canaston Bridge in Pembrokeshire were destroyed in a war of attrition in which gates were felled as quickly as they were replaced, the intervals between destruction and replacement lengthening all the time as the trusts' resistance flagged in the face of failure by the authorities to make any significant arrests.

One of the problems facing the magistrates was the absence of any pattern in the attacks and the impossibility of deploying to

[1] *Report of the Commissioners of Inquiry for South Wales, 1844*: evidence of James Rogers.

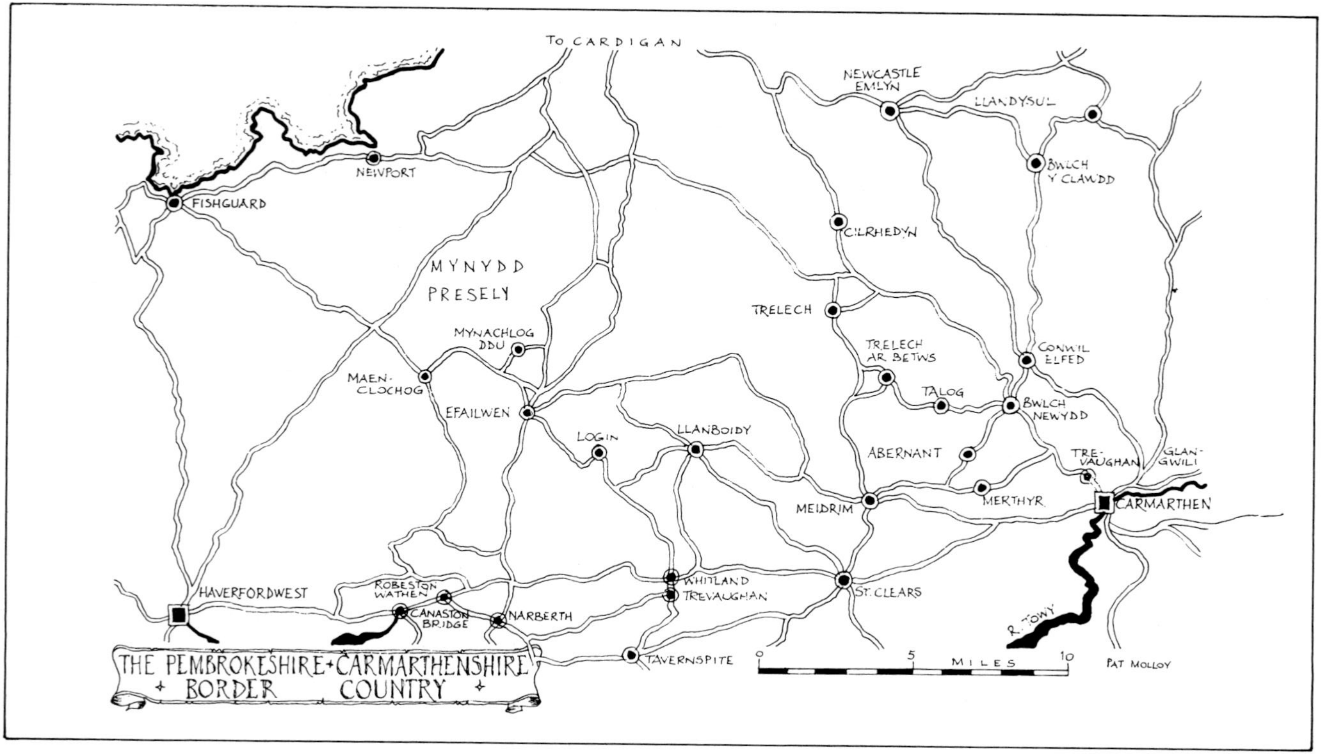
THE PEMBROKESHIRE + CARMARTHENSHIRE BORDER COUNTRY
To CARDIGAN
NEWPORT
FISHGUARD
MYNYDD PRESELY
MYNACHLOG DDU
MAEN-CLOCHOG
EFAILWEN
LOGIN
LLANBOIDY
NEWCASTLE EMLYN
LLANDYSUL
BWLCH Y CLAWDD
CILRHEDYN
TRELECH
TRELECH AR BETWS
TALOG
CONWIL ELFED
BWLCH NEWYDD
ABERNANT
TRE-VAUGHAN
GLAN-GWILI
MERTHYR
MEIDRIM
CARMARTHEN
HAVERFORDWEST
ROBESTON WATHEN
CANASTON BRIDGE
NARBERTH
WHITLAND
TREVAUGHAN
ST. CLEARS
TAVERNSPITE
R. TOWY
0
5
MILES
10
PAT MOLLOY

any useful purpose what few men were willing to be sworn as special constables. And they were few indeed because such was the service that Rebecca was performing for the local farmers that most of those summoned for service were only too happy to pay the fine rather than be sworn in and risk spoiling the good work! As Timothy Powell, J.P., told the Lord Lieutenant, Lord Dynevor, '. . . it is quite certain that any civil force which locally the Magistrates can command will not be able to put down these lawless and daring proceedings or bring the offenders to justice. All parties have been so influenced by interest or fear that we find it impossible to gather evidence necessary for a conviction.'[2]

The response of the magistrates in west Carmarthenshire to this new campaign was reasonable enough to begin with as they went through the usual procedures of offering rewards and summoning special constables, but it very soon assumed the shape of panic under the combined pressure of the failure of their rewards, the collapse of their efforts to mobilise a sufficient force of special constables, and the realisation of the size of the bill for repair of the gates that would inevitably fall to the county rates. And panic was not long in coming.

Within six days of the attack on the Mermaid gate (on 18 November), four gates were down in the six miles from St. Clears to Whitland. And then, during the night of Monday 12 December, Rebecca made a dramatic descent on the village of St. Clears and destroyed every gate around the place, not only terrifying the inhabitants in the process, but holding to ransom everyone returning towards Carmarthen from Narberth Fair:

> The leaders of the mob were disfigured by painting their faces in various colours, wearing horse-hair beards and women's clothes. We understand that these depredators had patrols in every direction, preventing all travellers from proceeding on their journeys during the time that the demolition was going on. We learn also that all the doors of all the houses in the neighbourhood were locked and the inhabitants confined within, not daring to exhibit a light in their windows. It is said that they had a *gentle* intimation from the mob to that effect, and from fear of being illtreated by them they obeyed their commands.

[2] Letter dated 13 December, 1842, Timothy Powell to Lord Dynevor: Public Record Office, File HO 45/265.

> On this day Narberth Fair was held and the mob stopped all drovers coming in the direction of Carmarthen and levied a contribution from them, stating that they had destroyed all the toll gates and that therefore they had no tolls to pay.[3]

And all this without any sign of either special constables or magistrates. Yet the very next day a letter was on its way by mail coach from Carmarthen to the Home Secretary, Sir James Graham, imploring him to send troops. But the government had no troops to spare to deal with such a trifling affair as three nights of rural toll gate breaking when its forces were so stretched in the 'Disturbed Manufacturing Districts' of England and in the now strike-torn valleys of Monmouthshire and Glamorgan where Chartism and talk of armed struggle had raised its head again. So it sent three Metropolitan Police officers from London.

Inspector George Martin and his two constables arrived in St. Clears on Tuesday 20 December, the day after the Mermaid gate had been destroyed yet again. Their journey at a time when the railway had only reached as far west as Bristol had involved a train journey from Paddington, a twelve hour paddle steamer voyage from Bristol to Tenby and a bumpy three hour coach ride from there to St. Clears. But tired as they were they had to walk through a crowd of onlookers to the Blue Boar Inn which was to be their lodgings, since their appearance in the village prompted a great deal of curiosity among the countrypeople. Their uniform—black top hat, high-necked silver-buttoned tail coat and white trousers—was a perfect novelty to them, for a regular police force was a luxury as yet unknown in Carmarthenshire or, for that matter, in the entire west of Wales, except in the Borough of Carmarthen, which had had its own small force for nearly seven years.[4]

Welsh speaking Inspector Martin had plenty of time to survey the scene because a fortnight elapsed before he had his first riot. He and his men saw through a peaceful and (being billetted in the Blue Boar Inn) convivial Christmas before their services were called upon for more active duty than seeking information about Rebecca. Needless to say, their efforts in that direction

[3] *Carmarthen Journal,* 16 December, 1842.

[4] Their story is told in *A Shilling for Carmarthen: The Town They Nearly Tamed* (Gomer Press, 1980).

'Their appearance prompted a great deal of curiosity': the uniforms of the London Metropolitan Police in the 1840s. *(Police Staff College, Bramshill)*

yielded nothing, for the name 'Rebecca' was spoken only in whispers . . . and never within earshot of the law!

By the first week in January, 1843, the magistrates had somehow managed to put fifty-four special constables under Inspector Martin's command, though that officer's first encounter with them the day after his arrival in St. Clears did not exactly fill him with confidence in their loyalty to the cause. 'I have now just seen several of the special constables,' he wrote, 'and I am sorry to say they appear determined not to assist and . . . I feel sure that if the two men and myself were to go out and come in contact with the mob that the specials would desert us and very likely assist the mob.'[5] Nevertheless he was saddled with them and he organised them so that at any given time in the night there would be nine men patrolling on foot in and around the village. But perhaps those special constables, lulled by the deceptive peacefulness of the preceding three weeks, were all on the eastward side of the village when Rebecca visited Pwll Trap gate again on Monday night 2 January, because they did not attempt to interfere with an elaborate performance enacted there with all the *éclat* of the best traditions of the *Ceffyl Pren*. Or perhaps they preferred not to act without their Metropolitan Police comrades, who at the time were cosily ensconced in the Blue Boar enjoying the hospitality of the landlord, Mr. Thomas.

It was about midnight when a large crowd, this time all on foot, dressed in a variety of garments, faces blackened, and armed with the usual array of weaponry, walked up to the gate at Pwll Trap. They halted a few yards short, and the lady Rebecca —stooped, hobbling, and leaning like an old woman on 'her' blackthorn stick—walked up to the gate. Her sight apparently failing her, she reached out with her staff and touched it. 'Children,' she said, 'there is something put up here; I cannot go on.' 'What is it mother?' cried her daughters. 'Nothing should stop *your* way.' Rebecca, peering at the gate, replied 'I do not know children. I am old and cannot see well.' 'Shall we come on mother and move it out of the way?' 'Stop,' said she, 'let me see', and she tapped the gate again with her staff. 'It seems like a great gate put across the road to stop your old mother,' whined the old one. 'We will break it mother,' her daughters cried in unison;

[5] Letter dated 21 December, 1842, from Inspector Martin to Lord Dynevor: Public Record Office, File HO 45/265.

'Nothing shall hinder you on your journey.' 'No,' she persisted, 'let us see; perhaps it will open.' She felt the lock, as would one who was blind. 'No children,' she called, 'it is bolted and locked and I cannot go on. What is to be done?' 'It must be taken down mother, because you and your children must pass.'

Rebecca's reply came loud and clear: '*Off with it then my dear children. It has no business here.*' And within ten minutes the gate was chopped to pieces and the 'family' had vanished into the night.

Here was the *Ceffyl Pren* in classic form: a public 'trial' of an offence against the community, the pronouncement of the judgement . . . and instant justice. A more effective and popular 'justice', it seemed, than any the people were likely to get from magistrates who appeared to have tied themselves so closely to blood-suckers like Thomas Bullin and his turnpike trusts.

Becca is come!

But the government still would not be budged in the matter of sending troops to pull the chestnuts from the fire for the Carmarthenshire magistrates. So, in evident panic and to the fury of the Board of Admiralty, the magistrates sent a messenger to the commander of the Royal Marines detachment guarding Pembroke Dockyard requesting urgent assistance. A company of thirty marines reached St. Clears on 15 January after a long day's march and they were immediately treated to a typical example of Rebecca's impudence. They received a note telling them that she intended attacking the gate at Trevaughan, six miles back towards Pembroke. When the marines arrived there after a counter-march of one and a half hours, they found the deed done. And as they marched back to St. Clears they passed the wreckage of two other gates, at Pentre and Maes Oland!

The Royal Marines were understandably pleased when after only five days they received orders to march the twenty-three miles back to their dockyard. The Board of Admiralty had found out where they were and wasted no time in ordering them back, and in ordering twenty-nine additional marines by steamer from Bristol to join them in guarding the dockyard arsenal, fearing some kind of armed uprising. It was a measure of the alarm created by the manner of the magistrates' response to what as yet

Pembroke Town *(Haverfordwest Library)*

was by national standards no more than a routine outbreak of unrest.

Having lost the marines, though, the magistrates immediately brought out the Castlemartin Yeomanry, on whom they could legally call without the authority of the Home Secretary and the War Office. Major Bowling rode out from Pembroke Town with Captain Bryant, Lieutenant Leach and twenty-six part-time cavalry troopers—armed with swords, pistols, carbines and

The Castlemartin Yeomanry Cavalry *(The Pembroke Yeomanry Trust)*

bayonets, and each carrying twenty rounds of ball cartridge—arriving in St. Clears late on Saturday 21 January. But Major Bowling found that he had nothing to do but put his men out in small detachments to patrol the lanes and guard the gates between Whitland and St. Clears on dark, wet and wintry nights on which nothing at all happened during the three weeks they were there. And to cap their misery, as soon as the Carmarthenshire magistrates found that they were going to get a bill for their services (on top of the £5.19s.6d. (£5.97½p) a day they were paying for the three London policemen), they sent them marching straight back to Pembrokeshire. They had no sooner trotted through the two gates at Trevaughan than Rebecca destroyed them. And this after a whole month of inactivity. Impudence indeed.

It was the attack at Trevaughan, though, that gave the magistrates a boost they badly needed, in the shape of two men said to have been involved in it. There was, of course, a reward of £50 (offered by the magistrates and the trusts) for information leading to the arrest and conviction of anyone involved in the destruction of toll gates, and Lewis Griffiths, a miller and pig dealer of Pantypark Mill in Wiston (thirteen miles west of Trevaughan) came forward to Inspector Martin to lay claim to it by informing on two men in whose company he had been on the night of Whitland Fair during the usual drinking spree in the Golden Lion there.

Thomas Howells, a farmer of Llwyndrissi, just on the edge of Whitland and a mile from Trevaughan gate, and David Howells, a miller and a relative and near-neighbour of his, were arrested on Tuesday February 21, eight days after the riot, and Inspector Martin took them to the magistrates court which was held in its usual place, the Blue Boar Inn in St. Clears. There was pandemonium outside the court and the special constables tried manfully to keep order while Lewis Griffiths the pig dealer was giving his evidence under oath. The two defending solicitors cross-examined him in a determined attempt to discredit him, but the magistrates accepted his evidence, refused large offers of bail for the defendants, and committed them in custody for trial at Pembrokeshire Assizes a month hence.

The crowd outside—mostly, it would seem, women and girls—were furious and it was deemed advisable, for his own safety, to send Lewis Griffiths to gaol as well! When he and the two prisoners were placed in the open carriage in which Inspector Martin was to convey them to Haverfordwest Gaol there was a riot. It was only the truncheons of the London policemen and the specials that cleared a sufficient path through the crowd to enable them to get out of St. Clears, clear the hill to Pwll Trap and get on to the open road for their three hour drive to Haverfordwest, twenty miles westward.

One of the magistrates who had committed the two Whitland men for trial—Timothy Powell of Penycoed, just outside St. Clears—soon had cause to reflect on the hazards of his calling in such troubled times. A few days after the hearing he had the first of several mysterious fires in the woodland plantations on his estates at Penycoed and at nearby Llangynin. It was a taste of the difficulties that would dog Timothy Powell and his fellow magistrates for many months yet as Rebeccaism tightened its grip on the countryside.

Shades of Efail-wen?

Over the first six weeks of this campaign the big question, the one that occupied much of men's thoughts, was what connection if any was there between these attacks and those at Efail-wen and Llanboidy three and a half years before. Certainly so far as distance is concerned the same people could be involved, and Inspector Martin had no doubt at all that those who attacked the St. Clears gates were 'farmers as well as their servants and chiefly I believe from the neighbourhood of Llanboidy.'[6] He had even taken out a warrant for the arrest of Robert Roberts, a Llanboidy miller, but nothing seems to have come of it. But the best evidence establishing the connection with Efail-wen comes in the person of William Phillips, Longford Farm, Clynderwen—thirteen miles, or about two hours on horseback, from St. Clears—who took part in the attack on the Mermaid gate on 18 November, 1842.[7]

William Phillips was an undiscovered member of the mob that had attacked the gate at Efail-wen and one of two farmers arrested for refusing to pay toll there whose successful action for damages had, ironically, led to the imprisonment of the two arresting officers who were unable to pay the compensation and costs awarded to the farmers.

But in the absence of fact, rumour abounded, and a favourite and very strong rumour was that the leader was (according to an observer at Trevaughan) English speaking, and (according to the old woman who kept Robeston Wathen gate) 'a person of most gentlemanly address and voice.' The identification of members of the higher orders with the struggles of the poor was by no means a new phenomenon in rural society and we have only to turn for a parallel to the legend of Robin Hood. Every country, every part of every country, and every age has its Robin Hood, and west Wales in the days of Rebecca was no exception. The germ of truth always lies somewhere in most of our folk tales, but such was the agitated state of the Welsh

[6] Letter dated 2 January, 1843, Inspector Martin to the County Magistrates: Public Record Office, File HO 45/265.

[7] This comes from a uniquely direct source—Mr. Thomas L. Phillips, grandson of William Phillips. In 1982, at the age of 85, he told the author of conversations he had with the old Rebeccaite, then aged 90, when he lived with him at Clynderwen in 1907 at the age of ten. This represents a remarkable link, spanning a hundred and forty years, and adds to information contained in contemporary records.

countryside in the spring of 1843 that many of the simple and superstitious people of the Carmarthenshire—Pembrokeshire border country even believed Rebecca to be not human at all, but supernatural! Not surprisingly, this belief gained even more ground when gates suddenly began to be demolished almost simultaneously at places forty miles apart.

The Fishguard Trust's Prendergast gate, on the northern edge of Haverfordwest, the Pembrokeshire county town, was the first to go, on Wednesday night 1 February. But the Prendergast gate simply disappeared without a sound, and only the stumps of its posts were left when the gatekeeper came out to open up in the morning. There was never a clue to who was responsible, but the Robin Hood myth soon surfaced again in the rumour that the Prendergast Rebecca was none other than Owen Tucker Edwardes, son of landowner and magistrate William Edwardes of Sealyham, seven miles north of Haverfordwest. After all, the Edwardes' were persistent and outspoken critics of the Fishguard Trust. But who wasn't? The only wonder is that the Fishguard Trust, which had committed just about every breach of turnpike legislation that it was possible to commit, had survived so long without attack.

Not that the gentry were above a bit of direct action themselves. The fiery Pembrokeshire landowner, Colonel Colby, for instance, sent a servant to pull down the chain across the road at Plaindealings, above Narberth, after Mrs. Colby had suffered the indignity of actually being asked to pay toll. Not only that, but he forcibly resisted an attempt to arrest his servant for removing the chain and went to Tenby court and abused the magistrates who committed the man for trial. True to form, though, the Grand Jury at the next Pembrokeshire Quarter Sessions decided that his servant had 'no case to answer' and he was discharged. It would not, of course, occur to the Gallant Colonel or his Lady that a lot of people might feel that there seemed to be one law for the rich and another for the poor.

The silent removal of the Prendergast gate at Haverfordwest contrasted just three nights later, and forty miles to the east, with an attack on the Kidwelly Trust's Garreg gate on the outskirts of Kidwelly. There, the style was exactly right: the sound of a 'great number of horses' reported by the many who locked them-

Narberth Market

(Haverfordwest Library)

selves in their homes, and all the familiar disguises reported by the few who ventured out to watch.

And at Llanddarog, six miles east of Carmarthen, the night of Thursday 16 February saw a neat piece of 'self-help' enacted under the banner of Rebecca, when:

> . . . a number of persons riotously and tumultuously assembled and pulled down the toll bar erected near the village, and not being content with that, the rascals set fire to the materials and totally consumed them, together with the toll box belonging to the said bar.
>
> On that day a person had applied to the tollkeeper and offered him five shillings [25p] for the passage of a wedding party which was to go that way on the Friday, which was refused, being under ten shillings [50p]. By next morning the whole had been destroyed and the wedding party passed scot free. We leave our readers to draw their own conclusions from that circumstance.[8]

I shall show no mercy

Back in Pembrokeshire, the trial of Thomas and David Howells for the attack on Trevaughan gate was drawing near, and Rebecca issued a very pointed message. In a noisy and well-supported demolition of the Robeston Wathen gate (eight miles, or about an hour and a quarter's ride from Trevaughan), Rebecca spoke to the bystanders and warned them that '*Should any harm happen to the two men now at Haverfordwest Gaol for trial on suspicion of having been concerned in these riots, I shall show no mercy to anyone, but harry the whole country.*'[9]

A week later, in the Shire Hall at Haverfordwest before the Honourable Mr. Justice Maule, Rebecca's warning bore fruit. Pig dealer and informer Lewis Griffiths was cross-examined strongly by Mr. John Evans, Q.C., for both defendants. The combination of Griffiths' drunkenness and evident greed for the £50 reward was in Mr. Evans' view a telling reason for his evidence to be rejected. Indeed, he drew from another prosecution witness, John Thomas, the landlord of the Golden Lion in Whitland, the statement that Griffiths 'was not sober in my sight. He drank a great deal. I had heard him say many times about the reward. Reward bills were stuck on my door. They were up before the gate was taken down. I heard Lewis Griffiths

[8] *Carmarthen Journal,* 24 February, 1843.
[9] *Carmarthen Journal,* 10 March, 1843.

Haverfordwest: The Shire Hall (where the Assize Court was held) is on the left.
(Haverfordwest Library)

speaking of the rewards on Tuesday or Wednesday', the attack being on the Monday.

But the gatekeeper, William Rees (mentioned by Griffiths in his account) could not be budged. He knew Thomas Howells as well as he knew anyone. He had known him for years. He had witnessed the demolition of his own tollhouse and Thomas Howells helping to demolish it. As the Judge was to say in his summing up, Griffiths' evidence was 'confirmed in many important particulars' by that of gatekeeper Rees.

Defence Counsel played the classic 'each-way bet', as had Chartist Thomas Powell's defender at Welshpool Assizes:[10] his clients had not been present and had not taken part in the affair, but, if they *were* there, and if they *did* do it, what they did could not have amounted to the offence charged. 'As the defendants were not present at the *commencement* of the work of demolition,' said Mr. Evans, 'and as the work was not *completed* in their presence there was not an *act* of demolition.' An imaginative

[10] A policeman's expression used to describe a line of defence used to this day by barristers in Crown Courts, e.g. 'I did not kill my wife . . . but if I *did,* I was provoked.' In the case of Thomas Powell in his trial for using seditious language it was claimed that he did not use the words alleged, but if he *did* they were not seditious words.

defence, to say the least. If the defendants were present and taking part only in the *middle* of the demolition and not at the beginning or the end they had not committed the *complete* crime of demolition. Not surprisingly, the Judge would have none of it, and over-ruled the submission.

Mr. Evans need not have taken the trouble, for Inspector Martin of the Metropolitan Police had already delivered Rebecca's message in the course of his own evidence as to his efforts to bring his other witnesses to Court: 'I have searched for Lewis Roberts but cannot find him, nor David Thomas, nor Benjamin Watts' servant girl. I had also subpoenas for two servant girls but could not serve them.'

It was enough. The jury very quickly returned verdicts of not guilty and Thomas and David Howells emerged from the Shire Hall to a rapturous welcome from a huge crowd. There was no need for thoughts of vengeance now . . . except to burn down a few more acres of magistrate Timothy Powell's woodland at St. Clears, just to reinforce the message!

A spreading flame

The night before the trial of Thomas and David Howells, a spark from the fire of Rebeccaism leapt across a gap of some fifteen miles of hill country to the north, to ignite a separate campaign, by a separate band of men, this time against the Newcastle Trust. The first attack on Bwlch-y-Clawdd gate five miles beyond the village of Trelech—now about to become a hot bed of Rebeccaism—was an isolated one, to be followed a month later by an attack on nearby Bwlch-y-Domen gate, and then the usual sequence of replacement and further demolition of both of them.

The Newcastle Trust would suffer the destruction of at least eighteen of its gates over the next two months.

In mid-May, what might be called the first phase of the 1843 outbreak came to an end, with the destruction of a gate on the edge of Fishguard town, completing a picture in which over a period of six months some twenty-six toll gates and side bars had been destroyed—some of them repeatedly—across a stretch of west Wales countryside measuring some fifty miles by thirty.

The sum total of arrests was two, and the sum total of convictions was nil—despite all that the Carmarthenshire and Pemb-

Fishguard: the view from just west of the town square towards the old harbour in Lower Town. *(Haverfordwest Library)*

rokeshire magistrates, their special constables, their three London policemen, their offers of rewards and their flirtations with the military could do.

Thomas Bullin had really started the ball rolling this time, for the activites of Rebecca were about to enter a phase in which the carnival aspect of her night rides was to become tainted by an unwonted violence, which would at last shake the government, almost as much as the past six months had shaken west Wales magistrates. And, for the first time, the doings of the peasantry of remote west Wales would be brought to the attention of people who had never given a second thought to their existence, let alone to their problems. The world would learn about them through the pages of the most powerful organ in the land . . . the 'Thunderer', *The Times* of London.

Chapter Three

AMBUSH

Any journey across south west Wales would bring the traveller into Carmarthen, the region's most populous town and its commercial and social centre; where the upper and lower roads from London converged at the first crossing of the River Towy from the sea, ten miles away, to give the place the strategic importance that had made it a garrison town for the Romans.

Fronted by its river to the south and backed by almost impenetrable hill country to the north, Carmarthen stood astride the southern route from England to Ireland in a manner that ensured a busy prosperity even in the most depressed of times. Serving a deep and extensive hinterland, its busy quay rattled and rang with the loading and unloading of paddle steamers and sailing ships, on a river swarming with small boats shuttling to and from the villages of the Towy estuary on the Bristol Channel. Its numerous coaching inns were scenes of constant bustle and noise as coaches from and to all points of the compass arrived and departed, were loaded and unloaded, their horses changed and rested and their passengers fed and lodged, in this, the hub of the west Wales communications network.

From miles around, the countrypeople flocked to Carmarthen's crowded provision markets above and below its eighteenth century Guildhall and to its livestock fairs, its makers of hats, harness, shoes and agricultural implements, and to its weavers, tanners and millers, while those who could afford it shopped in a town which boasted the height of fashion and the most modern in household gadgetry. Its merchants imported and exported every conceivable commodity, and its foundries made the best iron and tin money could buy and exported it the world over.

But like the country as a whole, Carmarthen, the home of ten thousand people, was a place of contrasts, from its magnificent town houses to its dark and insanitary slums; from the opulence and high social doings of the visiting gentry to the destitution,

Carmarthen

(Illustrated London News)

drunkenness and early deaths of the lowest of its poor; from the Carmarthenshire Hunt banquet in its Boar's Head Hotel to the black bread and gruel of its crowded workhouse; from the well-fed comfort and affluence of its traders to the footsore misery of ragged, ill-rewarded sellers of small country produce. And it was a town with a far-flung reputation for drunkenness and violence, possessed of a class of people—the notorious 'Carmarthen Mob'—who welcomed any opportunity for boisterous behaviour, from a wild and noisy Christmas Eve 'Torchnight' to a good old-fashioned fight with their town's five-man police force, who themselves were almost as troublesome to their Chief Constable as many of the town drunks.

Carmarthen was also a town surrounded by the toll gates of no less than five turnpike trusts whose boundaries met there, with all the potential for trouble that that implied.

The traveller coming in on the Swansea road would suddenly get his first sight of Carmarthen as his coach topped Llangunnor Hill before beginning its descent to the Pensarn turnpike gate on the southern end of the town bridge. He would look down and be struck by the quaint beauty of the little town, its castle ruin and Norman church nestling alongside the winding River Towy, and by its backdrop of hills, rising one on another in an arc to the north of the town. What he probably would not know was that in the folds and clefts of those hills, in one-roomed cottages on tiny patches of land and on small hill farms in and around the villages of Trelech, Abernant, Talog, Cilrhedyn, Newchurch, Merthyr and Cynwyl, lived nearly six thousand people, many of whom had reached such a pitch of desperation as would soon cause the town of Carmarthen to be shaken to its foundations.

A deceptive quiet

A deceptive quiet reigned in Carmarthenshire and Pembrokeshire in the second half of May, after the isolated attack at Fishguard and the opening shots of the campaign against the Newcastle Trust, and the reasons for it are far from clear. The causes of the disturbances were as pressing as ever, though the efforts of the Whitland and Tavernspite Trusts to explain what they believed to be misunderstandings about their affairs and their conduct seemed to have taken at least some of the heat out of the conflict. That the first attacks at Llanddarog and Kidwelly in east Carmarthenshire owed more to some isolated local annoyance than to the general discontent exhibited further west is indicated by the fact that in each case several weeks elapsed before those gates were visited again.

Quite clearly, other influences were at work apart from the campaign element—apart, that is, from the deliberately thought out, carefully planned and well disciplined operations typified by those against the Whitland Trust. For one thing, the 'irritant' factor, as it may be called, can be seen in the coincidence of the times and places of the attacks on gates and those of the livestock fairs, where the vast amount of drink traditionally consumed by drovers and buyers played no small part in the incidence of spontaneous attacks.

Attacks on toll gates occurred for all kinds of odd reasons outside those which motivated the true Rebeccaites—like the anger of the wedding party at Llanddarog at the refusal of the toll keeper to accept a joint payment, and like the Gallant Colonel Colby's reaction to the shock of a toll collector actually having the nerve to demand payment from his wife. And such caprices, encouraged by and in imitation of Rebecca's example, would continue to occur. Indeed, that might well have become the shape of things after mid-May, but what happened in Carmarthen on 26 May was to determine otherwise. It would bring troops and more troops; it would lead to three months of almost daily attacks, in concentrated areas moving gradually eastwards across Carmarthenshire and northwards into Cardiganshire and Radnorshire; and it would lead to dismay and disarray among many erstwhile sympathisers and supporters as the movement began to attract criminals and descend to the level of vendetta.

Water Street

Water Street gate was only a matter of two or three hundred yards from the very centre of Carmarthen, across one of the two turnpike roads from Carmarthen to Cardigan, both of which were managed by the Newcastle Trust. The trust had built the second road—from Glangwili at the eastern end of town—in 1842 and had quite naturally kept its toll gate on the old one because of the equally natural tendency of travellers to seek out ungated roads (where they could find them!) in order to avoid paying. The problem in this case was that people living right on

Carmarthen Market *(National Library of Wales)*

the edge, or within only a few miles, of Carmarthen and having regular business there found the town gate in Water Street a particular irritant. There was no way around it and people who lived in the hill country above Carmarthen, already feeling hemmed in by the gates around Newcastle Emlyn and Llandysul to the north of them—gates which had already felt Rebecca's axe,—showed an increasing reluctance to pay. The results showed in the magistrates' court room in the town's Guildhall, where more and more farmers and villagers were fined for refusing to pay or for abusing gate keeper Henry Thomas. Such prosecutions served only to stoke the anger of a people who could actually find themselves returning on a ten mile walk from Carmarthen market with far less in their pockets than the value of their produce after being squeezed for tolls at the town gate.

But then Rebecca took a hand.

Henry Thomas lived with his wife and small child in the stone-built house by the gate. So busy was his gate and so annoying was it to so many people, in and out of town, that he had become quite philosophical about the hazards of a gatekeeper's life. Saturdays—market days—were the worst, and it would be

Saturday tomorrow, but as midnight came on Friday 26 May and the noisy drunks began to clear the streets, he settled himself down for a quiet night's sleep, to be ready for whatever the morrow might bring. Rebecca was certainly not on his mind, for it was common knowledge that she and her family did not venture into towns like Carmarthen.

He settled onto his bed fully clothed in anticipation of having to turn out for the odd late night traveller, and sure enough, at ten minutes to one, there came a knock on his door—a man returning to town with a horse and cart. The man paid and passed through, and Henry Thomas closed the gate, went back into his house, and finally got to sleep.

And then came his nightmare. It was like one of those dreams that come in the first, deep, sleep, from which the frightened sleeper fights his way to consciousness as from black, turbulent depths. Henry Thomas fought his way up through noise like thunder, overlaid with demonic sounds like the squealing of pigs and the sounding of the last trump, and suddenly he was up and across the room instinctively towards his door. It burst inwards as he reached it, and framed in the gap were the objects of his nightmare—two large, black-faced figures wearing long, loose and wide gowns, with turbans topping large, ringletted golden wigs. That would have been more than enough, but Rebecca and her 'sister' Charlotte were brandishing cavalry swords!

With his wife and child screaming in the bedroom behind him, Henry Thomas' reaction was instantaneous—almost as if long practised. 'Oh, Becca is here!' he cried. 'Go on with your work, you are quite welcome.' 'Do not be alarmed,' said Rebecca, 'we will do no injury whatever to you.'

The sound of axes outside told him his gate was already doomed, and the gunfire and shouting suggested that the destruction of the house itself would not be far behind. He begged Rebecca to spare his furniture, and pleaded for the safety of his wife and child who were crying in their bed. Rebecca responded by going to the door—followed by Henry Thomas—and addressing the crowd of about three hundred white-gowned, bonnetted figures, most of whom were armed with guns and on horseback. She ordered them to demolish only the gate and the house roof, but not to damage the ceiling for fear of injuring the woman and child. And her daughters set to work with a will. The noise was tremendous and Henry Thomas saw at least a dozen of the mob standing abreast across the street firing shotguns towards Catherine Street and the town centre. Others sent blasts of gunfire in other directions to deter interference from the terrified residents of Water Street, several of whom heard the shots whistling past them as they leaned out of their windows.

Rebecca's daughters swarmed all over the toll house on ladders they had brought with them, and in the act of stripping the roof one of them fell through the ceiling, to the further terror of the gatekeeper's wife and child. Rebecca's apology for this was only barely heard above the crash of axes and sledgehammers, the rasp of cross-saws and the cheers of her daughters. The neighbours, who were also enduring all this, must have wondered where the town's police were, since the police station was only five hundred yards away in Cambrian Place and the noise was deafening. In fact, Chief Constable John Pugh and his four constables, Nicholas Martin, David Woolcock, Thomas Evans and Robert Awberry, had already come running along Catherine Street with truncheons drawn. But as soon as they showed their noses around the corner of Water Street, Rebecca's dozen 'sentinels' sent blasts of birdshot whistling over their heads and thudding into the walls . . . which served as shelter for them until Rebecca and her followers had departed far beyond pursuit.

Thanking Henry Thomas with the utmost courtesy for his lack of resistance, and apologising to him for the inconvenience she had caused, Rebecca shouted the order to mount, and away they went, cheering, shouting, firing and blowing their horns. Away beyond Fountain Hall—where they paused to fire a farewell volley—and up through Trevaughan village, back into the hills of Newchurch, Abernant and Talog, their shouts and gunfire fading as the hills enfolded them. And as the first streaks of dawn appeared in the sky, there was not a man among them who did not reflect that this was *one* Carmarthen market day when they would get their produce to the market place toll free!

Eight miles to Talog

As Carmarthen filled for that market day, the shattered gate and roofless toll house in Water Street were the objects of a good deal of interest by the happy, non-paying countrypeople come down through Trevaughan; by a crowd of sightseers; by the town's policemen now recovered from their fright, and by the Borough Mayor and his fellow magistrates. This was the town magistrates' first taste of Rebeccaism, and they were furious. They were furious with their police above all and they returned from the shambles of Water Street to their chamber in the Guildhall to hold an immediate enquiry, to which they called Chief Constable John Pugh and his four men. The Mayor lashed into them and threatened dire consequences in the event of any further failure to do their duty. It was to no avail that John Pugh reminded them of the little problem of the gunfire from Rebecca's dozen 'sentinels', and the Mayor, brushing all excuses aside, ordered his town clerk to record in the minutes of the Watch Committee that the police had been,

> . . . severely reprimanded by the magistrates for their cowardice in not making an attempt to put a stop to the lawless proceedings and capture some of the gang.[1]

The people did not have long to enjoy the absence of a gate at Water Street, though, because there was a new one by the following Monday and Henry Thomas was back on duty with his money bag and toll book. But Rebecca had taken due note and word quickly spread of a notice in Welsh found pinned to the door of Bwlch Newydd Chapel, four miles up the road from Water Street:

> This is to give notice that the goods of all persons who will henceforth pay at Water Street Gate will be burned and their lives will be taken from them at a time they will not think—Becca.

The notice was timely because Wednesday was the next market day and many were the rows at the gate and much the abuse hurled at the keeper on that day as a result of it. Out of all the people with whom he had trouble that day, Henry Thomas reported three Talog men to the magistrates and summonses were issued against them for refusing to pay tolls. They were John Harries of Talog Mill, Thomas Thomas, the owner of the shop at Talog, and Samuel Brown, a farmer, who lived at Brynmeini, just outside the village. In the Guildhall on the following Saturday, 3 June, Henry Thomas gave evidence against them and the magistrates fined them £2 each and ordered them to pay

[1] Watch Committee minutes, 27 May, 1843 (in private hands).

8s.6d. (42½p) costs. £2.8s.6d. (£2.42½p) was a massive imposition when one considers that a good ploughboy or a 'good strong servant girl' would be paid £2.10s.0d. (£2.50p) a year, with keep. But it was not that which worried the three men so much as Rebecca's threat that their goods would be burned and their lives taken from them if they paid. So they refused, and the magistrates, with what even then was indecent haste, issued 'distress' warrants for the seizure of goods to the value of the unpaid fines and costs. In even more indecent haste, and going over the head of their Chief Constable, they swore in four special constables and sent them off on foot on the eight mile trek to Talog to execute the warrants.

But word spreads remarkably quickly in the Welsh countryside, and the specials had got no further than Blaenycoed village (a mile and a half short of Talog) when they heard the sound of horns and were suddenly surrounded by forty of fifty black-faced men wielding scythes, sticks and pitchforks. No more persuasion was needed. The four unhappy specials walked back to Carmarthen empty-handed, while the mob who had turned them back went on to nearby Trawsmawr, the home of county magistrate Captain Davies who had countersigned the warrant to give it legal effect outside the borough, and pulled down part of his boundary wall.

To their credit, and unlike some of their brother magistrates in the county, those in the borough continued to rely on their own resources and forebore to ask the government for military assistance. They resolved on a show of strength in the form of a large armed posse but, again, they cold-shouldered their 'cowardly' Chief Constable, this time by putting their men under the command of—of all people—their road surveyor, David Evans, whom they swore in as a special constable for the purpose.

During the evening of Sunday 11 June, David Evans gathered his forces in a Carmarthen buzzing with speculation and rumour to such a degree that all hope of secrecy was lost. Ten special constables, twenty-eight elderly army pensioners and the four Borough Police constables were paraded and given their orders, and all but the army pensioners (who were given truncheons) were armed with a brace of pistols each—a special issue, in line with the philosophy of the 'new police' system that its officers should carry firearms only when they were likely to face armed criminals.

It will be of interest at this point to consider the calibre of the men comprising road surveyor David Evans' posse. There were the ten non-too-willing special constables, for whom the only alternative to service was a fine; the twenty-eight Chelsea 'out-pensioners', most of whom were in their sixties and worn out by hard soldiering; and the four Borough Police constables—P.C. David Woolcock, who had served time in Carmarthen Gaol for playing a leading part in the 1831 'Reform' election riots in the town and who would shortly be sacked for drunkenness, P.C. Robert Awberry, another who would lose his job through drunkenness, P.C. Thomas Evans, yet another hard drinker, who would lose his job through cowardice, and the doyen of all Carmarthen's policemen—tough, illiterate, amiable Irishman Nicholas Martin, the only surviving founder-member of the force (of only six years' standing for all that!). He would go on to complete what in those days was an amazing twenty-five years service, while clocking up at least *forty-four* disciplinary convictions for drunkenness and indiscipline on the way. All hardly calculated to inspire the confidence of the townspeople, or, more to the point, frighten the big lady on the white horse who had made such a thorough job of Water Street gate.

The posse began to muster by the gate just after midnight and the roll was called. But of P.C. Thomas Evans there was no sign. P.C. David Woolcock was sent to find him, and he did, cowering in a shop doorway in Lammas Street. As he reported to the Watch Committee later:

> . . . he told me not to be so foolish as to go to Talog or we should be murdered. I then desired him to deliver up his pistols, which he did. I did not see him afterwards. Evans told me he was unwell.[2]

So, without the 'ailing' P.C. Thomas Evans, the posse marched off, out of the comforting glow of the Water Street gas lamps and into the darkness; up through Trevaughan, climbing high above Carmarthen and into the steep, winding lanes of the hill country, on their three hour walk to John Harries' mill at Talog, eight miles away.

John Harries seemed to be expecting them when they arrived

[2] Watch Committee minutes (in private hands).

in broad daylight at half past five in the morning. And so did the forty or so people who gathered around Talog Mill after a gun had been fired, apparently as a signal. No-one raised any objection to the seizure of Harries' furniture, which was placed on the posse's handcarts in a hushed atmosphere of the greatest foreboding. They went to Thomas Thomas' shop in the village, only to find that he had a receipt for his fine, paid the previous Saturday to avoid upset to his pregnant wife. And then they went looking for Samuel Brown at Brynmeini but, suddenly, Thomas Thomas the shopkeeper came running from behind, pleading with them that if they cared for their own safety they should return John Harries' furniture and his fine would be paid. But he was too late. There was a blast from a horn and as if from nowhere Rebecca appeared in all her regalia, mounted on her large white horse and surrounded by some four hundred black-faced men, at least a quarter of whom carried loaded shotguns.

Outnumbered ten to one, the forty-two men in the posse were quickly over-powered, searched and forced to empty their muzzle-loading pistols by firing them into the air, and then hand them over. To their credit the three regular policemen did not give up without a struggle, but the odds were overwhelming and it was soon all over. Then they were all lined up for inspection by Rebecca. She was most polite to the army pensioners, whose long and loyal service to the Crown she applauded and whose coming unarmed had, she explained, saved them from some very unpleasant consequences. To the policemen, though, she 'manifested considerable animosity'[3] and demanded to know if Parish Constable David Rees[4] and P.C. Thomas Evans were present. They were not, which, said Rebecca, was as well for them because 'had they been there their lives would have been taken away from them.'[5] It seems that P.C. Thomas Evans had known what he was about all right when he went into hiding in Lammas Street rather than come to Talog and (as he said) be murdered!

The disarmed posse was then ordered to march, and the regular and special constables received a good deal of rough-

[3] *Carmarthen Journal,* 16 June, 1843.
[4] Ibid.
[5] David Rees was a Parish Constable who was known to be infiltrating the Rebeccaites to collect the rewards then on offer. He died 30 years later at his home in Mill Dam Street, Carmarthen, at the age of eighty-two.

handling as they did so. They were marched to Trawsmawr, the home of Captain Davies, J.P., where the horrified constables were ordered to complete the destruction of the walls begun by the Rebeccaites the day before. They hesitated. Rebecca threatened to shoot them dead. They demolished the walls.

The defeat and disgrace of the party sent by the Carmarthen magistrates to overawe Rebecca was complete. They were lined up again and the ever-polite Rebecca walked down the line shaking hands with the army pensioners. 'Go to your homes,' she told them, 'and you will not be molested.' Her message to the officers of the law was delivered in a very different fashion—by a parting volley from a hundred shotguns, which hastened them on their way by showering them with a cloud of gunshot.

The disconsolate party of law enforcers shuffled off on the four mile walk back to Carmarthen, the beautiful sunshine and early morning bird song failing to penetrate their deep gloom. What were they to say when they got back? They had failed to execute the magistrates' warrants; they had been disarmed and were lucky to have their pistols back; and they had demolished the walls of a prominent county magistrate!

A gathering storm

The fury of the Carmarthen authorities now knew no bounds, as the fiasco brought ridicule from all sides. Even the ragged urchins of the town took to taunting the policemen on their beats that Becca was coming to get them, and the embarrassed army pensioners felt obliged to defend their own honour as soldiers by giving a public explanation of their part in the affair:

> *To the Editor of the Carmarthen Journal.* Sir; We, twenty-eight out-pensioners of Her Majesty's Royal Hospital, Chelsea, now resident at Carmarthen and its vicinity, present the following facts for information of the public as well as for the justice due to ourselves relative to an affair whereby our courage as veterans has been called in question.
>
> The charge of cowardice preferred against us cannot be substantiated. We feel we do not deserve it. What service could be rendered by twenty-eight decrepit individuals with no other weapons of defence other than constables' batons against such an armed number of able-bodied, active and incensed rustics?
>
> We spent the prime of life in the service of our country, we fought hard against its foes and bled in distant lands. The fact of our being

pensioners corroborates this assertion and are we now at this stage of life (most of us upwards of sixty years of age) to be branded as cowards because we did not cause ourselves in an undefended state to be slaughtered?

We trust that this will satisfy all generous minds, and any duty we owe to our Sovereign and our Country we will always perform to the utmost of our ability. GOD SAVE THE QUEEN.[6]

Quite clearly the 'civil power' was unable to cope alone, so throughout Monday 12 June clerks wrote frantically as witnesses were examined by the magistrates and letters dictated to accompany their statements to the Home Secretary. The Mayor wanted him to have the full picture as quickly as possible so that he could send troops to Carmarthen as a matter of urgency. All the paper work was completed and a light carriage was on its way towards Brecon by early evening, to connect with the earliest available mail coach for London.

Excitement and anticipation of further outrages was at fever pitch in Carmarthen already, but what happened in the hill country on Wednesday 14 June sent another express heading in the direction of London with an even more urgent appeal for troops. Somewhere up there, in Trelech, Talog, Blaenycoed or Cynwyl Elfed, Rebecca called a meeting of the farmers of the Hundred of Elfed. And when Rebecca called there were few who did not answer. The number of farmers who attended was estimated by magistrate Lloyd Davies to be about two thousand, but it would more likely have been in the hundreds since there were only just over four hundred farmers in the whole area. At all events, the message from the meeting was clear enough: the farmers unanimously adopted a resolution demanding that the Newcastle Turnpike Trust produce a detailed financial statement covering the previous eighteen years. If they found it 'fair and correct' and were satisfied that the tolls had been 'fairly laid out on the roads', all well and good, and the Water Street gate would not be interfered with again. In fact if all this were satisfactory and if in addition the Water Street tolls were reduced, Rebecca and every farmer in the parishes represented at the meeting would add their strength to that of the forces of law and order to put down the disturbances.

But if not, the Water Street gate would be immediately

[6] *Carmarthen Journal,* 23 June, 1843.

smashed and the toll house finally reduced to ruins. Bad enough news in itself, but the orders issued to the meeting hard on the heels of that resolution really put fear into the hearts of the authorities in Carmarthen: all male householders of the Hundred of Elfed were to assemble at the Plough and Harrow public house, two miles outside Carmarthen, at eleven o'clock next Monday morning, 19 June, to march on Carmarthen for the purpose of presenting their demands to the Mayor and magistrates. Whether rich or poor, *all* must attend; in case of illness a substitute must be sent, or the house and barns of the absentee would be burned; and all those with horses must be mounted. This was clearly to be Rebecca's biggest and most open demonstration so far of the forces at her command and her determination to see that she had her way.

In their deliberations and demands to the authorities, the farmers covered the whole range of their grievances, including, of course, the Poor Law, on which:

> It was proposed to pull down and destroy the [Carmarthen] workhouse. The bias in the minds of all present seemed to be to raze it to the ground in the month of August. That question was, however, adjourned to their next meeting.[7]

In this connection, the events of Monday 19 June 1843 were to demonstrate yet again the gap that opens up between intention and execution when it comes to controlling highly emotional popular demonstrations.

The meeting ended, the farmers left for home, and before that night was out the Newcastle Trust, whose affairs had dominated the discussions, had lost two more gates, both on roads out of Newcastle Emlyn (one on the Carmarthen side of the town and one at Felindre Siencyn on the road to Llandysul) . . . and both within an hour's ride of Trelech and Talog. And over the next succeeding three nights the trust would lose four more, on the Cardigan Road and at Bwlch y Clawdd and Pont Tyweli.

The meeting had decided that two of its members should take its resolutions to a Newcastle Emlyn attorney, Edward Crompton Lloyd Hall, to seek his advice on the legal implications of their cause and to have their grievances and demands put in legal form. It was clear from what had been said at the meeting

[7] *Carmarthen Journal,* 16 June, 1843.

that the majority of the farmers had a great deal of respect for him and considerable confidence in his judgement, and the following afternoon not two but twenty farmers arrived at his home. Edward Crompton Lloyd Hall's reaction was to sit down and write a letter to the Home Secretary as soon as his visitors had gone:

> On my return home this afternoon [15th June, 1843] I found a deputation of about twenty farmers, residing in six or seven different parishes in this neighbourhood, waiting to consult me on ye steps I should deem it most advisable for them and those whom they represented to pursue in consequence of a number of letters having been sent by or in ye name of ye organised band known as Rebecca and her daughters, commanding them to appear at Carmarthen on Monday next, the 19th of June, with their servants and under-tenants, on pain of having their houses pulled down if they dare to absent themselves.
>
> The men appeared quite terrified at ye threat, and with reason, as 'Rebecca' is almost nightly at work pulling down ye turnpike houses, and one house belonging I believe to Mr. Saunders Davies, M.P. with all ye furniture was burnt to ye ground three or four nights ago in consequence of ye tenant having done something to give offence to Rebecca.[8]

It was not that Lloyd Hall was unsympathetic to their cause. His flirtation with radical politics was well enough known and he was on that account not altogether popular among his fellow landowners, particularly in view of his harassment of inefficient magistrates, with whom he frequently clashed when defending in the lower courts. But he knew his public duty when he saw it. Seeing the disintegration of society going on around him he added his own assessment of the situation, summarising the true and sorry nature of the disturbances with a rare insight, and cautioning those in London that:

> If Her Majesty's Ministers think there is nothing more in these disturbances than a mere local impatience of Turnpike Tolls, they are deceived.
>
> To judge of ye Welsh and their feelings and modes of thought and action by anything with which an Englishman is acquainted would only lead to error. That they have had great local injustices in many things is too apparent, and unfortunately there is no middle class in

[8] Letter to Home Secretary, 15 June, 1843: Public Record Office, File HO 45/454.

the country districts to bind society together. Ye few gentlemen resident here are widely scattered, their homes being in but few instances less than four miles from each others. Ye consequence is that each amongst his own tenantry is a petty prince, whose word, be it right or wrong, has hitherto been law; and there being hardly any distinction between ye farmers and their labourers, and their language isolating them from ye rest of ye Kingdom, they have scarcely emerged from ye state of comparative barbarism and poverty induced by ye internal troubles of this part of ye country.

This being ye case, and ye unfortunate measures of ye Government having fallen upon us with a severity unknown to ye rest of England [sic], ye farmers are pinched in their means, and as ye Turnpike tolls are most extraordinarily heavy and ye gates placed upon ye most catching system throughout this country, they naturally endeavour to relieve themselves of that burden. There being a custom in this part of ye country called carrying 'Ceffil prens' (derived from ye old Welsh law abolished by ye introduction of ye English law in ye latter part of ye reign of Henry ye 8th), ye mode of getting rid of such a grievance by nocturnal violence is perfectly familiar to their minds.

As to getting evidence against them, that is hopeless. In ye best of times it is difficult to make a Welshman speak ye truth, either with or without an oath, no doubt attributable to ye curious provisions of ye old Welsh laws, traditionary reminiscences of which still remain. Ye offer of a reward, however great, has I believe never been known to produce any effect in this country.

If this state of things is not repressed very shortly, ye efforts of Rebecca will, I have no doubt, be directed to other matters; for ye dissatisfaction with ye mode of administering justice and ye laying on of taxation of all kinds is such throughout ye whole of this part of ye country that it is quite palpable they only want leaders to effect a thorough revolution.

The people have thus discovered their immense power without knowing how to use it constitutionally.[9]

Being the shrewd man that he was, Lloyd Hall held his letter back for nine days, until 24 June, endorsing it with the words 'Copy of a letter written but not sent to ye Home Office till ye 24th, lest it should be ye cause of irritating ye country people if they should find I had been ye means of bringing down soldiery.'

Lloyd Hall's letter was the first of a long series with which he bombarded the Home Secretary during the remainder of the

[9] Author's italics.

summer. None of them received even the courtesy of an acknowledgement; and Lloyd Hall would undoubtedly have written fewer of them had he known that they were merely serving to reinforce the suspicion of some people that he was the real brain behind the Rebecca Riots! As it was he was invited—nay commanded—by Rebecca to take part in an attack on the Newcastle Trust's gates. He received a letter in Welsh telling him to be there with all his servants, armed with guns, swords, mattocks and pickaxes—or to take the (unspecified) consequences. His reply, an open letter published the day after the invasion of Carmarthen, was intended to leave no doubt whatever of his attitude to Rebecca's style of doing things:

> Welshmen; You have sent me a letter *commanding* me to appear on Wednesday night at Blaennant Lane armed and disguised. That your object is to obtain redress for some of the grievances with which you are oppressed is evident. But this is not the way to obtain such redress. Do you think I can countenance or join your riotous proceedings? I tell you No. And what is more, though I have fought, am fighting, and will continue to fight your battles until I can obtain perfect justice and political regeneration for you and your children, I am and will always be the first man to keep the Queen's peace and prevent any rioting or disturbance.
>
> Why will you hinder me from fighting your battles in the only way in which we can be successful, and by your violence and absurdity, which can do no good, turn me from a friend to an enemy? Your conduct is childish and absurd and not like men who have great objects to attain. Why will you exhibit folly when wisdom is required? A hundredth part of your strength properly applied will do more for you, and without risk, than a thousand times your power wasted in the absurdities you have lately indulged in. Be guided by me. Do what I tell you and you must be victorious in the end. If you do, peace and prosperity will be sure to return to you. If you do not, I shall leave you to enjoy the results of your ignorance and folly.[10]

But although he disobeyed Rebecca's command, Lloyd Hall could not resist going quietly along that night with some of his servants and following at a distance the several hundred strong body of Rebeccaites as they marched around the town of Newcastle Emlyn, occupying it for hours without challenge and destroying its five gates and their toll houses. The military style and

[10] *Rebecca and Her Daughters,* by H. Tobit Evans, 1910.

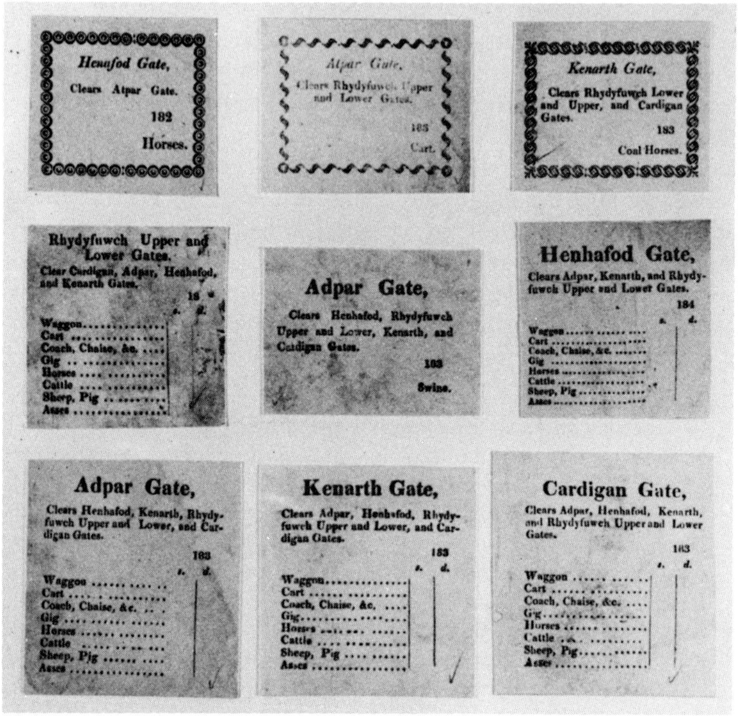

Toll tickets of the Cardigan Trust *(Nat. Library of Wales)*

precision of their progress impressed him most forcibly as he observed that:

> Three men went first armed with guns. Then an advanced guard (also with guns) of from fifteen to twenty. Then ye main body, some with guns, ye rest with axes, saws and in short all sorts of weapons, and ye rear was brought up with an afterguard of from twenty to twenty-five armed with guns. They took up their positions in ye order of march, ye advance and rearguards forming across ye road. The words of command were all given in English, such as 'Stop', 'Go on', 'Half form in order', in a fine manly voice.[11]

Reporting all this and more in detail to the Home Office, Lloyd Hall concluded with the biting comment that '. . . no

[11] Letter dated 22 June, 1843, E. C. Lloyd Hall to Home Office: Public Record Office, File HO 45/454.

magistrates as far as I can learn took any steps towards keeping ye peace.'

I have no force at my disposal

By letter, public notices pinned to chapel doors, horse messenger, and even, it was said, announcements from church and chapel pulpits, Rebecca's orders for the Plough and Harrow rendezvous were spread through the parishes, and word of what was brewing in the hills reached the Mayor of Carmarthen. His request for troops following the Talog ambush had already been met by the despatch of a troop of the 4th Light Dragoons from Cardiff, but they had still not arrived when information was received about the intended march on the town which prompted another letter from the Mayor to the Home Secretary. The Rebeccaites, he told him:

> . . . have within the last two or three days held meetings, most numerously attended, at which it was determined—for the purpose of intimidating the Magistrates by a display of physical strength and inducing them to return the fines which had been paid for refusing payment of toll at the Water Street Gate—to enter the town on Monday next at noon to the number of many thousands. I have no force at my disposal adequate to preserve the peace unless the promised cavalry arrive here tomorrow [Sunday 18th June].
>
> The country in which the Military force will have to act is in many parts hilly and much covered with wood and with high fences, which would render it rather impracticable for Cavalry to act unless assisted by Infantry, and I beg leave most respectfully to submit to you the expediency of sending down immediately a company of Infantry as well, the parties whose illegal proceedings we have to suppress being very formidable from their armed number and extensive organisation.[12]

It was indeed a 'very formidable and extensive organisation' that prepared for the gathering at the Plough and Harrow at eleven o'clock on Monday 19 June, 1843. But it was not only Rebecca that the Carmarthen authorities had cause to fear. In their own town was a body of people who had even more to complain of in terms of poverty and harsh living conditions and who had a tradition of violence going back a lot further than Rebecca's. The 'Carmarthen Mob', at least, would make a lively day of it.

[12] Letter to Home Secretary, Saturday 17 June, 1843: Public Record Office, File No. 45/454.

Chapter Four

INVASION

Monday came—sunny, still and hot—and as the horns sounded the call through deep, narrow valleys, the countrypeople gathered in their hundreds in the lanes and fields around the Plough and Harrow. Rebecca was there in a fantastic horsehair wig of long, golden ringlets and mounted on her large white horse in the centre of some three hundred other horsemen.

The authorities never did learn the name of that commanding figure who sat aloof as her subordinates marshalled her children into some kind of order. Nor did anyone recognise her among those captured that day or later, which was itself eloquent testimony to the reign of fear that so effectively deterred would-be informers. The tradition that she was a Trelech farmer named Michael Bowen of Cwmlleiniogau Isaf has gained popular acceptance, but that 'tradition' was not born until fifty years later, in 1893, when a local historian claimed that he had recognised him as he rode through the streets of Carmarthen. As a boy of fifteen, he wrote,[1] he had stood among the crowds of onlookers as the horsemen passed, and Rebecca, whom he recognised as Michael Bowen, winked at him. That Michael Bowen was in the procession seems not to be in doubt because his wife never forgot how pale and shaken he looked when he returned home that day after walking the ten miles without his horse. Whether he was Rebecca is another matter. If a wink from a man with a blackened face under a large horsehair wig fashioned into ringlets can be taken as evidence of identification, so be it. But another account, written by the Vicar of Newchurch—the heart of this particular Rebecca country—tells another story.[2] In 1910, an old man named Thomas, the 'gaffer' on the Green Park estate, told the Rev. T. M. Morgan that he had taken part in the attack on Water Street gate and in the march on Carmarthen,

[1] Alcwyn Evans, MS 12368.E., National Library of Wales.

[2] *The History and Antiquities of the Parish of Newchurch* by the Rev. T. M. Morgan, Vicar, 1910.

and that Rebecca and Charlotte were both of the Parish of Newchurch. They were, he said, the Rees brothers of Rhydymarchog farm—only a mile from Bwlch Newydd Chapel where Rebecca's warning about the consequences of paying toll at Water Street had been pinned to the door. The Rees family had moved there from Cardiganshire shortly before, to remain at Rhydymarchog for about two years, and, according to gaffer Thomas, they had brought with them three long trumpets such as were used in Cardiganshire to call in the harvesters. It was these, he said, that had been heard at Water Street gate, before the ambushes at Blaenycoed and Talog, and were now calling the countrypeople to the Plough and Harrow rendezvous—all within five miles of Rhydymarchog farm. Furthermore, Captain Davies, J.P., whose boundary wall around Trawsmawr had been demolished by the police under Rebecca's orders, was the Rees' neighbour—just three hundred and fifty yards away.

Neither the 1841 Census nor that of 1851 shows a Rees family at Rhydymarchog, but the Tithe Roll of 1844 does,[3] which supports Thomas' story of their short stay and adds credibility to his identification of the brothers as the leaders.

Lovers of justice are we all

The crowd around the Plough and Harrow swelled to about two thousand—men, women, boys and girls—and only the leaders wore Rebecca's customary apparel. Rebecca looked behind her, waved her hand in the air, and her army marched for Carmarthen, behind a band of music and a huge banner proclaiming:

'CYFIAWNDER A CHARWYR CYFIAWNDER
YDYM NI OLL'
('Justice, and lovers of justice are we all')

with a profusion of other banners scattered through the procession and bearing such inscriptions as 'RHYDDID A GWELL LLUNIAETH' (Freedom and better food) and 'TOLL RYDD A RHYDDID' (Free tolls and Freedom).

It was pure carnival: the band was playing, a hot sun was shining in a blue and cloudless sky, children ran about laughing and screaming in and out of their mothers' long and flowing

[3] Dyfed Archive Services, Carmarthen.

skirts. The whole crowd was infected by an atmosphere of fun and a tingle of anticipation which seemed to banish all the hardship, fear and intimidation that had brought them there—just as the presence of Rebecca and her mounted entourage, splendid and awe-inspiring in their dress and equipage, seemed to banish any trepidation they might have felt at the prospect of a confrontation with the town authorities and the soldiers that were rumoured to be there. Truly, as Edward Crompton Lloyd Hall had told the Home Secretary, the people had discovered their immense power.

The police, still without the troops for which the magistrates had been pleading for several days, were out early that morning, they and the special constables having been ordered by the Mayor to assemble at the Guildhall at eight o'clock. Chief Constable John Pugh was there with his four-man borough force, but the magistrates' orders to them were to lie low and allow the procession to pass through the town if no breach of the peace were occasioned.

The town magistrates were joined by a large number of their county colleagues two of whom, Captain Evans of Pantycendi and J. Lloyd Davies of Blaendyffryn, actually went up the road to meet Rebecca and her followers near the Plough and Harrow to make a last minute plea to them to think again. The sight of such a huge number appalled them and the temper of the crowd, in which voices could be heard calling for them to be murdered, put them in considerable physical danger. But though they failed to persuade them to desist, they did at least persuade them to leave their firearms behind and take only their sticks and bludgeons. There would undoubtedly have been a different story to tell of that day had the Rebeccaites not stacked their one hundred and fifty shotguns in a barn near the Plough and Harrow before heading for Carmarthen.

The streets of the town were by now crowded with townspeople and visitors from the surrounding country, and it did not go unnoticed that the familiar elements of the 'Carmarthen Mob'—the coraclemen and other 'idlers of the town'—were not only on the streets but actually streaming out of town to meet and join the procession, several of them jumping onto horses to sit behind their riders. All the shops and business premises were closed and the whole town held its breath as the faint sounds of the harvesting horns carried over the clear air from the hills above Trevaughan.

And then, at half past noon, the massive banner came into sight around the bend up by Fountain Hall, leading the band of music, the mounted leaders and their huge and noisy following down through the hated Water Street gate.

Carmarthen was an ancient town of very narrow streets and nothing had ever been seen there like the press of people—marchers and spectators—that now squeezed through them on their circuitous march. Down Water Street, into Goose Street and up Picton Terrace they went; around General Picton's monument and back, down Lammas Street, into Blue Street and along the quay, to climb Castle Hill to Spilman Street and Saint Peter's Church. Here they seemed to hesitate, as if unsure what they were doing in Carmarthen at all. One way (Little Water Street) led to the workhouse. The other (King Street) led to the Guildhall, where any representations to the waiting magistrates would have to be made.

It was King Street they chose, and as Rebecca and her vanguard rode into a tightly packed Guildhall Square loud cheering broke out, but such was the struggle to pass through—made no easier by the pressure of two or three thousand people in the far-stretched procession behind—that more confusion ensued. There should, according to all the rumours, have been troops in town and everyone was keyed up for the confrontation. But there were none. There weren't even any policemen in sight, and the expected confrontation had evaporated, to provide an anti-climax for which the leadership had not bargained. And in the confusion, the main object of the whole affair was forgotten and the list of grievances and demands was not presented to the magistrates who were waiting somewhere behind the crowd to receive it.

It was then that the leadership passed from Rebecca to the 'Carmarthen Mob'. The fact that at least a hundred 'idle townspeople' were already loitering about the workhouse on Penlan Hill and that no attempt was made to seek out the magistrates before the procession made its unexpected turn from Guildhall Square into Red Street, directly towards the workhouse, puts this beyond doubt.

To the Bastille

The countrypeople had plenty of cause to fear banishment to the Union workhouse far away in Carmarthen when utter desperation drove them 'on the parish', but the townspeople had that grey and forbidding edifice right on their doorstep, ever before their eyes, and they despised it with all the passion with which the revolutionary Parisians had despised their Bastille.

Carmarthen's workhouse was administered by the Carmarthen Union, a grouping of parishes brought about by the Poor Law Act of 1834 to improve the administration of the 'Poor Rate'. The system which the unions had replaced had become an expensive shambles under the strain imposed by the tremendous social changes of the late eighteenth and early nineteenth centuries. Things had reached the state where able-bodied men and their families were thrown onto parish relief in such numbers as to swamp a system designed only to provide for the sick and the aged.

How could the parishes be relieved of the able-bodied poor? Simply, so the theory of the new Poor Law said, by ending their parish relief (for which, at least, the community had got some

The men's ward of a typical workhouse *(Illus. London News)*

Carmarthen Workhouse: iron grill for grading rocks. Each able-bodied pauper's daily quota of 1½ tons had to be broken up small enough to pass through the apertures. *(Carmarthen Museum)*

useful work out of them, on hedging and road-mending for example) and giving relief to them and their families only in the workhouses, where they would repay it in honest toil. As a deterrent to poverty it was thoroughly effective; husband and wife were separated within the workhouse, tobacco and alcohol were banned, the diet was sufficient but basic, the regime prison-like, and the 'honest toil' for the able-bodied men consisted of breaking stones—a daily quota of fifteen bushels, or about one and a half tons! Refusal to work on the stone-breaking brought the offending pauper before the magistrates and onto the tread-wheel in the gaol for a month or two, and that such cases were common is shown by a comment in the *Carmarthen Journal* (under the heading 'Refractory Paupers') that:

> The germs of incipient rebellion and treason on a small scale would appear to lurk in the workhouse of the Carmarthen Union. Since the Christmas holidays, when the inmates rejoiced in the 'seasonable liberalities' which the press—not the paupers!—boast of everywhere, there has been nothing but risings and mutinies against the stonebreaking. Within the last week about half a dozen paupers were committed to prison for refusing to break them.

Small wonder that none but the most desperate sought relief within the walls of that workhouse, and it is not surprising either that it soon acquired all the infamy of the Bastille. And now there was a chance to do something about it.

By the time the procession reached the workhouse there were several hundred ahead of Rebecca and they attacked the stout wooden gates with their fists demanding admittance, which the master Ray Evans at first refused:

> . . . but when the master saw the door on the point of giving way he opened it as he knew it would be forced in less than a minute. Hundreds of rioters immediately entered the yard and soon found their way into the house by breaking every lock which impeded their progress.
>
> Some of them laid hold of Mrs. Evans, the Matron, by the arms and pushed her against the wall and ordered her to deliver the keys of the house or she would be a dead woman in an instant, and the workhouse children screamed out in a most piteous manner 'Oh dear mistress; don't kill our dear mistress.'
>
> Several of the others attacked the master and wrenched two keys from his hand and one of them knocked him down. Some of them proceeded to the men's yard, ordered them out of the place and

attempted to enter their bedroom, where they were resolutely opposed, the men saying it was out of their power to better their circumstances, and they succeeded in stopping the rioters entering their own bedroom.

They then ordered the children out of the place. When Mrs. Evans remonstrated with them and said 'Where do you expect the poor children to go, they have no homes in the world?' they answered 'We'll find them a home' and all the children and women were turned out into the road, where a poor woman of this town was severely hurt.

Others of the rioters had proceeded direct upstairs into the children's bedroom, being led by a woman who had lately been discharged from the workhouse,[4] and immediately commenced throwing the beds, blankets and pillows out through the windows into the yard. In fact the whole place was now in their possession. They had forced their way into the bedroom and were dancing on top of the tables and beating them with their staffs in a furious manner.

We have no doubt that had it not been for the special intervention of Providence the whole place would have been fired or razed to the ground in a very short time.[5]

'The special intervention of Providence' came in the form of Major Parlby's troop of the 4th Light Dragoons, who were proceeding towards Carmarthen at a walk, climbing the hill from Pontardulais eighteen miles away at the moment that Rebecca led her followers through the Water Street gate. The dragoons were approaching Cross Hands when a breathless messenger on a foam-flecked horse came riding hard towards them. Major Parlby reined his horse and brought his troop to a halt. The message was that Carmarthen was being invaded by thousands of insurrectionists. The order was given and the 4th Light Dragoons began what must have been the longest gallop in their history—an incredible dash of fourteen miles in an hour and ten minutes under a blazing sun, up and down the sides of several steep valleys, a dash that caused two of the troop's horses to drop dead of exhaustion when they arrived in Carmarthen.

They crossed the town bridge at a furious pace and galloped up Castle Hill into Spilman Street, drawing rein by the Ivy Bush

[4] Frances Evans, a servant girl, who had been discharged from the workhouse after giving birth to an illegitimate child. She lived and worked at Cilgwyn Uchaf, a mile from Bwlch Newydd.

[5] *Carmarthen Journal,* 23 June, 1843.

The 4th Light Dragoons, pausing for refreshment on the march.
(Regimental Museum, Queen's Own Royal Irish Hussars)

Hotel, where a borough magistrate, Thomas Charles Morris, already mounted on his own horse, awaited them. He paused only to tell Major Parlby that the workhouse was under attack before wheeling his horse to take the lead and with a wave of his arm taking them off at the gallop towards the field of action.

Meanwhile, Borough Councillor James Morse had arrived at the workhouse amid the wild rampaging of the mob and, climbing to a bedroom window, he called on them in a loud voice to desist. Incredibly, many of them did—enough at least to give him a hearing as:

> . . . he pointed out that their present unjustifiable conduct would only bring upon them the consequent punishment arising from offending against the law of the land, and that once the Riot Act was read their lives would not be safe. He therefore entreated them to return to their respective homes.[6]

While this was going on, most of the rioters were continuing their work of destruction and were engaged in furious fighting with the borough policemen and special constables, who had been brought up by the Mayor and his fellow magistrates. But the 'respectable portion of the multitude' at least heard

[6] *Carmarthen Journal,* 23 June, 1843.

Councillor Morse out, gave him three cheers and turned their horses' heads towards the workhouse gates to leave what had become a scene of mindless destruction and a travesty of all that Rebecca was supposed to stand for. They were too late.

The dragoons were already charging at full tilt up Penlan Hill, sabres flashing in the brilliant sunlight, in the first full-scale charge in their regiment's history. Their next would be with the Light Brigade at Balaclava![7] This was what a man joined the cavalry for. The charge, with all its blood-rousing exhilaration that drove out every thought and every object save the thrill of the gallop and the sight of the enemy. It was a thrill that had already communicated itself to Magistrate Morris who, entering fully into his unaccustomed role, earned a stern rebuke from Major Parlby by waving his top hat in the air and shouting 'Slash away, slash away!'

The mob outside the workhouse heard the thunder of the horses' hooves on the earthen surface of the road, saw its whole width filled with charging cavalry and then fled in all directions. But the dragoons crashed into them, felling a number with sabre cuts and trampling others under their horses' hooves in a melée that caused chaos in the courtyard, where men, women, children and horses were packed in an inextricable, struggling and panic-stricken mass. The dragoons immediately divided into two bodies, one going off in pursuit of those fleeing through the cornfields and the other surrounding the workhouse walls to contain the unfortunates penned inside.

The flight of those not confined in the yard reminded the *Carmarthen Journal* reporter on the spot of nothing less than the flight of the French from the field of Waterloo—hardly surprising in view of the almost poetic touch given to the occasion by the fact that the cavalry had charged to Penlan Hill up Waterloo Terrace! '*Sauve qui peut* [save himself who can] was the order of the day', he wrote, while flattened fields of ripening corn, tattered hedges hung with shreds of torn clothing, dozens of riderless horses wandering aimlessly about never to be claimed by their owners, a litter of abandoned sticks, bludgeons and

[7] Major Parlby would be at Balaclava too, and take part in the charge of the Light Brigade. By then he was a Colonel. In the aftermath of that disastrous charge and following the return of Lord Cardigan to England, William Parlby was promoted to Brigadier to take command of the remnants of Cardigan's Light Brigade, which included his old regiment, the 4th Light Dragoons.

banners, and scattered groups of crying women and children and dazed old men, bore stark witness to the scale of a disaster that was to end for good Rebecca's interest in the town of Carmarthen. And when those gathered up by the dragoons outside were added to the eighty or so trapped in the workhouse yard, some one hundred prisoners shuffled miserably into line for inspection by those who had witnessed the attack on Water Street gate and the ambushes at Blaenycoed and Talog.

The most prominent capture was Talog miller John Harries who, to add to his problems over his unpaid toll and his all-too-evident part in the attack on the workhouse, was identified as one who had spread Rebecca's call to take part in the invasion. He was proved to have delivered letters and indeed to have been the author of one of them, and the parish clerk of Abernant told how Harries had obliged him under threat to read out Rebecca's letter from the altar steps with the parish notices after Divine Service on the day before the march on Carmarthen. And as if that were not enough, John Harries and four others were identified as having taken part in the Talog ambush.

The magistrates wasted no time in setting the machinery of justice in motion. They set up a court on the spot (in the workhouse schoolroom) and the prisoners trooped through one by one in a procession that occupied the rest of the day. John Harries and the other four were committed in custody for trial at the next Carmarthenshire Assizes, but so pathetic were the pleas of most of the rest—their stories of threats and intimidation and their evident unfitness for the real work of Rebecca—that the magistrates released them on condition that they should appear at the Assizes 'should an indictment be laid'. The vast majority heard no more of the matter.

Thus, in the eyes of the magistrates at least, was Carmarthen's firm stand against Rebecca vindicated, and they were unstinting in their praise of the contribution of Her Majesty's 4th Light Dragoons. From Mayor Edmund Hill Stacey to the Home Secretary, with a copy to Major William Parlby:

> Sir; I have the honour . . . to inform you that the Cavalry arrived just in time to prevent the destruction of the workhouse. This they did in a most spirited yet temperate and judicious manner. The mob amounted to between four and five thousand who were in a few

An officer of the 4th Light Dragoons (*National Army Museum*)

minutes dislodged from and about the premises and fled with all the haste terror could add to their legs, leaving prisoners to the amount of nearly one hundred in the hands of this gallant troop.

My reason for troubling you with this is to show to the Government that by active endeavours on the part of the Magistrates of the County, backed by the Military power which will be at their disposal, this insurrectionary spirit can be crushed, if not annihilated.[8]

The mayor's optimism can be excused, but he and his fellow magistrates in Carmarthenshire were to have another think coming. Yet the note of relief was genuine enough and was echoed throughout the town. This from Major Parlby in reply:

Gentlemen; I had the pleasure of reading to my troop on parade this evening your letter expressing your approbation of their conduct yesterday. We beg to return to you our sincere thanks for the flattering manner in which you have acknowledged our services. I have the honour to be, Gentlemen, Your most obedient Servant, W. Parlby, Major, 4th Light Dragoons.[9]

But there was still a large blot on the Carmarthen escutcheon, and the mayor and magistrates wasted no time in removing it. At a meeting of the Watch Committee in the Guildhall on Thursday 6 July, Chief Constable John Pugh was dismissed for cowardice, though at the same time 'the conduct of the other police officers was overlooked on the grounds of their not having an efficient person to lead and direct them.' As the members of the Watch Committee explained, 'as the ratepayers were heavily taxed they had the right to insist that an efficient force be established.'[10]

Pugh had been conspicuous by his absence from much of the rioting, though he was in action in the workhouse yard arresting a number of people pointed out to him by the magistrates. He was assaulted by several of the rioters, including David Thomas, a twenty year old farmer and member of Rebecca's 'Band of music'—who hammered Pugh with his bassoon! But he had not done enough, and anyway someone had to be sacrificed to assuage the anger of the respectable people of the town, so he

[8] Letter from the Mayor of Carmarthen to the Home Secretary, 20 June, 1843; Public Record Office, File HO 45/454.

[9] Printed in the *Carmarthen Journal,* 23 June, 1843.

[10] *Carmarthen Journal,* 7 July, 1843.

ceased to act forthwith. None other than Constable Nicholas Martin was selected to act as Chief Constable during the interval before a successor was found. It was a brief moment of glory for this tough, illiterate, hard-drinking but immensely popular Irishman—he of the forty four disciplinary convictions for drunkenness, absence from duty, disobedience and insubordination![11]

Nothing to lose but their lives

As the Carmarthen authorities were congratulating themselves on their victory over Rebecca, the doings of the people of west Wales became for the first time the subject of an editorial in *The Times* of London.[12] And a scathing one it was:

> The Welsh special constable is a timorous animal, more so it would appear than the Welsh rioters.[13] The last ten or twelve years have furnished the world with two or three examples of what these preservers of the peace are worth . . . and it has long been plain that the ordinary police force of the country was absolutely incompetent to deal with the skilful and daring 'Rebecca'.
>
> It was the duty of the Government at once to vindicate the efficiency of the law; at once to crush such an open and triumphal defiance of all authority. Whatever was necessary for this purpose ought to have been done at once. That and no less. *Nothing however was even attempted.* At last came what might have been thought a climax . . .

The editorial went on to describe the attack on Water Street gate and the ambush of the police and army pensioners at Talog, concluding that:

> They thought themselves lucky to get off with whole skins. This final and complete victory over the majesty of Welsh law truly alarmed the magistrates and might have been expected to infuse some life into the Government. After a few days they [the Carmarthen authorities] heard from the Home Office that a force

[11] So popular was Martin that when he was dismissed in 1840 (after only four years service) for being drunk on duty, a petition signed by well over a hundred 'respectable inhabitants of the town' persuaded the Watch Committee to reinstate him.

[12] *The Times,* 22 June, 1843.

[13] In the area of south west Wales so far affected, none of the counties and only one town (Carmarthen) had police forces of the pattern of the London Metropolitan Police Force, which the government was trying to encourage everywhere. The old parish and 'Special' constable system prevailed elsewhere.

was 'coming' . . . and from the countryside that a mob of some thousand men was to parade Carmarthen on Monday the 19th 'as a demonstration'.

The mob entered the town and proclaimed their grievances, comprising inter alia of turnpike gates, tithes, the poor law, church rates and high rents. They then set to work by pulling down the workhouse.

Fortune has played our cards for us better than Sir James Graham [the Home Secretary] and we hope that this discomfiture and the presence of the 4th Dragoons will effectively stop Miss Becca's gambols for some time.

Outbreaks of this kind sometimes assume one pretext, sometimes another, but the cause which lies at the bottom is usually physical hardship. Men who have nothing to lose by disorder but their lives, and whose lives are not comfortable enough to be worth much forethought. These are the combustibles on which rebellion and tumult live. Oppression or injustice is the spark which fires them. Without entering here into a disquisition upon the Poor Law we must beg to observe that as the law stood prominent among the catalogue of their grievances, so their most daring and—judging from the multitude of their forces—their most popular act has been the destruction of the Union workhouse.

What will be the result in Carmarthenshire and Glamorganshire? What will be the result when these thousands of men already disposed enough to find fault with the Poor Law *are brought under its actual operation?* When the ranks of Becca are recruited from multitudes driven from their avocations by the ebbing of commercial prosperity and indignant of the provision which the law offers for their support, will the Home Secretary secure the country from the outrages of these new rebels by more [poor] relief or by fresh troops of cavalry?

It is in no triumphal or hostile, or even reproachful spirit that we ask these questions. We ask them before the evil arrives in order that those upon whom the task lies may be prepared with an answer, and whatever that answer is, whether conciliation or force, may they exhibit it soon and not leave South Wales a prey to that anarchical tyranny to which they have almost abandoned Carmarthen!

Thus spoke The Thunderer. *And when The Thunderer spoke, governments listened.*

Chapter Five

IF THE LAW IS VIOLATED . . .

Home Office, London, Monday 19th June, 1843.

To Lord Fitzroy Somerset, Military Secretary to the Commander in Chief, War Office, London: My Lord, I am directed by Sir James Graham [the Home Secretary] to request that you move the Duke of Wellington to give directions that a company of Infantry may immediately proceed to Carmarthen and that Colonel Love may be instructed to repair to Carmarthen to take charge of the troops employed in Carmarthen, Cardigan and Pembrokeshire, and to communicate with the magistrates upon all matters relating to the public peace on which they may wish to consult him. I have the honour to be, my Lord, &c.[1]

Thus, at the very moment that Rebecca's hosts were being scattered through the cornfields on Penlan Hill by the sabres of Her Majesty's 4th Light Dragoons, did the government acknowledge the failure of civil power to contain the Rebecca Riots and the need for firm and decisive action by the military. And thus was fifty-four year old Colonel James Frederick Love, Knight of the Hanoverian Order and holder of the Waterloo Medal, launched on a new experience, something which neither he nor those who knew him would have thought possible after almost forty years of such soldiering as he had seen.

He had fought and bled on every major field of battle seen by the British army from Corunna to Waterloo and he was an infantryman through and through. He had been an officer of the élite Light Division—the pride of the army—in the days when its individuality, dash and skill at arms had played such a crucial part in the rout of Napoleon's armies. And his reputation as a leader of them was formidable indeed. In Spain under Sir John Moore he had shared in the rigours of the retreat to Corunna, fighting the rearguard action and keeping his face to the enemy throughout the retreat until the last of the army had embarked. He had fought at Busaco and Fuentes D'Onoro. He had been at

[1] Public Record Office, File HO 41/17.

James Frederick Love, K.H., in later years, when he was a Major General.
(The Crown Estates Commissioners)

the head of the light infantry stormers in the bloody and costly assault on the fortress of Ciudad Rodrigo, an affair of the bayonet in which the light infantrymen climbed the scaling ladders under murderous fire with rifles unloaded, having been told by their commander that 'If we do not do the business with the bayonet we shall not be able to do it at all.'

He had been shipped across the Atlantic to fight the Americans in the ill-fated seaborne attack on New Orleans, where, coming up against sharpshooters as skilled as his own light infantry—General Andrew Jackson's Tennessee mountainmen—he had had two horses killed under him and had been carried wounded from the field. Given immediate promotion to Major he had been shipped back again to Europe in time to rejoin the 52nd Regiment of Light Infantry to share in its finest hour, under Wellington at Waterloo. The 52nd, who had put the seal on the rout of Napoleon's Imperial Guard when their commander, acting without orders but in the true tradition of light infantry unorthodoxy and opportunism, had suddenly wheeled his regiment out of the line to face the flank of the Imperial Guard and to pour into it their own special brand of rapid and deadly accurate fire. And Major James Frederick Love had survived four more dangerous wounds in the service of his King and Country.

What great days they had been under Wellington all those years ago; and with the 52nd—'a regiment never surpassed in arms since arms were first borne by men.'[2] But he was to fight again for Wellington. This time against what seemed to be his country's new enemy . . . *its own people.* His battles with them over the past twelve years or so had made him familiar enough with that kind of warfare. There was, he had learned, nothing like the cold steel of the bayonet and a volley by disciplined ranks of redcoats to thin a riotous mob. He had learned it back in 1831 when the country had been racked by riots and seemed to face revolution in the course of attempts to persuade Parliament to allow a modest extension of the vote. By then the country had a Prime Minister who was probably the best proof ever of the adage that great soldiers rarely make good politicians . . . his old chief, the Duke of Wellington himself. He had very firm ideas when it came to talk of democracy: 'I have never read or heard of

[2] *History of the War in the Peninsula,* Sir W. Napier, 1834-40.

any measure,' he had told the House of Lords, 'which in any degree satisfies my mind that the state of the representation in Parliament can be improved. As long as I hold any station in the government of the country I shall always feel it my duty to resist such measures when proposed.'[3]

No wonder that in a country whose people were straining at the bonds of an electoral system which allowed the vote to only about one in thirty of them and the parliamentary seats only to the powerful men of land and property, the Great Duke should again stand in need of his army.

Violence and near insurrection had gripped all the major towns of the land, and Love had seen action in most of them. In Wales, Merthyr had been held by the iron workers for a whole week, and Colonel Love had commanded the troops in the bloodbath that ended it. But it was the great riots in the city of Bristol that had most alarmed the government, when even repeated cavalry charges had failed to clear the rioters from the burning city centre. Only Love's dash with the 11th Regiment of Foot from Cardiff, across the Severn estuary, had saved Bristol from total destruction.

Distinguishing himself yet again in the Canadian insurrection of 1831, he had returned to Britain in time to take command of the troops who put an end to John Frost's march on Newport. And here he was, four years later, keeping the lid on the valleys of Glamorgan and Monmouthshire, where Chartism had again got up a head of steam. But now, Colonel James Frederick Love was about to take on the most frustrating assignment of his long life as a soldier.

To cross the Loughor

Being the prudent commander that he was, Colonel Love had placed himself and a detachment of the 73rd Regiment of Foot at Swansea—hitherto the westward limit of his jurisdiction—in anticipation of an order to cross the River Loughor into Carmarthenshire. That order reached him on the evening of Wednesday 21 June. By first light next morning a carriage and escort were ready to take him and his aide-de-camp, Lieutenant Wardlow, on the four hour journey to Carmarthen, while his infantry

[3] *The Duke,* Philip Guedalla, 1931.

mustered and prepared to march the twenty-eight miles in two five hour stages. The workhouse there was earmarked already to serve as their barracks.

By 9 a.m. on the 22nd, Colonel Love was in Carmarthen and he went straight to the workhouse to set up his headquarters and discuss the situation with the magistrates and Major Parlby, whose dragoons were already billetted about the town. The situation reports presented to him showed that events had moved swiftly since Monday's invasion of the town. In fact on the very evening of the invasion the gate at Llanfihangel-ar-arth (thirteen miles north of Carmarthen) had been smashed by about a hundred and fifty men in the usual garb of Rebecca and her daughters, thus keeping a promise they had made when attacking the gates at Newcastle Emlyn and Felindre Siencyn on the previous Wednesday. And as at Newcastle Emlyn and Felindre Siencyn, Rebecca had a bit of sport with the special constables standing guard over the gate. Overwhelming them from all sides, she ordered them to join in, but since they had no tools to do the job she was content to oblige them merely to strike at the gate with their truncheons as a gesture.

Where had this band of Rebeccaites come from? The fact that the attack at Llanfihangel-ar-arth occurred within hours of the *débâcle* at Carmarthen workhouse, where a hundred were under arrest and many others had left their horses behind to face a three or four hour flight home on foot, suggests another band at work. But there was yet another group, also able to operate independently and not only within easy reach of and contact with the other two groups but also working within the operational area of the original Rebeccaites of Efail-wen and Llanboidy, much further west.

It will be remembered that William Phillips of Longford Farm, Clynderwen, who took part in the attack at Efail-wen in 1839, also took part in the first attack on the Mermaid gate in St. Clears (fifteen miles to the east) in November, 1842, and Inspector Martin had already reported his belief that a great many of them had come from Llanboidy and the hill country north of St. Clears from where the invasion of Carmarthen had been launched. And there is even some evidence to suggest that the brothers Rees of Rhydymarchog farm, who led the attack on Water Street gate and the invasion of Carmarthen in May and

June, 1843, were related to Thomas Rees (Twm Carnabwth) of Mynachlog-ddu, the Rebecca of Efail-wen in May, 1839![4]

The continuing existence of Rebeccaites in the direction of Efail-wen became clear enough on the very day after the Carmarthen invasion. In a dramatic daylight return to the gates surrounding St. Clears after an absence of seven weeks:

> . . . Rebecca and a great number of her daughters assembled at Meidrim [three miles north of St. Clears] about four o'clock in the afternoon and stopped there some hours. They were nearly all dressed in women's clothes and Rebecca was on horseback, elegantly dressed.
>
> They called at the Wheaten Sheaf, where they cleared the cellars of all the ale and porter, and about ten o'clock departed for Saint Clears. They went to several gentlemen in the village demanding money, saying Rebecca and her children could not carry on their work without having something to eat and drink.
>
> They assembled at Saint Clears from all parts of that country, most of them armed with guns and other destructive weapons, and immediately levelled with the ground the gates leading to Saint Clears from both ends. Mr. Thomas of Clyngarthen, a respectable farmer, refused to join the depredators and on that night the cattle from the mountain were turned into his wheat field, which was completely destroyed.[5]

Where Inspector Martin, his Metropolitan Police officers, his special constables and his supervising magistrates were during the ten hours of Rebecca's rampage through Meidrim and St. Clears, history does not record. Moreover, while all this was going on, the side bars at Llandeilo Rwnws[6] and Dryslwyn Bridge, nearly twenty miles east of St. Clears and out beyond Carmarthen, were being removed without a sound.

[4] Rebecca was accompanied by her 'sister' Charlotte on only two occasions in the whole history of the riots—at Carmarthen and Llanwrda, 20 miles to the east. The rarity of the name Rebecca in those days was matched by that of Charlotte, but one of the only two Rebeccas found in a random sample of 3,000 women's names in the 1841 Census lived in Maenclochog (3 miles from Mynachlog-ddu, with her sister Charlotte, and their name was also Rees. The name Charlotte was also given to Twm Carnabwth's first grand-daughter and there has been a Charlotte in every generation since. Furthermore the Rees brothers of Rhydymarchog came from and returned to Cardiganshire, the border of which passes within 12 miles of Twm Carnabwth's home village, and there are descendants of Twm Carnabwth living in Cardiganshire to this day.

[5] *Carmarthen Journal,* 23 June, 1843.

[6] Typical of this period, the spelling is phonetic. It should be *Llandeilo yr Ynys,* the name of a farm by the Towy bridge at Nantgaredig.

To complete the picture presented to Colonel Love, several other incidents served to show that it was not only toll gates and workhouses that attracted the attention of Rebecca or those acting under her umbrella. For example, only nine miles outside Carmarthen, at about the time of the Colonel's arrival there:

> . . . a distress for rent was levied on a man named Lloyd living at the Albion Tavern, Llanstephan, and a bailiff of the name of Rees took possession of the goods, but previous to the day of the sale Rebecca and a great number of her daughters paid him a visit, horsewhipped him in a brutal manner and kept him in safe custody until the furniture was entirely cleared from the house. When he was let loose he found nothing but an empty house, Rebecca and her followers having made their exit.[7]

And only six days earlier the tithes had been causing trouble again, when Rebecca had reacted angrily to the almost incredible behaviour of the Rev. John Hughes, Vicar of Penbryn, a village about seven miles up the coast from Cardigan. A resident of his parish who was not even a member of his congregation but a chapel-goer, was either unable or unwilling to pay an increased tithe and the Vicar took legal action and sent in the bailiff. The warrant authorised the seizure and sale of the debtor's property to the value of the amount owed and the bailiff seized the only article in the house of a value that would pay the tithe. Of all things, the man's family Bible!

Rebecca was furious and threatened dire revenge. Writing from Penyrherber near Newcastle Emlyn she warned the Vicar that if he did not return the man's Bible and return to all his parishioners the cash difference between the new tithe and the old she would come with three or four hundred of her children and take it out of him in pain and suffering. 'I will break two of your limbs,' she wrote, 'one leg and one arm, and I will put all your goods on fire. Remember not to deceive yourself; the above thing is as certain to take place as there is life in your body.'[8] It did not, but a much chastened Vicar spent many worried nights locked in his guarded Vicarage from then on.

A troublesome triangle

That Colonel Love was facing at least three, and possibly

[7] *Carmarthen Journal,* 23 June, 1843.
[8] H. Tobit Evans, op. cit.

four, interconnected groups of Rebeccaites was made plain to him by Friday 23 June, the day after his arrival. On that day his infantry marched into Carmarthen to the beat of fife and drum at half past ten in the morning 'having marched from Llanon with their muskets, knapsacks, etc., in the short space of five hours—a distance of nearly eighteen miles, *being at the rate of three and a half miles an hour,* a difficult task to perform in this hot weather.'[9] And on that night the town of Cardigan, twenty-eight miles away (and only eleven from the scene of the previous night's attacks at Newcastle Emlyn) was occupied for several hours and its gates attacked with a vengeance, without the least impediment from the authorities. The *Carmarthen Journal*'s description of the affair cannot be bettered:

> The inhabitants of Cardigan were greatly alarmed on Friday evening by Rebecca and her daughters paying a visit to the Pensarn turnpike gate on the Aberystwyth road and the Rhydyfuwch gate on the Llangoedmor road. About eleven o'clock a large party were seen coming down Cardigan Common preceded by about six horsemen exceedingly well mounted, the rest being on foot. The horses were on the full gallop and those on foot running after them at a rapid pace. They were all disfigured, having their faces blackened and wearing some women's clothes, others with smocks, etc. and otherwise disguised, carrying with them guns, swords, scythes, pitchforks and other weapons of destruction, intended no doubt as self defence in the event of their being attacked.
>
> Immediately on their arrival at the Pensarn gate the work of demolition began and the sounds of saws and hatchets were distinctly heard and whilst the work of destruction was being carried on several shots were fired, followed by a tremendous shouting.
>
> The gate and the hedge soon disappeared, but the toll house being strongly built, the roof and walls being of the best materials as to stone and mortar, it appeared that it was a difficult task for them to destroy it. They then left and came down through the centre of the town to the Cross, then turned down Saint Mary's Street, over Pontycleivon to Rhydyfuwch gate which, with the walls thereunto attached being old, immediately vanished.
>
> We are told that one of the leaders went to the toll house kept by a widow who remonstrated with him and expressed the hope that none of her furniture would be damaged or injured, when Becca replied 'Be not alarmed. Shut your door upon you. Your house and furniture will not be touched. We only want the gate and walls.'

[9] *Carmarthen Journal,* 30 June, 1843.

Cardigan, looking north from the Guildhall towards the Pensarn Turnpike Gate. *(Mr. Donald Davies, Cardigan)*

After finishing the work the horsemen galloped away and the rest all dispersed.[10]

So, after six months of toll gate riots and a variety of other outrages, what evidence could the authorities produce to Colonel Love as to the identity of the leaders? None. Or the instigators? None. Or the means whereby the attacks were being coordinated? Again none, except the obvious conclusion to be drawn from the coincidence between the holding of the meeting of the farmers of the Hundred of Elfed (on Wednesday 14 June) and the sudden surge and spread of activity which had followed it. The Home Office had not yet told Colonel Love of their misgivings about Edward Crompton Lloyd Hall, while Hugh Williams, 'the instigator and undiscovered leader of the Rebecca movement', had not yet even appeared on the stage, his activities having been thus far confined to Chartism and the campaign to abolish the Corn Laws, at least so far as was known. So, in the absence of any evidence on which to break the movement on the basis of its past crimes, the Colonel's first priority was to be the

[10] *Carmarthen Journal,* 30 June, 1843.

deployment of his forces in a preventive role. And this happened quickly.

Within five days the Castlemartin Yeomanry had been mustered, one troop under Captain Leach being sent to Newcastle Emlyn and one under Captain Mansel to St. Clears, while the third remained in reserve at Pembroke. The Government steamer *Confiance* had sailed from Pembroke Dock to Cardigan carrying a hundred and twenty Royal Marines under Major Whylock—sixty to garrison that town and the remainder to march to Newcastle Emlyn and join the yeomanry there. With a hundred and fifty soldiers of the 73rd Regiment of Foot and fifty men of the 4th Light Dragoons holding Carmarthen, and a reserve of some five hundred Royal Marines and sailors at Pembroke Dockyard, Colonel Love now had a force of nearly nine hundred under his command, and he proceeded to split the operational elements of his force into smaller detachments to patrol and guard gates, workhouses and other vulnerable points.

And it worked, to a degree, because after the attacks in Cardigan on 23 June, nothing else occurred within that triangle for some fourteen days . . . during which time the troubles outside had spread as far west as Fishguard and, more ominously, over the eastern boundary of Carmarthenshire into Glamorgan, where Colonel Love had thought he had only the Chartists to contend with. But at least his troop dispositions seem also to have saved Narberth workhouse from the same fate suffered by that at Carmarthen. Still showing her traditional boldness, Rebecca had publicly marked the place for destruction, but when she and her six hundred followers approached in typical carnival fashion they found the Yeomanry there already. The reserve troop under Major Bowling had galloped there from Pembroke and though her daughters outnumbered the cavalry by twenty four to one, Rebecca retreated, her band dispersed in all directions towards the Presely hills—and Narberth workhouse was never threatened again.

From our own reporter

In the meantime, and only a few hours behind Colonel Love, there was another important arrival in Carmarthen. Thomas Campbell Foster, a reporter for *The Times* of London had received instructions from his editor late on Tuesday 20 June, as

Royal Marines, with a government steamer in the background.
(Royal Marines Museum, Portsmouth)

Pembroke Dock *(Haverfordwest Library)*

Thomas Campbell Foster in later years, as a Q.C. and a Master of the Honourable Society of the Middle Temple. *(National Portrait Gallery)*

soon as news had been received of the invasion of Carmarthen. And a shrewd choice of correspondent he proved to be, this scholarly student of the law, this compassionate observer of the trials and tribulations of the common people, this newspaper reporter with the uncommon gift for what would to-day be called investigative journalism.

Foster left London at once, taking the Great Western Railway to its terminus at Bristol, from where he crossed the Severn by steamer to Cardiff, to travel the remaining seventy miles across south Wales by coach. He did it in only thirty-six hours and was in Carmarthen by Thursday evening, installing himself in the Ivy Bush Hotel, outside which two armed dragoons stood sentry 'while groups of wondering and curious boys and idle men were standing at a respectful distance looking with aspects of awe at their carbines and accoutrements.'[11] He wrote his first dispatch that evening, giving his first impressions of what he had seen and heard on his journey:

The riots at Carmarthen and the state of South Wales.
From our own Reporter: Carmarthen, Thursday evening.

Immediately upon learning of the occurrence of the riots I left for Carmarthen and on my route collected some information on the state of the country.

In the mining districts of Glamorgan and Monmouthshire the depressed state of the iron trade has caused a degree of wretchedness and discontent which must be seen to be fully appreciated and the population is in so excited a state that a very slight event might produce great danger to the public peace. In Carmarthenshire, Pembrokeshire and Cardiganshire the Rebeccaites traverse the country from end to end and level the gates and commit other outrages with perfect impunity, added to which the whole country is suffering from the effects of the new poor law, against which there appear to be universal feelings of detestation.

On the road between Swansea and Carmarthen every person I spoke to sympathised with the rioters and upon my asking what the attack upon the Carmarthen workhouse had to do with the turnpike gates the reply was 'Oh that is another monstrous oppression, to rob and imprison the poor who are badly fed and do not even get one half of what is collected for them.'

The main cause of the mischief is beyond doubt the general poverty of the farmers. They have become thereby discontented at every tax and burden they have been called upon to pay. If to this cause, increasing poverty and discontent, can be added an unjust imposition [the road tolls] you have the crowning climax, however trivial it may appear in itself, which has fanned this discontent into a flame.

Incredible as it may appear, I have been informed by several persons likely to be acquainted with the fact that taking the whole county of Carmarthen, on average there are not three miles of road without a toll bar. From Pontardulais Bridge at the boundary of the county to Carmarthen, a distance of only nineteen miles, I myself counted no less than *eleven* toll gates, or rather ten and the clean-swept foundations of where one stood last week.

The farmers of the county, a most peaceable, quiet and orderly population, are roused to such a pitch of indignation by this abuse that at length, under a leader more daring than the rest who

[11] *The Times,* 26 June, 1843.

Rebeccaites, or 'Beccas' *(Illus. London News)*

assumed the name 'Rebecca', several of these newly set up gates were pulled down. Emboldened by success and neither checked by the strong arm of the law nor appeased by timely remedy of the abuse, and having the silent sanction and approval of the mass of the population, these at first insignificant acts of lawless violence have assumed an importance and have led to results which may end in serious disaffection amongst a population of the most inoffensive and peaceable in Her Majesty's Dominions.

In those cases where there has been a show of resistance and policemen and special constables have been arrayed, they have not been determinedly and properly led, and esteeming 'discretion the better part of valour' they have quietly looked on, peeped around corners and even, it has been said, been 'compelled' to do Rebecca's own work for her.[12]

Let me beg of you my men

Yet another leading actor in the drama arrived in Carmarthen on that same Thursday. Colonel The Honourable George Rice Trevor, M.P. (son of the Lord Lieutenant of Carmarthenshire, Lord Dynevor, and his father's Vice-Lieutenant) arrived from London to take over from his ailing father the responsibility for law and order in the county. And he was very soon briefed by Colonel Love and the magistrates. Nor did he waste time in getting to the heart of the matter. The very next day he took the chair at a public meeting in the Salutation Inn, Newcastle Emlyn, where he not only appealed for calm and the repudiation of violence, but spelt out in clear terms the consequences of the failure to do so:

'I have represented the county for twenty-three years,' he said, 'and I now endeavour to induce you not to place yourselves in collision with the law, nor offend against it. If you do so you may escape for a time, but depend upon it the government will send such a force into this country as will put down these outrages.' Turning to the causes of the troubles Colonel Rice Trevor said, 'I am told that you complain of certain grievances. When I say that the magistrates and myself, who have spent the greater part of our lives in the county are both willing and anxious to redress all grievances which may be proved to be so, I am sure you will believe us.' But now came the warning, quietly but firmly: 'The magistrates have had a force of troops put at their disposal by the government and though they are willing to redress all that is amiss they cannot give way to force and must put down all disturbances, the government being ready to increase the number of troops if necessary. It would give me the greatest pain,' said Colonel Rice Trevor, 'to use those troops against men to many of whom I am under deep obligations and in whose houses and cottages I have often received refreshment, for believe me I am always proud to go into the houses of my countrymen and can say that whatever may be their conduct in other respects, their hospitality is proverbial. Let me beg of you my men not to force me to do that which I shall do, however much I regret it, if it is

[12] *The Times,* 24 June, 1843.

Col. The Hon. George Rice Trevor, M.P., Vice-Lieutenant for the County of Carmarthen. *(Nat. Library of Wales)*

necessary to the performance of my duty, nor to force me to order those troops to fire upon you. Cast away those busy meddlers who have interfered with you and thus led you astray, for that these are not your acts I know. But remember, if the law is violated it must be vindicated. If it is violated and force be used, remember the troops must resist force by force. If you have grievances we are ready to redress them. Then come with your complaints to the gentlemen [the magistrates] who are your neighbours and you may depend upon their being attended to, but for your own sake avoid attending nightly meetings and committing acts of outrage which will be ruinous to you.'

The farmers listened intently and Colonel Rice Trevor congratulated himself on the effect his warning seemed to be having on them. But that was the night when Rebecca and her daughters rampaged through Cardigan only eleven miles away, and there can be no doubt that some of the Colonel's audience were among the most enthusiastic of the participants!

Chapter Six

READY FOR ANY MISCHIEF

For both Thomas Campbell Foster and Colonel Love the next two weeks were fully occupied with the process of getting the feel of the country and its people, of discovering the causes of the disturbances, and of working out possible solutions.

Foster spent hours in the saddle every day, listening, talking and making notes, before making for the nearest decent inn to take his evening meal and then sitting late into the night drafting his almost daily dispatches by flickering candle or lantern light, ready to catch the London mail coach at break of day. Employing interpreters, he spoke to the poorest of the countrypeople, and putting a few gold sovereigns about where they might do the most good, he found his way into the most remote communities and meeting places—creating opportunities for communication with the ordinary people denied to others of his station in life and like himself ignorant of the language and ways of the rural Welshman. They were opportunities which very soon gave him a rare and penetrating insight into the situation and which enabled him to deliver his assessment of it to his twenty thousand readers with an unassailable authority. It would not be going too far to compare his errand and his efforts with those of his co-reporter on *The Times,* William Howard Russell, who eleven years later found an affinity with the ordinary soldier in the Crimea and a standpoint from which to expose the scandalous mismanagement of that war and bring down a government.

As for the Colonel, he had made his basic troop dispositions, he had given his subordinate commanders a brief from which they could decide upon the tactical use of their men, and now he could turn his attention to the broader issues—in the short term the identification of those responsible for the trouble and in the longer term the removal of the causes. He too would travel widely, for his command stretched the whole length of south Wales—well over a hundred miles, from Pembroke Dock to

Newport—and he would cover as many as seventy miles in a day on his enquiries and inspections.

But for both Foster and the Colonel there would be the immediate task of almost daily toll gate attacks to investigate and to report upon, Foster to his readers and Love to his three Lords Lieutenant and his government. Their first full week saw seven gates demolished on four nights, beginning with the attack on the Penygarn gate (six miles east of Carmarthen on the main London road) in which two or three hundred black faced men in women's clothes swooped down from the steep hill above the road and to a roar of gunfire smashed house and gate to pieces. In the true tradition of the newspaperman Foster was there first thing next morning getting the old gate keeper's first hand account of what had happened 'so close under the noses of the military' as Foster put it.

'When I went to the spot,' wrote Foster, 'I saw the poor man and his family sitting houseless by the wayside.' He sat down alongside gate keeper Griffith Bowen—ex Grenadier Guardsman, veteran of Wellington's army in the Peninsula and at Waterloo—pulled out his notebook and wrote the old pensioner's story:

> About a quarter before twelve o'clock last night I was standing at the door of the tollhouse smoking my pipe, but looking up the hill upon hearing some talking I saw two men at a distance of about fifty yards. After the men had talked a little I saw a body of them to the number between two and three hundred, disguised and with their faces blackened, and most of them had women's caps on and they had Rebecca at their head.
>
> Many of them were on horseback but they dismounted at the top of the hill and left their horses there. They then marched down the hill and I could see that they were armed with guns and pistols, pickaxes, sledgehammers and all sorts of offensive weapons. Being much alarmed, my wife and myself fled from the house and I hid myself behind an ash tree a short distance off, from which I could observe their motions.
>
> Upon their reaching the gate, Rebecca called out 'Hello, Hello gate.' After a short interval he gave the word of command 'Come on' and the work of destruction immediately began. The whole of the mob fell to work pulling down the gate and sawing off the posts, which were of solid oak and each four feet in circumference. Some of them also entered the toll house and having thrown out the furniture

> on the roadside and tore down the bedstead they began pulling down the walls of the house [which were two feet thick] and left them and the gate in complete ruins.
>
> They kept firing guns and pistols at intervals during the whole period, which occupied upwards of an hour, and then at the word of command marched up the hill and disappeared, taking with them my Waterloo Medal and about twelve shillings [60p] in silver which was in my desk.

And then, in Foster's words, the rioters 'escaped without detection although they must have marched more than two miles each way upon the main London road to and from the scene of the outrage',[1] a road supposed by now to be regularly patrolled by the dragoons.

The next night, toll gate wreckers struck fifty miles to the west, in and around Fishguard, a small harbour town in north Pembrokeshire. This time the target was the notorious Fishguard Trust, of whom it had been said that though they had gates each side of the town 'they have not repaired any of the roads in the Parishes of Fishguard, Dinas and Newport through which the trust leads, but all the burden of making and keeping the roads in repair falls entirely on the Parishes, *and it appears that the Act of Parliament for taking the tolls at those gates had expired now several years.*'[2] At Scleddau, two miles below Fishguard, the gate posts, walls and toll board (on which the various toll charges were listed) were broken into pieces 'so small that in the morning there was not any piece of timber larger than would make matches',[3] and the mob went off towards Haverfordwest. This was in the opposite direction to Fishguard where later in the night the toll gate on Fishguard Hill and the bar and house on the Newport side of the town were damaged by about a dozen other men who were undoubtedly fortified by the drink they had consumed on the way home from Newport Fair. No sign of the trappings of Rebecca here. Merely another bit of 'free-lancing' on the way back from another fair.

And on the next night (Wednesday 28 June) the pendulum swung right back again for a similar escapade a full seventy miles to the east where, in the aftermath of Llandeilo Fair, 'someone' broke down a gate in Llangadog.

[1] *The Times,* 30 June, 1843.
[2] *Carmarthen Journal,* 12 May, 1843. Author's italics.
[3] *Carmarthen Journal,* 7 July, 1843.

But now, at the end of June, came the beginning of the campaign against the Kidwelly and Three Commotes Trusts, a campaign that would engulf the Gwendraeth Valley and the Carmarthenshire/Glamorgan border country in a welter of violence totally at odds with the true spirit of Rebecca; violence that would gradually sicken her erstwhile supporters and help to bring an end to the movement. It happened suddenly, with an impact heightened by the fact that Rebecca had not touched that part of Carmarthenshire for well over four months. *'More Gates Destroyed'* cried the *Carmarthen Journal,* before going on to express its sorrow that:

> . . . the destructive spirit of Rebeccaism has now spread itself over the whole of the Three Commotes District, a great number of gates and bars having been demolished this week in that part of the country. Amongst others Pontyates, Meinciau, Pontyberem and both the gates at Kidwelly have been destroyed.
>
> On Friday night [30th June] a visit was paid by Rebecca and her children to the village of Llanddarog, about six miles from Carmarthen. They mustered about five hundred, armed with guns, swords and pickaxes. Notice had previously been given that Rebecca intended paying a visit to the above gate and accordingly, about midnight, this renowned lady and her daughters fulfilled their promise. When they arrived at the gate they enquired of the toll collector what was to be paid, to which the frightened gentleman instantly replied *'Nothing for you ma'am.'* Rebecca having acknowledged the politeness of the collector desired him to go into his dwelling and shut himself in, which he immediately did and her orders were given for the destruction of the gate. In a short time it was levelled with the ground amid the exultation of the 'family' and the firing of guns.
>
> They then proceeded to Troedyrhiw gate, which met the same fate.[4]

A strict enquiry

In the midst of all this, Colonel Love received his first detailed instructions from his political masters in London, in a letter posted under confidential cover on 22 June, the day he arrived in Carmarthen. It is a letter which reflects only too clearly the government's incredulity that 'a mere local impatience of turn-

[4] *Carmarthen Journal,* 7 July, 1843.

pike tolls' (Lloyd Hall's words) could have caused such trouble as now required the presence of so many hundred soldiers:

> Sir; I am directed by Secretary Sir J. Graham [the Home Secretary] to request you as soon as convenient to obtain for him information as to the causes of complaint on the subject of the toll gates and tolls which have led to the late violent proceedings. The points to which Sir J. Graham would direct your attention are whether any new gates have been made, new tolls imposed or old tolls increased; whether complaints have been made respecting the tolls demanded and what has been the course adopted by the authorities in these matters upon these points, and any others which you can suggest with a view to ascertaining the cause from which such a spirit of insubordination and violence has arisen. Sir J. Graham is very desirous of obtaining by your means as complete information as you may be able to procure.[5]

That the Home Secretary's enquiry had to some extent been prompted by Edward Crompton Lloyd Hall's letter of 15 June was indicated by the postscript to his letter: 'I am also to enclose a letter received from Mr. Hall, of whom nothing is here known. You may be able perhaps to obtain some information respecting the writer and as to the truth of the statements.'

On 26 June, within two days of receiving the Home Secretary's request for information and within only four days of assuming his new command, Colonel Love delivered his first assessment of the situation, following it up over the next fortnight or so with other letters giving his more fully considered views and his ideas on how solutions might be sought. They are letters which deserve more attention than they have so far received from the historian. The perspicacity they show is remarkable; the influence they had on the course of events was profound. And this from a soldier. A man more used to putting down disturbances than curing them.

He gave examples of how the trusts had put up gates and charged tolls on roads repaired by the parishes; of how they had operated in other ways outside the bounds of their legal powers and how they had bent to the will of the 'toll farmers' by putting gates or bars or chains across every little side road found to be used by farmers to carry their lime and produce free of toll. He

[5] Letter dated 22 June, 1843, Home Office to Colonel Love: Public Record Office, File HO 41/17.

told how tolls had been increased by fifty per cent in only six years, and how:

> The hostile feeling of the farmers to the payment of the tolls (exorbitant in many instances) was materially increased by the distress of the farmers themselves caused by the high rents, poor and church rates, which together with the very great depreciation in the agricultural produce of the country left them in many instances unable to meet the demands against them, or leaving them without any money after having done so. The increased tolls therefore became a greater hardship, as, from the want of money, instances occurred where the farmer having purchased lime could not transport it to his farm from the expense of the tolls.[6]

Commenting wryly on the stock answer of the trusts to complaints about the sharp rise in toll charges, which were claimed to have led to a general improvement in the west Wales roads, Colonel Love wrote:

> It is contended that from the improved state of the roads, two horses can now do the work of three, and one horse the work of two, which brings the toll charges nearly to what they were before. But this is very difficult to make the Welshman understand, *particularly those who have only one horse.*[7]

And then he turned on the magistrates, at whose door he firmly laid the blame for the fact that a problem which at the outset should have been well within their capacity to solve had been allowed to get so far out of hand:

> This [the burden of exorbitant and unjustified tolls at a time of unprecedented hardship] made the people reckless and from the destroying gates with impunity they proceeded to acts of greater violence and mixed up what had only in the first instance been a simple case of complaint (*which if taken in time might easily have been settled*) with the poor laws, tithes and rents, and there is now I regret to say a spirit abroad ready for any mischief—one which nothing at present but the presence of a military force can suppress or keep down.
>
> Nearly the whole of the agricultural inhabitants of the surrounding country sympathise with the rioters, even those who do not join them. Under these circumstances the magistrates, from finding a

[6] Letter dated 11 July, 1843, Colonel Love to Home Office: Public Record Office, File HO 45/453.

[7] Letter dated 11 July, 1843, Colonel Love to Home Office: Public Record Office, File HO 45/453. (Author's italics).

> great difficulty in obtaining special constables, are naturally less energetic than we could wish, *and rely too much on the military.*[8]

From that view of the magistrates' failure to face up to their responsibilities it was not difficult for him (two months later) to conclude that the system of peace-keeping which they represented had had its day anyway. He put the problem in a nutshell:

> The great cause why the outrages have arisen to such an alarming height may be attributed to the total absence of any Civil Force whatever in the three counties most disturbed, and it is only by creating such a force, *backed* by the military, that we can hope to put them down.
>
> Heretofore the military have been called upon to take the initiative instead of *supporting* the Civil Power, from the obvious reason of their being no civil force to support.[9]

The Colonel had, in fact, already asked for more policemen to be sent from London. 'I consider,' he had written, 'that Metropolitan Police officers would be of the greatest service at this moment, as the town police would be much more efficient if they had someone to lead them.[10] It would, however, be advisable not to send anyone that had been here before and they should have some clothes by which they might be disguised if necessary.'[11] This was very quickly done and within a few months he had been sent a hundred and fifty Metropolitan Police officers, of whom a number were eventually used as a nucleus around which was created the Carmarthenshire Constabulary, the first rural force of 'new' police in west Wales.

By 12 July, the Colonel had formed very firm views on the toll question and in putting them forward to the Home Secretary he made a suggestion that was to have far-reaching consequences:

> . . . sufficient has transpired to convince me that the whole affair of the Trusts demands a strict enquiry. That in general there has been great maladministration is evident, and in very many instances double the toll authorised by Law has been levied by the collectors. It is not for me to suggest what should be done, although I am

[8] Letter dated 11 July, 1843, Colonel Love to Home Office, Public Record Office, File HO 45/453. (Author's italics).

[9] Same, dated 30 September, 1843. (Author's italics).

[10] The Chief Constable of Carmarthen, John Pugh, had been totally discredited and would soon be dismissed.

[11] Letter dated 25 June, 1843, Colonel Love to Home Office: Public Record Office, File HO 45/453.

> strongly of the opinion that a strict enquiry would be beneficial to the public and tend perhaps more than anything else to allay the discontent so generally felt by the farmers.[12]

'*The whole affair of the Trusts demands a strict enquiry.*' Within fourteen days of receiving this letter the Home Secretary had sent two investigators to prepare a preliminary report on the state of the Welsh turnpike trusts. Within less than three months the government had set up a Royal Commission, whose massive report and collection of evidence were published only five months later. And within a year of Colonel Love's arrival in Carmarthen Parliament had passed a new turnpike roads act correcting every one of the defects in the old law which had led to all the trouble.

If the speed of the government's response to this problem was not unique, it would be hard indeed to find a parallel.

The Chartist Spectre

But that was for the future, and when Colonel Love wrote his assessments his problems were still very real—and not simply problems related to toll gate riots, as his report of 12 July went on to show:

> The accounts from the Monmouth hills are by no means satisfactory, and if the Ebbw Vale works which have lately failed should be suddenly stopped, great distress and consequent disturbance may be anticipated.
>
> I have ascertained for certain that people connected with the Rebeccaites have been to Merthyr Tydfil and that some Chartists from that place have been into North Wales, as well as here, also that people from Ireland connected with the agitators in that country have been to Merthyr and the Neighbourhood. There are some Chartists in this Town, [Carmarthen] but I do not believe that the farmers have as yet anything to do with them.
>
> There is a report prevalent amongst the people both in this and the Mining Districts (but possibly without foundation) that a general rising is to take place in the middle of August, when it is supposed that the state of Ireland will give more than sufficient occupation for the Troops, and all the speeches of the Chartists tend to this belief.
>
> Under these circumstances I am careful not by any movement of

[12] Letter dated 25 June, 1843, Colonel Love to Home Office: Public Record Office, File HO 45/453.

the Troops to uncover or reduce the force now stationed in Glamorgan and Monmouthshire, particularly as it would be desirous in case of any rising to prevent the union of the people in this country [west Wales] with those in the Glamorgan and Monmouth hills. I also consider it necessary that Carmarthen, Narberth in Pembrokeshire, Newcastle Emlyn and Cardigan should be at least for some months, or until more general quiet is restored, occupied by Troops.

It would also be of great service if I could have a couple of pieces of artillery, for besides the effect of such an arm on the fears of the peoples, it would enable me in the event of any serious disturbance to put it down at once and before it could possibly spread, which it would be most necessary to prevent.[13]

It is hard to imagine what turn the Rebecca Riots could take which would call for the use of field artillery and, indeed, some civil servant in the Home Office wondered too. In the margin, he wrote 'Is this necessary? I doubt it.' But the guns were sent—a six pounder field gun and twelve pounder howitzer, with men, ammunition and equipment from the army's field train at Woolwich. No doubt the Colonel shared the view of his old adversary Napoleon Buonaparte on the efficacy of 'a whiff of grapeshot' for scattering a riotous mob.

As to the Colonel's concern over a possible connection between Rebeccaism and Chartism, he had already been given food for thought by a report sent to him from Merthyr Tydfil on 2 July by Captain Napier, the Chief Constable of the two-year old Glamorganshire Constabulary. Passing on details of the proceedings at a Chartist meeting held at the Three Horseshoes in Merthyr and infiltrated by his informer, the Captain told him that two Rebeccaites from Carmarthenshire were lodging with one David Rees, and that they were in the area seeking to persuade the Chartists to 'join in union with them.'[14]

Unless all hope for struggling be gone

In the meantime, Thomas Campbell Foster was pursuing his own investigations and coming up with some very interesting findings. In his travels through west Wales Foster conversed

[13] Letter dated 11 July, 1843, Colonel Love to Home Office: Public Record Office, File 45/453.

[14] Public Record Office, File HO 45/453.

with any and every person who would talk to him and many were the stories he was told about the effects of those hard times on the rural population and in particular the effects of the new Poor Law. As a Llandeilo farmer told him:

> . . . agricultural labourers receive a shilling [5p] or ninepence [3½p] a day, but in the winter they are perhaps not employed for many weeks and when employed have only sixpence [2½p] a day. These people have a small cottage each to reside in and a little garden, and many of them arrive at actually the starvation point with their wives and children rather than apply for poor relief, knowing that if they do so they will be dragged into the Union Workhouse, where they will be placed themselves in one yard, their wives in another, their male children in a third and their daughters in a fourth, and thus completely separated they cannot even see one another except through the kindness of the Governor of the Union Workhouse, who perhaps would get reprimanded for allowing the indulgence, and in the meanwhile their little furniture, their cottage and their garden fall into hopeless ruin.[15]

Being the thorough investigator that he was, Foster always sought verification of what people were telling him. 'I have taken no man's "They say" for granted,' he wrote:

> . . . but have been myself over the workhouse and examined and tasted their bread, have obtained from the matron their diet table and have seen numerous orders for admission into the workhouse for applicants for relief who have been refused such relief unless they and their families enter the workhouse. I have seen a bundle of those orders which have been refused by the applicants, who preferred to starve or live by begging rather than break up their cottages, their only homes, and enter the workhouse.
>
> I enquired of the relieving officer the rent a man would have to pay for his cottage. He said 'Perhaps a shilling or one and sixpence [5p or 7½p] a week.' I asked what would become of the cottage if he and his family entered the workhouse. 'Oh' he answered, 'he would lock it up for a few days until he got work.' 'Suppose' I said 'he should not obtain work for a week, would the Union pay his rent?' 'Oh no' said he. 'The landlord must distrain on [seize and sell] his furniture for that.'
>
> Can it be wondered at, unless all hope for struggling be gone, every spark of honest and independent feeling be extinguished, that a poor man should spurn the offer to give him bread on condition

[15] *The Times,* 24 July, 1843.

The pious face of charity: a typical workhouse *(Illus. London News)*

The female ward of a typical workhouse *(Illus. London News)*

Women and children segregated in their yard of a Union Workhouse
(BBC Hulton Picture Library)

that he and his family should become outcasts by thus consenting to the breaking of the strongest tie to honest industry, his own fireside?[16]

Turning to the workhouse diet, which in the interests of journalistic truth he sampled for himself, he began with the bread, of which each man was allowed one pound and each woman fourteen ounces a day:

The bread which I saw and tasted is made entirely of barley and is nearly black. It has a gritty and rather sour taste. I have since

[16] *The Times,* 27 June, 1843.

The other nation: the gentry attend church (St. Peter's) in Carmarthen

ascertained that some of the poorer farmers use this bread and that 'it acted as a laxative and was therefore recommended as from its gritty nature it had a scouring effect.'

It struck me that taken as the chief food with only three and a half ounces of meat on Sundays and Wednesdays and the soup and milk gruel diet the rest of the week, its 'scouring' properties might not be desirable for the strongest man.[17]

As to the diet generally he found that apart from the allowance of meat on Sundays and Wednesdays only, the food allowed consisted solely of porridge (three parts water to one part milk), soup (in quantities of one and a half pints), potatoes (at one and a half pounds a day) and, on Mondays and Thursdays only, an ounce and a half of cheese for supper, with a salt herring apiece on Fridays.

A prison-like regime? Foster went to find out:

I will now turn to the dietries of the Borough Gaol of Carmarthen,

[17] *The Times,* 27 June, 1843.

and also the County Gaol, each of which places I visited and saw the rations served out, and leave you to compare the amount of food allowed to the criminals confined with that given in the workhouse to the poor. [Here he set out the prison diet tables, which were far more generous and wholesome than those of the workhouse.]

Can you wonder, on a comparison of these several diet tables, that the poor should complain that they are underfed in the workhouse and that the Union workhouse should be unpopular among them?[18]

And Foster's view of the law which governed this treatment of the poor?:

A law framed for the idle and dissolute and put in force against the sober and industrious, labouring under distress and misfortune, is an insult and an oppression. As the law stands it presumes the generality of the poor to deserve its harsh enactments—imprisonment, separation from family, hard work and starvation diet. No doubt there are among the poor, as there are in every class, those who are a disgrace to it, but they are exceptions. The great majority of the poor are only to be pitied and it is only adding insult and cruelty to their poverty to treat them as vagabonds.[19]

Burning questions

Colonel Love, as we have seen, was very concerned about the possibility that political agitators associated with the Charter movement were either directly involved in the west Wales disturbances or were using them to advance their own cause, and that the troubles in Ireland might also be influencing events in Wales. Foster very soon formed an opinion on those questions. In the dispatch written on his second day in Carmarthen he wrote of rumours of an Irish connection:

A radical journal here to-day having published various rumours as to a cart load of arms being received in the neighbourhood of Talog, a small village about nine miles from Carmarthen and situate in the centre of the mountains, and that offers of assistance to the Rebeccaites have been made by the [Act of Union] Repealers in Ireland, I have endeavoured to be enabled either to authenticate or contradict such reports and have to-day visited on horseback Talog, Bwlch Newydd, Conwil and other places in the mountain district.

From the best information that I could collect on the spot I am

[18] *The Times,* 27 June, 1843.
[19] *The Times,* 10 August, 1843.

happily enabled to say that the rumour of such an importation into Talog is completely unfounded.

In the course of my enquiries I met with an intelligent person between sixty and seventy years of age and in answer to my enquiry as to whether it was true that the Rebeccaites were in communication with any persons in Ireland he replied 'Sir, you may depend upon it they are not, for they do not like either the Irish or their conduct, and they have no wish to be disloyal to the government or to oppose any of their acts. They only wish to get rid of the local grievances with which they are oppressed.[20]

And then Foster considered one of the burning questions of the hour—the connection, if connection there was, between Rebeccaism and Chartism. Prompted by the view expressed in a *Carmarthen Journal* editorial[21] that the Rebecca Riots arose from 'a deeply seated and widely diffused spirit of political disaffection', he set out to see if this were so. 'With all their distress,' he wrote:

. . . though they murmur at the payment of exactions whilst they and their families are starving, though they hate the new poor law bitterly and complain that they do not get more than half the price for their produce which they used to do, *yet I am convinced that there is nothing like political disaffection, opposition to the government or any Chartist crotchets instigating the present disturbances.*

Only distress, growing distress and want are at the bottom of it. I do not think that anything beyond the hope of shaking off an intollerable load and burdens too great for them to bear influences them. I have never whilst here heard anything whatever approaching to political disaffection.[22]

Indeed, at about the time Foster wrote this dispatch there was a meeting of farmers in Narberth at which a visiting Chartist speaker was noisily and angrily 'hooted out' of the hall, so unpopular was his message.[23]

The watchful eye

So, if there was no connection between Rebeccaism and Chartism (and neither Colonel Love nor the government shared

[20] *The Times,* 27 June, 1843.
[21] *Carmarthen Journal,* 23 June, 1843.
[22] *The Times,* 30 June, 1843. (Author's italics).
[23] Letter dated 15 July, 1843, J. H. Allen to Home Office: Public Record Office, File HO 40/51.

Foster's confidence in this), where stood the man who has been seen by so many as the link between the two—the Carmarthen lawyer, Hugh Williams, who has so far been conspicuous in the Rebecca story more by his absence than anything else? By now resident in Carmarthen, having married a wealthy old lady from St. Clears and moved from London where he had spent most of his time since leaving his native Machynlleth, Hugh Williams made his first public appearance in the anti-toll gate cause three weeks after the Carmarthen invasion.

On Thursday 6 July a man named David Thomas Howell was obliged to pay what he considered was an exorbitant toll at Water Street gate and he decided to do something about it. He went to see Hugh Williams at his Carmarthen office and retained him to act for him in a private prosecution against Henry Thomas, the embattled Water Street gate keeper who would eventually decide that the toll gate game was not worth the candle and who would give it up to join the Carmarthen Borough Police. The case came before the magistrates in the Guildhall on 12 July and Hugh Williams delivered a masterly, almost surgical, analysis of the procedure by which the Newcastle Trust had imposed the increase in toll, and on this highly technical legal argument, proving that the Newcastle Trust had acted outside its legal powers, he won the day.

This case was the making of Hugh Williams so far as the local farmers were concerned, for he made himself the great expert on the intricacies of the turnpike acts. Thenceforth he was in great demand, not only for similar private prosecutions but also for the drafting of petitions coming out of the public meetings that were soon to become such an important feature of the anti-toll campaign. He would also become the man to whom those arrested for toll gate riots would turn first for their defence, having already been retained for the defence of those arrested for the Talog ambush and the workhouse riot. Altogether quite an extensive involvement in the Rebecca affair, which would bring him under the closest scrutiny by the authorities. Yet when it comes to the assertion that 'he, himself, had probably instigated' David Thomas Howell's prosecution against gatekeeper Henry Thomas[24] there is not one shred of evidence. Hugh Williams'

[24] David Williams, op. cit.

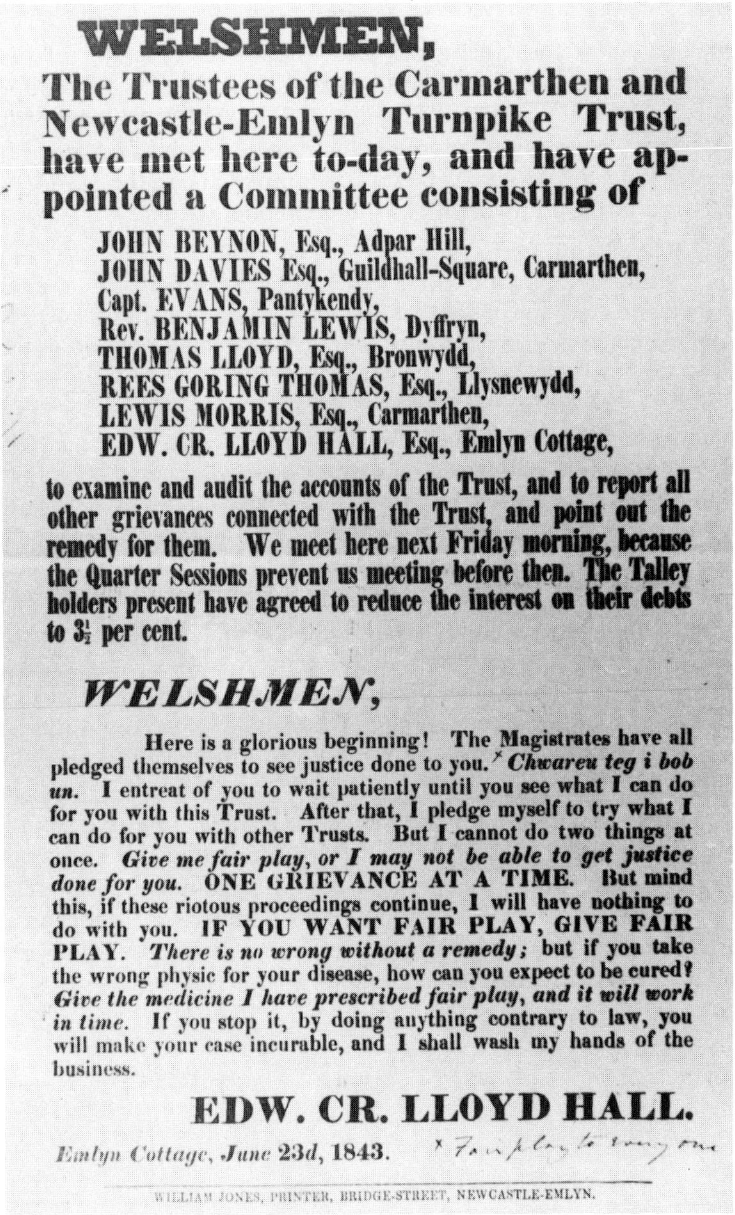

WELSHMEN,

The Trustees of the Carmarthen and Newcastle-Emlyn Turnpike Trust, have met here to-day, and have appointed a Committee consisting of

JOHN BEYNON, Esq., Adpar Hill,
JOHN DAVIES Esq., Guildhall-Square, Carmarthen,
Capt. EVANS, Pantykendy,
Rev. BENJAMIN LEWIS, Dyffryn,
THOMAS LLOYD, Esq., Bronwydd,
REES GORING THOMAS, Esq., Llysnewydd,
LEWIS MORRIS, Esq., Carmarthen,
EDW. CR. LLOYD HALL, Esq., Emlyn Cottage,

to examine and audit the accounts of the Trust, and to report all other grievances connected with the Trust, and point out the remedy for them. We meet here next Friday morning, because the Quarter Sessions prevent us meeting before then. The Talley holders present have agreed to reduce the interest on their debts to 3½ per cent.

WELSHMEN,

Here is a glorious beginning! The Magistrates have all pledged themselves to see justice done to you.× *Chwareu teg i bob un.* I entreat of you to wait patiently until you see what I can do for you with this Trust. After that, I pledge myself to try what I can do for you with other Trusts. But I cannot do two things at once. *Give me fair play, or I may not be able to get justice done for you.* ONE GRIEVANCE AT A TIME. But mind this, if these riotous proceedings continue, I will have nothing to do with you. IF YOU WANT FAIR PLAY, GIVE FAIR PLAY. *There is no wrong without a remedy;* but if you take the wrong physic for your disease, how can you expect to be cured? *Give the medicine I have prescribed fair play, and it will work in time.* If you stop it, by doing anything contrary to law, you will make your case incurable, and I shall wash my hands of the business.

EDW. CR. LLOYD HALL.

Emlyn Cottage, June 23*d*, 1843. × Fair play to every one

WILLIAM JONES, PRINTER, BRIDGE-STREET, NEWCASTLE-EMLYN.

Edward Crompton Lloyd Hall (The 'Pacificator') shows a somewhat premature optimism *(Public Record Office)*

reputation as the 'Instigator and undiscovered leader of the Rebecca movement' is liberally sprinkled with such innuendo.

But Colonel Love had already marked Hugh Williams for attention. A fortnight before the hearing of Howell's court case, replying to the Home Secretary's enquiry about the status of Edward Crompton Lloyd Hall, the Colonel wrote:

> The 'Pacificator', for so he calls himself, is a barrister and practises at the Quarter Sessions at Cardigan. He is an ultra radical in politics and his conduct has lost him the respect of his friends. He is extremely vain and self-sufficient, having unbounded confidence in his legal talents and ability. It is for the purpose of bringing himself into notice that he has adopted his strange line of conduct.[25]

And then he mentioned 'his connection with a Mr. Hugh Williams, who was connected with the disturbances at Newport under Frost' and told the Home Secretary, 'This man I shall recommend to the watchful eye of the Metropolitan Police when they arrive.' Though well connected with the Newport Chartists, Williams had had nothing to do with the planning or execution of the march on Newport, which resulted in a number of deaths by shooting and the arrest of some forty of the marchers. The reference to Hugh Williams' involvement related to the finding on one of the prisoners of a printed tract containing a poem entitled 'The Horn of Liberty', a tribute by Williams to the Chartists who had risen at Llanidloes. The poem, a stirring call to action was, like many a Chartist message, one that could mean all things to all men in terms of the means by which the end might be achieved—the curse of the Chartist movement—but even at a time when what would be considered to-day as the most innocuous political writings could bring a charge of sedition, no such charge was considered against Hugh Williams.

[25] Letter dated 26 June, 1843, Colonel Love to Home Office: Public Record Office, File HO 45/453.

Chapter Seven

THEY ARE ALL SPIES UPON THE SOLDIERY

Had young Daniel Lewis not been so in love with Elizabeth Williams he would never have shared his great secret with her. Surely the scandal that was about to break would put beyond doubt the conviction of her parents—pillars of respectability in the Goppa Chapel congregation—that she could do better for herself among the far more eligible sons of respectable and God-fearing farmers like her father. But the young Pontardulais weaver whispered his secret to her. The quite stunning news that he was going that night with a band of men to destroy the Bolgoed gate, a mile into Glamorgan from the village of Pontardulais on the Carmarthenshire border. Stunning enough in itself. But he was to be Rebecca!

Elizabeth made up her mind there and then. She would see in real life the spectacle that was on everyone's lips, and have the added thrill of knowing that the commanding figure at the head of the band was her own true love. And so, late in the night of Thursday 6 July, 1843, she and one of her mother's servant girls crept from the house and made their way to the Fountain Inn[1] where, at an upstairs window overlooking the Bolgoed gate, they settled down trembling with excitement to watch.

Two hundred of them came up the hill from Pontardulais, with Rebecca in the lead, astride a white horse and arrayed in the gleaming, starched whiteness of his mother's dress, lent to him despite the conflict between her strong chapel connections and the knowledge that she was thereby encouraging her son to break the law. Life would be difficult for her during the months that followed, but her Bible would be her strength, and Genesis, chapter 24, verse 60 her refuge.

Rebecca rode up to the tollhouse and demanded that the gate-keeper should come out. He did, and, polite and considerate as ever, Rebecca commanded her daughters to bring out all his belongings, stack them on the roadside and mount guard over

[1] Still open for business.

them. And then, turning in her saddle, she called out 'Come, come my daughters; there is work to be done,' upon which dozens of axes, crowbars, pickaxes and sledge hammers began hacking the gate to pieces and reducing the house to a pile of stone, timber and slate, amid the ritual cheering and firing of guns. Elizabeth and her servant girl looked on wide-eyed, and though other eyes peered from the windows of the few cottages in the neighbourhood, not a soul ventured outside while Rebecca's work was in progress. Within minutes it was over and two hundred men had vanished into the night.

The attack on the Bolgoed gate was the first incident of any real consequence in Glamorgan and great was the activity of the Glamorgan Constabulary (formed two years before) under their first Chief Constable, Captain Charles Frederick Napier, who,

Capt. Charles Frederick Napier, the first Chief Constable of the Glamorganshire Constabulary *(South Wales Police Museum)*

like Colonel Love, was an ex-light infantryman of some distinction.[2] A Scotsman, now aged thirty nine, he had spent seven years in the 95th Regiment of Foot—the legendary Rifle Brigade—but had given up the army to try his hand as a Chief Constable at a time when this was a natural progression for an officer and when a Chief Constable's job was to say the least rather different from what it is to-day. He and his men scoured the countryside for information and some very tempting rewards were offered, but for more than a fortnight there were no takers, and even when the information came it was not really the offer of money that brought it.

Sabbath fury

Daniel Lewis had a rival for the affections of Elizabeth Williams and the thought occurred to that rival, John Jones of Cwm Scer, Llangyfelach, that if Daniel Lewis were to be transported the thirteen thousand miles to Australia the field would be clear for him. So, on Saturday 22 July, two nights after a fresh attack by the Pontardulais men under Daniel Lewis (at Rhydypandy, five miles from Bolgoed) he went to see Police Inspector Rees in Swansea and told him all. A delighted Inspector Rees swiftly hid John Jones where no one could get at him and brought two magistrates to question him, with the result that warrants were issued for the arrest not only of Daniel Lewis but also of the brothers William and Henry Morgan of the Parish of Llandeilo Talybont, Matthew Morgan and David Jones of the Parish of Llangyfelach, and Griffith Vaughan, landlord of the Red Lion Inn, Pontardulais.

Captain Napier thought a party of four would be sufficient to do the job so he took with him Inspector Rees and Police Constables William Jenkins, No. 9, and Henry Lewis, No. 13. They set out from Swansea on horseback at midnight, armed with swords and a special issue of pistols, and covered the eight miles to Pontardulais in about two hours. There, at about half past four in the morning, they took Matthew Morgan at his home, and at five o'clock David Jones at his. By seven o'clock they were back in Swansea with their prisoners, whom they left under

[2] His brother, Robert, was also a soldier, earning distinction in the Indian Mutiny and being created Baron Napier of Magdala for his conduct of the campaign in Abyssinia (Ethiopia) in 1868.

guard at the Police Station House. By seven thirty they were back on the road and on arriving at Llangyfelach they arrested William Morgan without any trouble. He was left in irons with the two constables while Captain Napier and Inspector Rees went to Cwmcille Fach farm near Velindre to pick up Henry Morgan. And that was where all the trouble started.

It was Sunday. The Sabbath. And though the law might allow a warrant to be executed on the Sabbath the people of that part of the world saw such an act as nothing less than a crime in itself, a profanation of the Lord's Day. Something that would dog this case right through to its conclusion and bring the town of Swansea to a state of riot.

When the two officers arrived at Cwmcille Fach at mid morning they found Henry Morgan sitting by the fire and, according to the policemen:

> He instantly suspected the nature of their visit and feigned illness. The warrant was then produced and he again feigned illness, protested that he was not able to move, and could not apparently be brought to comprehend that it was necessary for him to accompany them to Swansea. Captain Napier then, in a firm and decided manner, requested him to submit and peaceably to accompany them, otherwise they would be reluctantly obliged to use force.
>
> The scene at once changed. The 'invalid', who had previously been unable to stir without pain, suddenly sprang up. His family surrounded him and expressed their intention to resist his capture to the utmost of their power, at the same time making use of the most bloody threats, desiring the officers of justice to stand off, at the peril of their lives.
>
> Captain Napier and Inspector Rees then laid hold of the man and endeavoured to get him out of the house. Two men and two women instantly laid hold of the Inspector, felled him to the ground and in spite of his efforts kept him there. The rest of the family, four in number, attacked Captain Napier. He again laid hold of Henry Morgan and succeeded in dragging him out of the house, but the instant he got out of the door he was violently thrown to the ground. Henry Morgan's father stood over him on one side with his foot upon his stomach, while one of the sons stood over him on the other side, both father and son having firm hold of Captain Napier's pistol and endeavouring to turn the muzzle towards his stomach and to fire if off. Fortunately the pistol was not cocked. After a lengthy struggle Captain Napier succeeded in turning the pistol towards them and conceiving his life to be in the utmost danger, his

assailants being armed with hatchets, sickles and hammers, he fired and hit John Morgan, who upon finding himself wounded started back for a second or two, and then advanced again, attacking the Captain with the utmost fury.

A third brother armed with a mason's hammer advanced towards Captain Napier and aimed a blow at him, which he avoided and in return knocked the fellow down. He sprang up in a moment and again struck out with his hammer. Captain Napier then closed with him, wrenched the hammer from him and finally threw him.

Mr. Rees during this time had a hard and hot engagement with his opponents who having thrown him down endeavoured by tightening his neckcloth to strangle him, but he being a strong and powerful man and accustomed to defending himself succeeded in regaining his feet. He had pistols with him and presented one of them often at different individuals but did not fire.

The women during the whole of the time fought with a most frantic violence. One of them attacked Captain Napier with a sickle and inflicted a very severe wound upon the side of his head. The other woman seized a saucepan full of boiling water which she threw at the officers but fortunately missed her mark.

The struggle had now lasted some minutes and both Captain Napier and Mr. Rees, having had to contend against such odds, began to feel exhausted, when succour arrived in the person of Police Constable William Jenkins who, finding Captain Napier bleeding at all points and Mr. Rees' condition scarcely better, he drew his sword, beat the crowd back and rescued his superior officers from certain destruction.[3]

Constable Jenkins had been attracted to Cwmcille by the sound of the shot from Captain Napier's pistol, but in leaving his comrade Constable Lewis with the prisoner William Morgan he had left that officer with troubles of his own. Morgan started shouting 'Help, help; lladdwch hwynt' ('kill them'), to which the whole neighbourhood responded lustily, giving Constable Lewis a very rough handling before he could get his man to Cwmcille and join the others. But despite all their bruises and bleeding wounds, Captain Napier, Inspector Rees and the two constables brought their two captives into Swansea and lodged them with the others while they went to get badly needed medical attention.

[3] *Carmarthen Journal,* 28 July, 1843.

He never lived so splendidly

As news of the arrests spread a vast crowd of town and countrypeople surrounded the station house noisily demonstrating their support for the prisoners, to such a degree that soldiers of the 73rd Regiment had to be called in to help keep order. The news of the shooting of John Morgan incensed the crowd even more and great was the disorder in Swansea throughout the remainder of that day. Morgan was in no danger, though, despite the erratic course of the bullet from the left side of his abdomen up and backwards into his ribs, and he slowly recovered under treatment in the prison infirmary behind the walls of Swansea Castle.

In the meantime the authorities showed their determination that the rest of the Morgan family should pay for their treatment of Captain Napier and Inspector Rees by sending a large party of well-armed police and troops to bring them all in—male and female. This time the Morgans saw that they faced overwhelming odds and came out with their hands raised in surrender. Morgan senior was not to be found, but the family gathering was made complete when he came to the station to enquire about them, and was promptly arrested.

The arrest of Daniel Lewis, the Rebecca leader, was delayed until the Monday by all the trouble surrounding that of the Morgans, and Superintendent Peake and Sergeant Bennett went with a carriage to take him at his home alongside Goppa Chapel in Pontardulais. His mother, aware of the fight at the Morgans' home and fearful of the shame which would be brought on her at the chapel if the same were to happen with her Daniel, pleaded with him to go quietly. He did. But with a certain dignity. 'Walk down here,' said Superintendent Peake pointing towards the narrow lane between cottage and chapel. 'Oh no,' said Daniel, 'you bring the carriage here. That is the law.' At least he believed it to be so, and Superintendent Peake (another ex-soldier not long a policeman) was unsure enough on the point to engage in a most difficult struggle to squeeze the carriage into the lane and up to the door. He managed it, and Daniel Lewis went off into captivity, head held high, through a large and admiring crowd of neighbours.

Along with him went Griffith Vaughan, landlord of the Red Lion, who had also been informed upon by John Jones and who

Swansea (*Illus. London News*)

was additionally charged with acquiring firearms and ammunition for the Rebeccaites—twelve shotguns, four pistols, a bullet mould and ten or twelve boxes of percussion caps. They arrived at Swansea station house as the magistrates were assembling and the other prisoners were being brought in through the immense crowd of onlookers, and the evidence against them was taken over the next few days amid considerable controversy over the magistrates' attempts to hold their hearings in secret.

The evidence of the police could not be shaken, despite the insistence of the prisoners and the universal belief among the thousands outside that they had started all the trouble by making the arrests on the Sabbath and by violently seizing their men without so much as an explanation. But the officers' wounds, it seems, spoke for themselves, and the prisoners were committed, on bail, to await their trial before judge and jury, four months hence.

The degree of support shown for the prisoners not only in the numbers who invaded Swansea and surrounded the station house and gaol during the hearings, but also in the constant stream of well-wishers bringing an abundance of country produce to the gaol, went far beyond any suspicion of the intimidation commonly attributed to Rebecca. 'He never lived so splendidly in his life' said Elizabeth in later years of her Daniel's time on remand. 'They came in droves, with the best of eggs and chickens. He was a man of great heart and he shared it all with the others.'[4] But the informer Jones would rue the day he betrayed the Rebeccaites, for informers could not hide in anonymity then as they can to-day. They had to stand in open court and give their evidence on oath.

A rising tide

During the seventeen days between the attack at Bolgoed and the arrest of Daniel Lewis, no fewer than twenty five gates were destroyed, in places as far apart as Carmarthen, Cardigan, Pumsaint, Llandovery, Canaston Bridge, Bolgoed (again) and many places in between. Clearly, given the fact that on one night

[4] I am indebted for these stories about Daniel and Elizabeth Lewis to Mr. Wynford Vaughan Thomas, the author and broadcaster, whose grandfather and grandmother they were.

alone toll gates were destroyed simultaneously at places more than fifty miles apart, Colonel Love had serious problems in deciding how best to stretch his resources. And stretched they were because it was equally clear that Swansea needed to be strongly garrisoned to cope with violent incursions by unemployed coal and iron workers and discontented country-people, as would Llanelli when the Gwendraeth Valley troubles reached their climax in the following two months. And all the time the Chartist threat hung over the industrial areas to the east. Thomas Campbell Foster saw it on one of his rides through the valleys to Merthyr:

> I find that the whole of Glamorganshire is equally with Carmarthenshire in a feverish and excited state, and that there is a general and growing feeling of disaffection and discontent.
>
> The people in the hill districts here, it should be remembered, are of totally different habits and character from those of Cardigan, Carmarthen and Pembrokeshire. There they are a simple agricultural people, while here the great majority of the population are violent Chartist politicians. In the Merthyr district I learn from undoubted authority that political meetings are held weekly and oftener and that there are some arms distribution clubs to which the men subscribe and by which they are supplied with a musket, bayonet, crossbelts etc. for £1.16s.0d. [£1.80p]. This state of things has been going on for some considerable time and I am informed by a public officer that in the event of an outbreak one district alone could furnish five thousand stand of arms, consisting of muskets, bayonets, rifles, etc.[5]

No wonder Colonel Love had to keep his weather eye turned eastwards, while trying to make the best use of his forces in the west. There, small detachments of foot soldiers shared watch with special constables at the gates while the dragoons patrolled miles of country roads every night, in between dashing all over the place on false alarms, which achieved the very purpose intended—the exhaustion of men and horses.

How in these conditions could one decide which gates should be guarded? And in which areas? More dragoons marched into Carmarthenshire, from as far away as Somerset, not only to reinforce their comrades but also to fill the gaps caused by the coming need to release the volunteers of the Yeomanry to get in

[5] *The Times,* 13 July, 1843.

The 75th Regiment of Foot *(Nat. Army Museum)*

their harvests. The 75th Regiment was brought by steamer to Swansea, to disperse through the countryside and to be followed within a fortnight by the 76th. All the market towns of the west were bursting at the seams with troops to such an extent that temporary barracks were being sought all over the place to relieve the pressure on publicans and householders who had by law to billet the soldiers.

The attacks continued, and not all Rebeccas were as polite and considerate as Daniel Lewis. Nor did they confine their activities to the hours of darkness:

> *Rebecca and her Daughters:* On Friday afternoon last [7th July] a mob of these lawless depredators assembled together mustering about a hundred strong in the neighbourhood of Nantgaredig, about five miles east of Carmarthen. They were on this occasion all disguised and had their faces blackened and wore something designed to imitate a turban. They were all dressed in smock frocks and carried with them various implements of destruction.
>
> Their first outrage commenced at Llandeilo Rwnws gate, which is attached to the bridge over the River Towy. At the time, a respectable young man, a farmer of the name of Nicholls, happening to be on the spot was placed under examination [by Rebecca] and charged with having on some former occasion volunteered to become a special constable with a view to aiding in quelling the riots. He had to endure the operation of a very severe horse-whipping, after which he was allowed to depart. A man of the name of Lloyd from Carmarthen attempted to escape but they pursued him and he shared the same fate.
>
> Lloyd and a person of the name of Evans [both special constables] had been placed at the gate to enter the names of all persons who refused to pay tolls and to take care that the gate man did not raise more toll than he was authorised to do, but on the first appearance of Rebecca, Evans started off at full speed towards Carmarthen, and being a remarkably swift runner succeeded in making his escape from the clutches of Rebecca. *He was so frightened of the appearance of the old lady, who was at least six feet high, with her face blackened and brandishing a large hay knife in her hand, that he protests he will never have anything more to do with turnpike gates.* [6]

Enter here Mr. William Lewis, a toll farmer who, like Thomas Bullin, was seen as the cause of all the trouble in the areas where he leased toll gates. On the previous Saturday he

[6] *Carmarthen Journal,* 14 July, 1843.

had had a number of people before the Carmarthen magistrates on charges of refusing to pay tolls, and Rebecca's joy knew no bounds when she found *him* hiding in the tollhouse:

> Lewis was brought out, and unfortunately having his horse whip in his hand he was at once overpowered, the whip in question taken from him and most severely and violently beaten. Rebecca was not however content with this, but on his bended knees she compelled him three successive times to swear by all that was sacred that he would never again have connection with the tolls or the turnpike gates.
>
> Then came the scene of destruction. Pickaxes, hatchets and saws were set in operation and the gate entirely demolished. *It is currently reported that Mr. Lewis resigned his trusteeship on Saturday last.*

At Gwarallt gate, near Llanybydder on the Lampeter-Cardigan road, Rebecca reacted yet again to the imposition of tolls on people attending country fairs. On Monday 10 July the fairs were on both sides of the gate—at Carmarthen and Lampeter—and Rebecca and about two hundred of her daughters opened the road to all, toll free. Here she outdid her counterparts in other districts by being 'dressed agilely in female attire and sporting a parasol' and did 'no other injury than merely destroying the gate and posts.' The solitary man arrested for that affair—David Evans, a farmer, of Penlan—suffered no other inconvenience than a short time in Carmarthen Gaol before being released on bail to take his trial at Carmarthenshire Assizes. A year later he was discharged after the jury had spent twenty-two hours considering their verdict and then disagreed. And the architect of his discharge was his defending counsel—Edward Crompton Lloyd Hall, the representative and champion of the farmers of that district.

How it is to end, God alone knows

While all this was going on the turnpike trusts were doing all in their power to reverse their previous disastrous policies and placate Rebecca, but those to whom they directed their newspaper announcements either did not read newspapers or did not believe there was any real change of heart or, quite simply, were enjoying their new-found power and importance. In fact, representations had been made to the Swansea Trust about the gates in the Pontardulais district on the very day before the attack at Bolgoed, giving negotiations no chance at all. And the attacks became more and more vicious. On the edge of Swansea, for example, the Tŷ Coch (or Red Lion) gate was destroyed on Thursday 3 August in:

> . . . circumstances of peculiar aggravation, one of the men having beaten the toll collector, an old woman, in the most cruel manner. She had rushed out of the house and screamed for assistance when one of the senseless brutes engaged in the work of demolition and who apparently was the ringleader pursued her and struck her with an iron bar on her arm with such violence as to fracture the bone, at the same time saying in Welsh 'Damn your bloody eyes you old hag of Satan; silence or else I'll smash you.' The woman fortunately knew the scoundrel and gave such a description of his person to Thomas Jones, an active and intelligent police officer of the town, that he, in company with Mr. William Rees (Mr. Inspector Rees' son) after a tiresome journey to some collieries in the Parish of Llansamlet, succeeded in apprehending the villain and bringing him to Swansea Police Station.[7]

The man they arrested 'twenty fathoms underground' at the coal face was David Jones, but the ordeal of Margaret Arnold, the old toll collector, was not over even when she had given the evidence before the magistrates that had him committed to the Assizes for 'cutting and maiming' her. In the court she:

> . . . seemed to suffer much from her injuries and was taken to Swansea Infirmary guarded by a party of policemen, the violent language and gestures of the relatives of the prisoner rendering it prudent to take this last precaution. In fact, on her way there she was followed by about a dozen blackguards who hooted and threatened her with further personal violence and seemed disposed to carry their threats into execution, when fortunately Colonel Cameron passed, who, perceiving the state of affairs, stepped between the parties and protested that he would knock the first man down who would advance in pursuit of the woman.[8]

Even by 22 July, a fortnight before this, Edward Crompton Lloyd Hall had become so concerned about the deterioration in the situation as to tell the Home Secretary:

> I am convinced that ye whole population of ye country is

[7] *Carmarthen Journal,* 4 August, 1843.
[8] *Carmarthen Journal,* 11 August, 1843.

becoming more reckless and dissatisfied. *How it is to end God alone knows.*[9]

Writing to the Home Office almost daily by now, he followed this up the very next day with a note of serious concern about the consequences of any collision between the troops and police and the armed Rebeccaites—something which had not yet occurred. What would be the consequences, he wondered, if the troops or police should open fire? And what effect was the worsening industrial situation in the east going to have on the troubles in the west?

> If ye ironworks throw back upon us [in west Wales] their thousands, ye present elements of mischief in ye country will be greatly aggravated and ye first blood drawn by ye soldiery and constables will I fear be ye signal for fearful acts of personal revenge against the particular individuals. The presence of ye soldiery will then be of little or no avail, for it will be perfectly out of ye question to garrison every house and even if it could be done for a time, *who shall outlive a Welshman's thirst for vengeance?*[10]

No sluggard when it came to lurid language, Lloyd Hall also had a curious facility for timing. On the very day he wrote this, John Morgan, struggling on the floor with Captain Napier and trying to turn his own pistol on him, was himself shot in the stomach by the officer, and the people's outrage reduced the town of Swansea to a state of riot for days afterwards.

Within a fortnight, though, came another and more serious gunshot wound, fired not by 'ye soldiery and constables' but by one of Rebecca's daughters. On Friday night 4 August:

> . . . New Inn gate about ten miles from Cardigan was attacked by a mob and the gate destroyed. The toll collector's wife on looking through the window was fired at by one of the savages and was wounded in the face *and blinded for life.* Seeing the toll collector's coat hanging inside the toll house, another of these miscreants under the impression it is thought that it was the toll collector himself, fired a gun at the coat and thirty slugs were found in it the next morning.
>
> Hearing the woman groan, they asked the toll collector if he was hurt. He said he was not but that they had murdered his wife. They said that was a pity and ordered him out of the house and made him

[9] Letter dated 22 July, 1843, E. C. Lloyd Hall to Home Office: Public Record Office, File HO 45/454.

[10] Letter dated 23 July, 1843, E. C. Lloyd Hall to Home Secretary: Public Record Office, File HO 45/454.

go with them to the Chapel keeper of a neighbouring Dissenting Chapel, whom they knocked up and compelled to give to the toll collector a bottle of the communion wine, which they told him to carry back to cure his wife with.[11]

This crime, like most of the others described so far, was never detected. Indeed there were no professional policemen to detect them in the three counties of Cardiganshire, Pembrokeshire and Carmarthenshire, apart from the growing number of officers from the London Metropolitan Police whose efforts had so far come up against a solid wall of popular support for the cause. Only in Glamorgan had the civil power scored any real success, in the shape of arrests for the attacks at Bolgoed and Rhydypandy. But there was a regular police force there. More and more did the civil power elsewhere demonstrate its impotence, and more and more did the evidence mount that the old system was dead and the tradition of relying on magistrate and special constable was discredited. At Carmarthen on Wednesday 2 August, for example:

> . . . the magistrates of the County attended the Guildhall to swear in the persons who had been summoned to act as Special Constables in the several Parishes in the immediate neighbourhood. For the several Parishes, *two hundred and thirty had been summoned,* but for the Parish of Abergwili *none answered to their names.* From Newchurch, *five appeared and three of them refused to be sworn.* From Llanpumpsaint and Merthyr, *none appeared.* Those persons who appeared and refused to be sworn were it is said afraid of Rebecca. Some of them stated that they had been warned the previous night not to take the oath or else their houses would be destroyed and their lives put in danger.[12]

And Thomas Campbell Foster, writing his dispatch in Carmarthen on the night of Wednesday 19 July, added his view of how the military were coping with the task of supporting this frail 'civil power':

> Although the Dragoons are in the saddle every night scouring the country here and there, they happen to be always in the wrong place, and the work of outrage continues not only undiminished but with increased and increasing audacity. This is the state of things here and there will not be a single gate standing in the country if a

[11] *Carmarthen Journal,* 11 August, 1843. (Author's italics).
[12] *Carmarthen Journal,* 4 August, 1843. (Author's italics).

different mode be not adopted to put an end to it. The government are pouring in troops. A detachment of artillery are marching by way of Brecon; a detachment of artillery are marching to Carmarthen by way of Swansea; the whole of the 4th Regiment of Light Dragoons are to be stationed in South Wales; three companies of the 75th Foot are to arrive in Carmarthen within the next two or three days; the Yeomanry are kept on permanent duty, and every military appliance of the government is exercised, yet not a single outrage has been stayed nor a single Rebeccaite captured.[13]

They laugh at the display of power by the government.[14]

Night ride

Two nights later Foster had the chance to see for himself the difficulties faced by the military in the territory in which they had to operate and the organisation of the Rebeccaites. Colonel Love allowed him to ride with him on a special patrol around the troublesome districts between the London mail road (Carmarthen to Llandeilo, on the south side of the River Towy) and the Gwendraeth Valley. The patrol was organised at short notice on information that Rebecca would be out that night (Friday 21 July), not only to mount attacks on toll gates but also to set fire to the whole village of Porthyrhyd. Earlier in the day Major Parlby had sent gallopers to Llandeilo and Llandovery with orders for the Dragoons stationed there to move out in a concerted patrol pattern, and the operation began in late afternoon with buglers blowing the muster call to turn out the men from their town and village billets. The dragoons were divided into six patrols:

> . . . who at once scoured the roads from Llandovery, Llandeilo and around Carmarthen. I myself [Thomas Campbell Foster] got on horseback and accompanied a troop of the 4th Dragoons which was headed by Colonel Love and the Vice-Lieutenant, Colonel Rice Trevor, and commanded by Major Parlby, in a ride around the country of twenty-seven to thirty miles. We left Carmarthen at half past five o'clock in the evening and were out upon the roads until nearly eleven that night.
>
> Our route lay through Llanddarog and Porthyrhyd, where we met another troop who had scoured the roads from Llandeilo by

[13] The arrest of Daniel Lewis and the others involved in the Bolgoed and Rhydypandy attacks were still four days away when this dispatch was written.

[14] *The Times,* 22 July, 1843. (Author's italics).

The 4th Light Dragoons: a patrol resting *(Nat. Army Museum)*

way of Penrhiwgoch and Middleton Hall, the mountain by Llaningithen, etc. We then traversed the Coalbrook and Pontyberem back to Carmarthen. The troop had not however traversed more than three miles on the road from Carmarthen before it became evident that we were watched from the hill tops, and shortly afterwards two signal guns were heard. A place called the Old Railway is the centre of some coal works and as we passed it it seems that a large meeting was to be held or was then holding in the coal levels, but all through the route everything wore the most peaceful aspect and few people were to be seen upon any of the roads. Of course it was imagined that the alarm had been a false one. This, however, was a mistake for within an hour after the troop of Dragoons had passed the Bethania gate, which is almost immediately below a hill called The Tumble and the road leading to Llanon, than a skyrocket was sent up from one of the hills and within a few minutes several large bonfires were lit on the various hills around as answers to the signal given by the firing of the rocket.

The consequences of these signals soon manifested themselves to the inhabitants of the surrounding country (though not, of course, to the soldiers) by the almost instantaneous appearance of about a thousand men—colliers and others—who appeared to be in a well organised condition. They commenced their operations by attack-

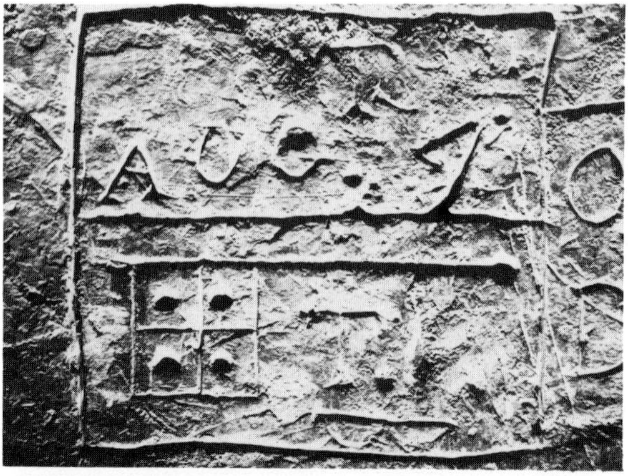

(a) Note the date, Aug. 43, the flag beneath it, and the trumpet (bottom right) below the initials T.P.

(b) 'Old boss Eye don't care a . . .' (The word 'Dam' has been all but obliterated.)

Graffiti carved by men of the 4th Light Dragoons in their billet, the cellar of what was then the George Hotel, Hill St., Llandeilo

(Pat Molloy—by courtesy of Mrs. M. W. Lewis)

ing and completely demolishing the Bethania gate, compelling the collector to seek safety in flight. They then walked in procession to Cwmmawr, through the village of Drefach and in fact through the entire neighbourhood, being accompanied in their procession by a species of 'rough music' consisting of a number of horns and drums and continuously firing shots as tokens of their triumph.

They then proceeded to demolish two toll bars on the road from Carmarthen to Llanelli, which exploit they accomplished in a very short time.

The scene throughout was remarkably striking, the bonfires burning on the hills, the firing of the rockets, the explosions from the guns, the beating of drums and the blowing of horns. The surrounding country in the meantime being beautifully illuminated by the light of the young moon, it was very striking in the extreme.[15]

You will repent of this

If further proof were needed of the extent of popular support for Rebecca in the area of the patrol, Mr. John Thomas of Cwmmawr could have supplied it. Being on the road as Colonel Love's patrol approached, he was unwise enough to put them right when they asked directions to Drefach and Carmarthen, and in the early hours of the following Wednesday morning he and his family were rudely awakened from their sleep when his parents' house:

> . . . was surrounded by a large party of Rebeccaites and colliers of the neighbourhood, who greatly alarmed the family by blowing horns and firing guns. A threatening letter was left pinned against the front door requiring the father to dismiss one of his workpeople, telling him that his son [John Thomas] was a marked man and saying that the next visit they paid to his house they would raze it to the ground.[16]

Another who had the temerity to direct a dragoon, in Carmarthen town itself, received his warning from a stranger in the crowd who shouted 'You will repent of this.' It was a warning reinforced the next market day when a visiting farmer said to him 'Ah sir, sorry to hear that you are against Rebecca.' 'Oh no, I'm *for* Rebecca,' he answered. 'What for then did you tell the dragoon to turn to his right and to his left for the workhouse on Monday last?' said the farmer. 'I did so, but who

[15] *The Times,* 25 July, 1843.
[16] *Carmarthen Journal,* 28 July, 1843.

Carmarthen peasantry *(Illus. London News)*

told you this?' asked the surprised townsman. 'I heard it at a meeting on the hills last night,' replied the farmer, 'and if you value your life you had better not come into my country, or if you do you will get your brains knocked out.'[17]

The lessons would be rammed home time and time again as the months passed. There never *would* be enough troops and the fragmentation into small detachments of an army created and trained to fight as a body was already having serious effects on both its organisation and morale. The civil strife that made this necessary throughout the Kingdom would eventually do untold harm to that army if no other way could be found to contain it. The truth was that no army could substitute for the civil power and that that civil power should be capable of coping with everything short of the catastrophe which would make involvement of the

[17] *The Times,* 30 July, 1843.

military a dire necessity and not just a matter of course. Things had gone too far and the civil power had failed to cope in the rural areas, and Thomas Campbell Foster realised very quickly that military action alone would never be enough to remove the crisis. Supporting the civil power in an emergency is one thing. Holding down an entire people is quite another.

'What is the effect of all this display of military force?' wrote Foster on the Monday night following his expedition with the cavalry:

> Ask the Dragoons and they will tell you they are knocked up with nightly marches and watchings, for they are sick of galloping nightly a dozen miles on false alarms to prevent outrages which they hear are threatened and which are never even attempted if they make their appearance and watch until daylight, but which are sure to be completed if they do not.
>
> But how is it that an effect so contrary to all reasonable anticipation is produced here? *It is because the whole country appears to be of one mind, and it is difficult to fight against a united people. They are all spies upon the soldiery.*[18]

[18] *The Times,* 27 July, 1843. (Author's italics).

Chapter Eight

TELL HIM THAT YOU ARE BECCA

By the end of July, 1843, Thomas Campbell Foster felt he was getting to the real root of the trouble; to the people who had instigated and were encouraging the activities of Rebecca. And on 27 July he began his long-running feud with the Baptist, Independent and Dissenting Chapels.

As early as 27 June (five days after his arrival in Carmarthenshire) he had heard how the name Rebecca had come to be chosen as the symbol of the people's struggle. He quoted Genesis, chapter 24, verse 60, and went on to say:

> The Welsh are a very religious people and with many of the ignorant and simple-minded peasants this opposition to the turnpikes is mixed up with the kind of fanaticism that they think they are doing a good and praiseworthy work in endeavouring to destroy that which they look upon as an oppressive injustice. I heard a Welshman myself say in allusion to a Dragoon being drowned while swimming in the river at Newcastle Emlyn 'Ah, you see, Providence is against them. They have had no luck since they have been here. They have had two horses die [at Carmarthen workhouse] and now there is one of their men drowned'.[1]

And travelling about the countryside on his investigations he came upon what he felt was more and more evidence of the deep well of religious belief from which all the passion of the Rebeccaite phenomenon seemed to have sprung. On a journey into Pembrokeshire, for example, which had seen him all day in the saddle speaking to one and another on the wayside, he arrived at Begelly, eleven miles short of Pembroke, at ten o'clock at night, and:

> . . . the road to Narberth being across country I procured one of the countrypeople as a guide and on the way conversed with him as to the general feeling of the people. He described to me in the most simple but forcible terms the miserable poverty they were suffering,

[1] *The Times,* 30 June, 1843.

The grave of Trooper John Kearns, 4th Light Dragoons, in Newcastle Emlyn Churchyard. He died one week after taking part in the charge at Carmarthen Workhouse, at the age of 25 years. His epitaph—'He fell not in the battle strife, nor on the sultry plain. Death did not meet the Warrior there, nor on the stormy main. But there, in Tivy's winding stream, on sunny summer's day, where bathing peacefully he sank, his spirit passed away. Mourn reader, with his comrades mourn, o'er one so young and brave, and trust in Him whose mighty arm from endless death can save.' *(Pat Molloy)*

and the sin, the wickedness and the oppression under which he said they laboured.

I ought here to remark that the lower orders in Wales have a considerable degree of religious fanaticism about them, are most of them Dissenters and are in the constant habit of quoting Scriptures for everything which they advance, and this man applied some text from Scripture to almost every observation that he used. He compared the present troubles to Daniel's vision, and as we passed the Union workhouse he said 'Ah sir, there is the house of oppression; them who God hath joined together let no man put assunder. Do you, sir, think it right that because we are poor they should take our children from their mother and me from my wife if I was compelled to go in there? And do you think it right that if a poor girl has been led astray she should be obliged to pay all for the child? That law has caused a pretty many babies to be put out of the way—it causes murder of the innocent—but nothing can stand that is against God, and this law is against God's word.'[2]

His broadside came a month later:

I was rather surprised to learn during my enquiries that the text I sent to you some time ago (the 24th Chapter of Genesis and 60th Verse) on which the Rebeccaites are said to found their proceedings, has frequently been preached in the Baptist, Independent and Dissenting Chapels and that the Preachers have advised the people to their outrageous proceedings. The Wesleyan Methodist Preachers, on the contrary, have pursued an opposite course and have urged the people not to break the law. This Sect however in Wales is not by far so numerous as the various sects of Dissenters.[3]

The storm broke, but within a week Foster was at it again, evidently playing the classic journalistic game of not firing off all his ammunition at once, but only in bursts, to keep his story going and his opponents guessing:

I have obtained, I think, pretty conclusive evidence that the Dissenting Ministers here are not undeserving the character they have obtained of fomenting these disturbances. The following is an extract from the last number of the Welsh monthly magazine called *Y Diwygiwr,*[4] published at Llanelli and edited by a Dissenting Minister and a leader and a kind of Bishop in his Church. I give you quotations from this magazine and I think you will say with me after

[2] *The Times,* 3 July, 1843.

[3] *The Times,* 31 July, 1843.

[4] Translated by Foster as *The Reformer.* It may be a measure of his bias against the magazine and its editor that he did not use the other translation *The Dissenter.*

'The deepwell of religious belief from which all the passion of the Rebeccaite phenomenon seemed to have sprung' (from the painting 'Salem' by S. Curnow Vosper) *(Lady Lever Collection, Walker Art Gallery, Liverpool)*

reading it 'No wonder the Dissenting Ministers should earn such a character.' After describing the outrages which have taken place during the last week, the article proceeds: 'We cannot regard these tumults, together with their like in other parts of the Kingdom, but as a direct effect of Tory oppression. Our wish, as we stated before, would be to see Rebecca and her children arrayed by thousands, clad with moral force for the suppression of Toryism. These are the only means to remove the burden from the back of the country. Fellow countrymen—be wise and firm, vindicate your principles in the face of day and in the eye of light. Avoid all measures which have placed you in your oppressors' fangs. Resolve to do your part to elevate the banners of freedom, civil and religious, everywhere,

> from the cabin of the poorest beggar in Carmarthenshire to Buckingham Palace.
>
> 'Seize the weapons you are sure to conquer with. Yours is moral force exclusively. Work it out, but the resource of your oppressors is physical force. They are much too strong for you on this ground. Resolve to see the sword of reason plunged in oppression's heart.'[5]

Though Foster did not touch upon their relevance to the Charter movement, which he had already dismissed as having no part in the Rebecca Riots, here once again were the catch-words that had brought about the riots in Llanidloes, the *débâcle* of Frost's march on Newport and all the Chartist disturbances in England over the past four years: '*Moral Force* or *Physical Force*.'

No doubt the Dissenting Ministers, too, protested that their words were intended to be taken *figuratively* and not *literally,* as had Thomas Powell, the Welshpool Chartist, in his trial for sedition. But Foster's reasoning was that the Dissenting Ministers knew better than Thomas Powell or anyone else in Wales the state of education among the masses, whose only source of education was the chapel and the Bible. And that they would know if anyone did how unlikely it was that their congregations would appreciate such subtle distinctions in the use of language.

But if the subtleties of language and the actual intentions of the author were matters for argument, as the flow of newspaper correspondence on Foster's views proved only too well, Foster himself was prepared to back up his side of the argument with some rather harder evidence—a written statement from one who claimed to have been in the congregation at Bethania Chapel, Llanon, when the crier William Jenkins read from the pulpit a notice from Rebecca warning the farmers among them not to attend and be sworn in as special constables, 'for if they would, Becca should visit them and destroy everything they possessed.' To William Jenkins' claim that he himself had read the letter under Rebecca's threat to destroy everything he possessed if he failed to do so, Foster replied, 'It is a clever way to get out of the hobble by saying such notice was left under the door.'

The controversy continued throughout August, drawing a letter to the editor of the *Carmarthen Journal* from the editor of *Y Diwygiwr,* the Rev. David Rees of Llanelli, who denied every allegation made by Foster and demanded specific proof of the

[5] *The Times,* 10 August, 1843.

Rev. David Rees, Llanelli, editor of the magazine *Y Diwygiwr* (The Dissenter)
(Nat. Library of Wales)

reading of Genesis, 24, 60 in any chapel. Foster's response, printed at the foot of his letter, was coldly dismissive. The Rev. Rees, he said, had 'completely shirked the charge against him of "fomenting and not repressing" the disturbances', while the editor of the *Carmarthen Journal* added his corroboration that when the St. Clears magistrates were having such great difficulty in swearing in special constables the previous February, a local Dissenting Minister, the Rev. Joseph Williams, had held the whip hand. Proclaiming himself the representative of the farmers, he refused on their behalf. Succeeding in wringing from the magistrates the promise to withdraw the Yeomanry, he gave his approval . . . and fifty of the farmers thereupon took the oath.[6]

Foster's final salvo—which he saw as his *coupe de grâce*—was delivered early in September when he quoted from the July issue of *Y Diwygiwr:*

> Rise up in arms together like men. Before the castles of oppression are laid low, before the high places of the church are

[6] *Carmarthen Journal,* 25 August, 1843.

> crushed and before the strongholds of Tory falsehoods are burnt, a devastating storm must be had. If you meet with an occasional Tory on your way to the poll, with his smiles from ear to ear and his arm stretched out shaking hands with everyone within reach, *tell him that you are Becca and that your profession is an opener of closed toll gates, or a destroyer of the same.*[7]

'This,' wrote Foster, 'from the organ of the Dissenters, published in their Chapels and read by them on the Sabbath after their prayer meetings. Is it difficult to see the result?'

By this time the disturbances had engulfed the very home of *Y Diwygiwr* and Foster concluded with a piece which positively glowed with journalistic self-satisfaction. His strictures on the Dissenting Ministers had, he felt, been totally vindicated and his worst predictions had come to pass:

> Before leaving Llanelli I would just remark that this town is a kind of Dissenters' stronghold. Here their Chapels abound. Here the people are blessed with the ministrations of the Rev. Mr. Rees. Here the Dissenting magazine *Y Diwygiwr* is printed and is extensively circulated in this town and neighbourhood; and here may be expected to be seen the chief fruits of Dissent. What are they? There is not a district in all South Wales more disturbed, or where cowardly malice and un-Christian revenge have proceeded greater lengths, than in the district six miles around Llanelli.
>
> Within the last four days toll houses have been demolished on all sides of the town, private property has been destroyed by incendiaries *and a poor old woman has been murdered by a body of ruffians.* 'By its fruits shall ye know it.'[8]

Phantom battles

But even if the disturbances *were* biblically inspired, even if they *were* encouraged from the pulpit, they were by no means always conducted with the dour earnestness of a religious crusade. There was no doubt about it; doing the Lord's work could be fun, and even Foster, for all his tirade against the Dissenters, could tell his readers 'There is also mixed in these outrages a degree of popularity and joke. Many think it fine fun to baffle both the authorities and the military, and from what I hear many join in these outrages for no other object.' As when

[7] *The Times,* 5 September, 1843. (Author's italics).
[8] *The Times,* 14 September, 1843. (Author's italics).

Rebecca, extravagantly attired in a ballroom gown and attended by a bewigged and stockinged 'negro' footman, was driven in a magnificent carriage into the farmyard of a 'respectable farmer' near Newcastle Emlyn, who, about two years previously, had made one of his servant girls pregnant and sacked her, obliging her to go into the workhouse to have her child:

> The facts of the case reached the ears of the now renowned Welsh outlaw Rebecca, who at once resolved on befriending the betrayed and deluded girl and correcting the evil under which she groaned, in a rather summary but ingenious way.
>
> About twelve o'clock on Friday night [11th August] the deceiving farmer was awoke from his slumbers by the rattling noise which intimated the approach of a carriage, and which was soon driven up his farmyard to his house, the door of which received a thundering rat-tat, giving him to understand that his presence was at once required. He immediately jumped out of bed, proceeded to answer the call and upon opening his door saw a black footman taking down the steps of the carriage and opening its door, when out came a lady very gaily attired with the child in her arms. She entered the house and introduced herself to the farmer by the name of Rebecca, saying she had brought with her his own child, which he was required henceforward to take care of and bring up respectably as he had been brought up himself, further adding that she, Rebecca, would keep a firm eye upon his conduct towards the child and should she find him wanting in the duties and obligations of a parent a second visit would be paid him, when he would be taught to rue his disobedience to this imperative direction.
>
> The astounded farmer at once promised obedience in the most implicit manner, when Rebecca delivered up the child to the father, who fondled and affectionately carressed it. Rebecca then expressed herself satisfied, shook hands with the farmer, stepped back into the carriage and rapidly drove off. The child remains still with the farmer and it is said he is treated as one of the family.[9]

Even the serious business of gate-breaking could have its lighter moments, as at Bwlch y Clawdd (near Llandysul) at around midnight on Wednesday 16 August, 1843, when two hundred mounted men armed with cutlasses and guns very quickly demolished the gate, and then:

> . . . to divert themselves they had a sham fight and the charges they made on each other were truly terrific. The guns were discharged in

[9] *Carmarthen Journal,* 18 August, 1843.

> all directions and the fire flashed from their swords as they met in combat, so that nothing was to be seen but fire and smoke. Some people who had assembled to watch their proceedings actually thought a conflict between them and the dragoons was taking place. They were all dressed in long white gowns girded about the middle with sword belts, and large straw hats on their heads. They had rather a warlike appearance.[10]

Clearly there was an element of fantasy in it too, the fantasy of a pitched battle in which the Rebeccaites employed against the cavalry tactics learned secretly from the ex-soldiers among themselves. It was intended to remain a fantasy and the whole of Rebecca's strategy of decoy and stealth was designed to that end. But could it last?

[10] *Carmarthen Journal,* 18 August, 1843.

Chapter Nine

A SWARM OF FLIES

'The fact is,' wrote Thomas Campbell Foster early in August, 1843, 'that the root of the evil is not the toll bars. They are only an aggravating oppression, which under different circumstances would have been borne by a quiet and inoffensive people without grumbling.' And the pattern of events around Carmarthen and further west during August and September would prove him right.

As the turnpike trusts in Pembrokeshire, Cardiganshire and west Carmarthenshire strove desperately to appease their tormentors, as ruined gates remained ruined, and as it became apparent from the arrival of two government investigators[1] that someone somewhere might be listening at last, so would Rebecca apply her lash more and more to the tithes, the Poor Law, high rents, bailiffs, bad landlords and unpopular magistrates. It was a turn of events that could only add to the problems of the hard-pressed District Military Commander, for Rebecca's activities became so sporadic, her targets so diverse and widespread and information so hard to come by that his efforts to pit his army against the Rebeccaites were best described in the words of one of the farmers Foster met on his travels: *'It is like firing a charge of shot into a swarm of flies'* he told him. And so it was because, for all the intense activity, large tracts of those three western counties were either untouched by it or affected only occasionally, a fact which struck Foster most forcibly:

> I have been almost constantly in the saddle, the stirring scenes around me having been so numerous and in such a variety and in such directions. Instead of being awed by the presence of the military the doings of Rebecca have become more daring and the disorganisation of society here more apparent. It is, however, equally strange that except where the outrages are actually being

[1] T. J. Hall and G. H. Ellis, the former a London Stipendiary Magistrate and the latter a solicitor with special knowledge of the Turnpike laws. Their mission will be examined in more detail later.

> committed, apparently profound peace reigns and persons can travel through the country in perfect security.[2]

An illusion indeed, for Colonel Love's resources were as stretched as they could be. At one end of his territory the rumblings of Chartism and unrest caused by the industrial depression demanded a strong military presence in the Glamorgan and Monmouth valleys, as did the frequent marches on Swansea by tens of thousands of foundry workers and miners affected by strikes, lock-outs, lay-offs and wage reductions. With what soldiers remained the Colonel garrisoned the main towns and villages of the west and guarded what gates he could. He kept the Castlemartin Yeomanry out in south Pembrokeshire and tried to stiffen the often shaky resolve of the magistrates and their special constables by spreading his small force of Metropolitan Police thinly among them, for despite all the pressure from the government, the Lords Lieutenant and himself, the magistrates of Cardiganshire and Pembrokeshire flatly refused to adopt the only remedy holding out any promise in the long term—the establishment of police forces in their counties. And even though those in Carmarthenshire allowed themselves—albeit under strong protest—to be bludgeoned into doing so in August by their Vice-Lieutenant, Colonel George Rice Trevor, it would not be before the end of the year that the man they appointed Chief Constable—Captain Richard Andrew Scott, late of the Royal Staff Corps—would be able to get his force together and deploy it. Too late, in fact, for the force to do anything of consequence in putting down the disturbances. In the meantime, Love's soldiers were easily outwitted at every turn owing to their inability to move without attracting attention, while the people's attitude to the civil authorities was little short of contemptuous.

Refusal to pay toll and taking conveyances through toll gates by force was becoming widespread and proving to be as effective in its way as gate-breaking. Farmers by the score were brought before the magistrates for refusing to pay toll, and the wheels of summary justice became bogged down in the whole process of inflicting fines and enforcing payment. Of course, wherever possible the names of those refusing would be taken by the gate-

[2] *The Times*, 24 July, 1843.

keepers, but Rebecca had an answer for that too. On Saturday 12 August, for example, in broad daylight, a band of twenty five white-gowned men on horseback arrived at the long-troubled Trevaughan gate in Whitland and forced the gate-keeper to hand over the books in which he had recorded the names of non-payers and to go down on his knees and swear that he would take no more tolls. Satisfied with this, the Rebeccaites galloped away, leaving the gate untouched.

I cannot fairly think I am in Wales

Meanwhile, in those two months of high summer, the 'flies' swarmed all over the three western counties and not even the long hours spent gathering the first good harvest for years under blue skies and a hot golden sun were allowed to deflect Rebecca from her purpose. Bailiffs seizing cottages, farms, furniture and stock were attacked and beaten and the goods and property restored to the defaulting tenants; animal pounds for storing the stock they seized were demolished, and in one case near Carmarthen the bailiff was himself confined in the cattle pound overnight and released only when the normal release fee of fourpence (1½p) had been paid. There may well have been some truth in the story that as a result of that experience, bailiff James Thomas became a leading advocate for the prevention of cruelty to animals and the abolition of solitary confinement in prison! Farmers as far apart as north Carmarthenshire and south Pembrokeshire were forced under threat of arson and murder to sell cheaply the corn they were hoarding against higher prices, and in one such incident at Haverfordwest Rebecca did the deed in her finest style. Arriving in a handsome carriage, dressed in a beautiful gown, wearing golden droppers on her ears and accompanied by a retinue of servants, she told the farmer of her desire that 'all the corn in straw should be threshed and the clean grain brought to market the following Saturday, that the poor labourer might have a chance to purchase it at a moderate price.' Her very word was his command.

Barns, outbuildings and cornstacks belonging to magistrates, suspected informers and unpopular landowners were burned; bastard children were united with their natural fathers and separated wives and husbands were forcibly reunited, in a campaign bolstered by a plague of Rebecca letters, some genuine, most not, but all couched in biblical language reinforced by biblical texts, and bearing all manner of threats. A farmer at Llandysul who took a second farm 'against the wishes of his neighbours' was beaten to within an inch of his life by a gang of disguised men, while the homestead of another at Gwynfe near Llangadog, and the outbuildings of yet another on the edge of Carmarthen town, were burned to the ground for the same reason. At Llanfihangel-ar-arth, thirteen miles north of Carmarthen, the house at Gwar y Graig farm was demolished stone by stone, merely because its owner, Mrs. Nicholls of Maesycrugiau, was encouraging would-be tenants to bid against each other for it.

The offence for which Rebecca's fury descended on Miss Jayne Walters of Glanmedenny, Newcastle Emlyn, was that she lacked a sense of humour. The crusty old spinster was at an open air wedding party when suddenly a ragged young farm boy ran up to her, threw his arms around her and kissed her . . . for a bet. The outraged lady took him to court for assault and the magistrate fined him £1 (the equivalent of nearly half a year's wages), whereupon Rebecca mustered her daughters and paid Miss Walters a riotous nocturnal visit, surrounding her house and threatening to burn it down with her in it if she failed to return the boy's pound. But this old maid was made of stern stuff and was one of the few to defy Rebecca and get away with it—though she bombarded the Home Secretary with letters of complaint for months afterwards.

At Llechryd, six miles away, three hundred men in full Rebecca regalia smashed a salmon weir belonging to Abel Lewes Gower of the mansion of Castell Malgwyn, a governor of the Bank of England. The Royal Marines at Cardigan had been decoyed away to the smaller weir at Felingigfran, and when one of them became detached from his comrades on the night march back he suddenly found himself right in the middle of three hundred fantastically garbed Rebeccaites marching from Llechryd. To show there were no hard feelings, the happy Rebeccaites, having first made sure that he had unloaded his musket, took him to a local pub and for the next two hours regaled him with as much ale as he could swallow, before escorting him to within easy reach of his Cardigan billet and bidding him a hearty goodbye. Within the space of twenty four hours and a distance of

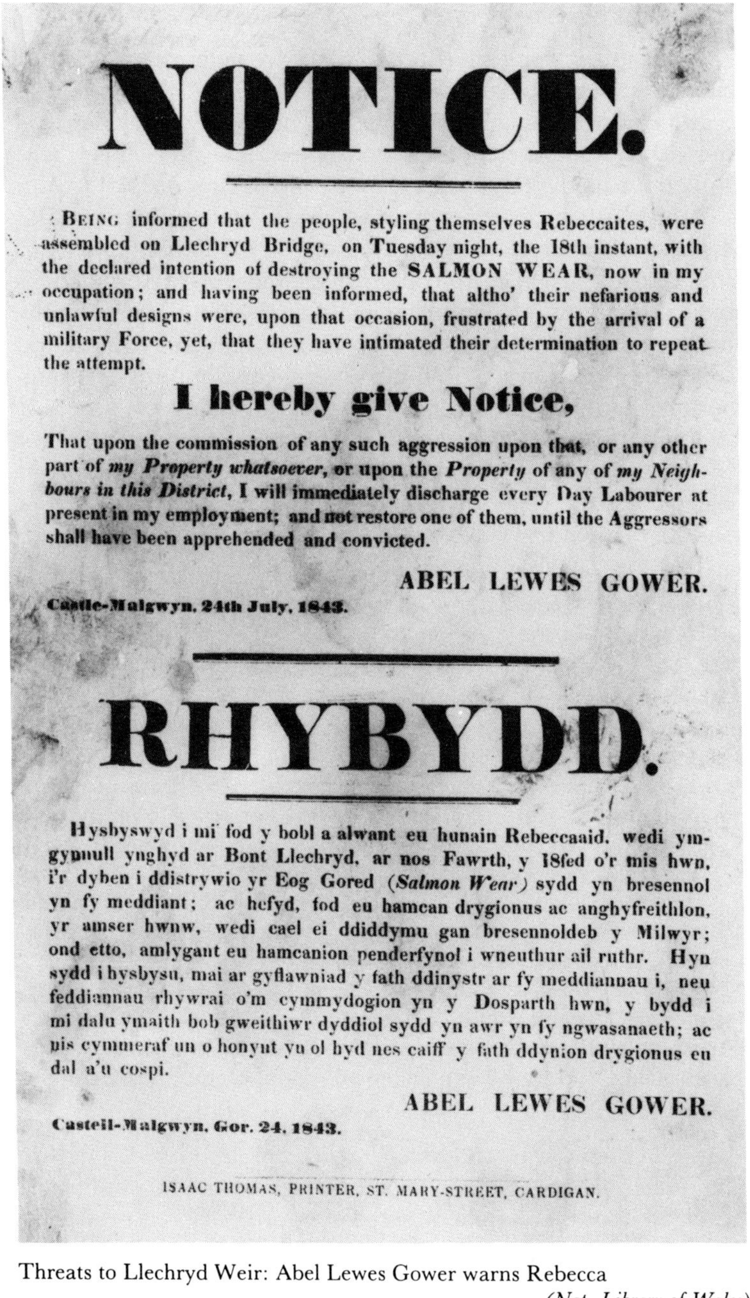

NOTICE.

BEING informed that the people, styling themselves Rebeccaites, were assembled on Llechryd Bridge, on Tuesday night, the 18th instant, with the declared intention of destroying the **SALMON WEAR**, now in my occupation; and having been informed, that altho' their nefarious and unlawful designs were, upon that occasion, frustrated by the arrival of a military Force, yet, that they have intimated their determination to repeat the attempt.

I hereby give Notice,

That upon the commission of any such aggression upon that, or any other part of *my Property whatsoever*, or upon the *Property* of any of *my Neighbours in this District*, I will immediately discharge every Day Labourer at present in my employment; and not restore one of them, until the Aggressors shall have been apprehended and convicted.

ABEL LEWES GOWER.

Castle-Malgwyn, 24th July, 1843.

RHYBYDD.

Hysbyswyd i mi fod y bobl a alwant eu hunain Rebeccaaid, wedi ymgynnull ynghyd ar Bont Llechryd, ar nos Fawrth, y 18fed o'r mis hwn, i'r dyben i ddistrywio yr Eog Gored (*Salmon Wear*) sydd yn bresennol yn fy meddiant; ac hefyd, fod eu hamcan drygionus ac anghyfreithlon, yr amser hwnw, wedi cael ei ddiddymu gan bresennoldeb y Milwyr; ond etto, amlygant eu hamcanion penderfynol i wneuthur ail ruthr. Hyn sydd i hysbysu, mai ar gyflawniad y fath ddinystr ar fy meddiannau i, neu feddiannau rhywrai o'm cymmydogion yn y Dosparth hwn, y bydd i mi dalu ymaith bob gweithiwr dyddiol sydd yn awr yn fy ngwasanaeth; ac nis cymmeraf un o honynt yn ol hyd nes caiff y fath ddynion drygionus eu dal a'u cospi.

ABEL LEWES GOWER.

Casteil-Malgwyn, Gor. 24, 1843.

ISAAC THOMAS, PRINTER, ST. MARY-STREET, CARDIGAN.

Threats to Llechryd Weir: Abel Lewes Gower warns Rebecca

(Nat. Library of Wales)

only five miles along the Cardigan Bay coastline, a magistrate who was an outspoken opponent of Rebecca was shot at, a vicar's curate was waylaid and beaten up for giving evidence at court, three toll gates were demolished and a gatekeeper's wife blinded for life by the powder blast from a shotgun.[3]

At his farm in Aberporth, magistrate Walter David Jones, M.D., of Llancych, Newcastle Emlyn, on holiday with his family, received a visit from an armed gang who surrounded his house intent on showing him the folly of publicly criticising the Dissenters and condemning Rebecca. Awakened by the sound of breaking windows, Dr. Jones took a candle to his bedroom window, to be met by a blast of shot whistling by him and thudding into the wall behind him. Understandably he did not wait to hear what it was that the crowd was shouting to him. But he delivered his reply to the people at large in the form of a handbill printed in Welsh:

> *To the persons who made a murderous attack upon me on Friday 4th August, 1843, at Pennar in the Parish of Aberporth:*
>
> I cannot fairly believe that I am residing in Wales; Wales, a country so noted for its religion, its loyalty to the Queen and its obedience to the laws of the land, the land that was at all times free from any disturbance, where we used to sleep quietly in our beds without a bolt or lock on the doors or windows.
>
> Is it possible that you are really Welshmen that could have accomplished such a foul deed as this? I cannot believe my own senses that you could have been guilty of such horrid deeds. Nay, you must have been misled by others; those that care nothing for your good name nor your character; who hide themselves behind the bushes, making use of you as their tools to keep themselves from being discovered.
>
> They tell you that the tollgates must be taken down and other oppressive demands must be done away with, but they are in fact a combined party endeavouring to oppose the laws of the land and their chief aim is to get an equal share of their neighbour's property.[4]

Here it seems was another who saw the hand of Chartism behind the Rebecca Riots; another magistrate who could not appreciate that there must be some extraordinary reason why a

[3] See page 192 for an account of this last mentioned incident.

[4] *Carmarthen Journal,* 8 September, 1843. (Author's italics).

peaceable and long-suffering people should resort to such violence and have such support among their fellows. The answer was all around them, and they still could not see how much they themselves had contributed to this sorry state of affairs through their own blindness and lack of touch with those whom it was their sworn duty to serve.

At the harbour village of Llangrannog, a little way up the coast, the Vicar, the Rev. Eleazar Evans, had long been under threat for his offences against Rebecca's law. It was not enough that his mainly Dissenting parishioners despised him anyway and resented having to maintain him with their tithes, but he chose to enrage them even more by building a schoolroom with money they had donated and then using it as a place of worship for his hated Church of England. And then he had the temerity to ignore Rebecca's demand that he 'give the money back, every halfpenny of it, otherwise if you do not, I, with 500 or 600 of my daughters, will come and visit you and destroy your property five times to the value of it and make you a subject of scorn and reproach throughout the whole neighbourhood.'[5] It was a warning reinforced by a classic demonstration of the *Ceffyl Pren,* in which one of the parish's tithe collectors was exhibited in effigy before a large crowd and auctioned by a man impersonating a well-known auctioneer. The buyer was the Devil himself! And there was yet another warning, this time in the form of a vicious assault on his young curate, who was ambushed on his way home one night and left with several broken ribs. The Vicar did not really need the letter he received the next morning drawing his attention to Judges, chapter 6, verses 27 and 28 in which Gideon, the Hebrew judge and warrior, threw down the altar of Baal in the night and a second bullock (his curate was the first!) was sacrificed. He sold his farm, his stock and virtually everything he had, repaid his parishioners and spent the rest of his short stay in Llangrannog barricaded with his family in the vicarage.

Across country at Llanfihangel-ar-arth near Llandysul, Rebecca took her customary interest in what seemed to be the unjust treatment of a claimant under a disputed will. Disguised in the traditional style and armed with guns and reaping hooks,

[5] *Rebecca and Her Daughters,* by H. Tobit Evans, published by subscription, 1910.

she and her daughters dragged the offending farmer, Daniel Harries, from his bed at Pantyfen farm and forced the terrified old man to sign a note in favour of the claimant, and then themselves departed from Rebecca's code by also robbing him and ransacking his house. In this case, though, the victim identified eight of his tormentors, five of them from the neighbouring village of Llanllawddog, one from Llanpumsaint, one from Trelech and one from Carmarthen. All were put into Carmarthen Gaol to await their trial at the Assizes.

But it is the distances from which they had come together as a Rebecca band that shows the extent to which the Rebeccaites of the various districts co-operated with each other. Their homes were spread over an area enclosed by a triangle measuring some ten miles by sixteen, and the furthest away from the scene of the attack faced a ride of some two and a half hours on horseback each way. It had been seen before, this overlap of activity and these distant connections covering the country between Carmarthen, Newcastle Emlyn and the Pembrokeshire border and it would be seen again elsewhere. Foster found evidence of it too, in the speed with which news of Rebecca's exploits and her calls to arms were carried across miles of difficult country. An informant of 'impeccable' veracity told him that on the morning after Lord Dynevor's corn stacks were burnt at Llandeilo he was told about it in Clydach, Brecknockshire, thirty seven miles away, 'though there is no regular mode of conveyance.' As Foster went on to explain:

> The farms here are small and the white cottages of the farmers are dotted all over the landscape. It rarely happens that any farmhouses are more than two or three miles apart.
>
> A note addressed to a far destination is delivered to a farmhouse, the farmers know what it means and are instructed what to do, and some man or boy on the farm runs to the next farm in the line, and so on, at about the rate of eight miles an hour.
>
> No wonder that the authorities find themselves baffled by organisation like this. The Dragoons with military tramp and parade travel along the road confident that they shall at last pounce on the Rebeccaites, whilst some ragged urchin takes the shortest cut over hedge and ditch with a letter in his breast to be passed on from farm to farm to the scene of action, and the Dragoons find they are just too late.[6]

[6] *The Times*, 5 September, 1843.

In an aside on the matter of Lord Dynevor's corn stacks, Foster mentioned that a grave dug to perfect dimensions had mysteriously appeared in the grounds of Dynevor Castle, followed by an anonymous letter to his son, Colonel George Rice Trevor, the Vice-Lieutenant of the county, informing him that it was for him and that he would be laid in it within the week! The distorted version of his Newcastle Emlyn speech published in the Dissenters' magazine *Y Diwygiwr,* which had it that he would 'blow out the brains of the servants and labourers of Carmarthenshire to serve as food for the birds of the heavens' would haunt the gallant Colonel for a long time to come.

Such widespread and gratuitous violence was bound to lead to tragedy, and when it did it did so in circumstances which demonstrated all too clearly how some of the deeds done in Rebecca's name had begun to depart from the true spirit of her movement; how that spirit was being perverted in the pursuit of self-interest and private revenge. It happened in Brechfa, a village enfolded by deep and narrow valleys high in the wooded hill country to the north east of Carmarthen, from where the twisting lane to the north crossed the moorland of Mynydd Pencarreg to the steep descent into Lampeter. A closed and isolated community, and an insular one where feelings ran deep, grudges were long-nursed and revenge often primitive in its ferocity.

Seventy one year old Thomas Thomas of Pantycerrig farm was a crotchety old man who resorted readily to the law to settle his differences with his neighbours. Towards the end of September, 1843, he had a prosecution going against Benjamin and Evan Jones, the sons of Brechfa's blacksmith, Benjamin Jones of Clunllydan, for stealing his sheep, and while the magistrates' warrants remained unexecuted because the boys had gone into hiding, old man Thomas became embroiled in another dispute. This one was with his neighbour on the other side, twenty year old David Evans, over damage done by Thomas' cattle in straying onto Evans' Byrgwm farm. Ten shillings (50p), take it or leave it, was the old man's offer to his neighbour. David Evans took it. But late that night Rebecca arrived at Pantycerrig to see justice done. A number of men with blackened faces and guns surrounded the house, forced their way in and dragged Thomas Thomas into his farmyard, where they formed a circle around him so that he might hear Rebecca's judgement. He must pay for the damage caused by his cattle, said Rebecca. He had paid, he protested. He had paid ten shillings. 'But the matter is now in the hands of Rebecca' was the reply, 'and you must pay £5, and £2 of that within nine days.' Amid much jostling and prompted by a few blasts of gunfire, he promised to do so and was then dragged down the valley to Byrgwm farm, the scene of the cattle straying, and there roughly manhandled by the white-gowned avengers. At length he was freed, and wended his bruised and painful way home—to spend the rest of the night wrapped in thoughts of his own brand of vengence.

Old Thomas Thomas was out again while Brechfa still slept and while the early mists still hung thickly in the clefts of the hills, on a two hour horseback ride down to Carmarthen to see the magistrates' clerk in the Guildhall and to swear out two arrest warrants—one for his twenty year old neighbour David Evans of Byrgwm and one for Evans' twenty five year old servant, James Evans. The charges were riot and assault. Their arrest by the parish constables five days later stunned the whole parish and had the old man not already slipped off quietly again, back to Carmarthen to give evidence before the examining magistrates, he might well have been lynched. As it was he received a warning strong enough to keep him in Carmarthen for the night. Which was as well, for on that night Rebecca put the torch to his farm, and in the frantic efforts of his servants to save his animals from the blazing outbuildings and drag his furniture from the roaring flames consuming his house, the clothing of one of his servant girls caught fire and she was severely burned.

It was to a smoking ruin that old Thomas returned the next morning, leaving the Evanses locked in Carmarthen Gaol, yet reflecting on how quickly the sweet taste of revenge had turned sour with the loss of nearly everything he owned. But still he stuck to his guns, and still the two boys he had charged with sheep stealing remained in hiding while he steadfastly refused to drop the charges. Just over two months later, in an effort, so he said, to reason with the old man, the boys' father, blacksmith Thomas Jones, invited him to Clunllydan on the afternoon of Monday 18 December. Old Thomas Thomas was never seen alive again.

His body was found next morning in the Marlais stream,

where it was crossed by the trunk of an ash tree fitted with a wooden handrail as it tumbled through Brechfa on its downward plunge to the nearby River Cothi and on to the Towy Valley, a thousand feet below. He had died not of drowning, said Carmarthen surgeon, Josuah Phillips, but of 'concussion of the brain' resulting from head wounds, a conclusion he reached on the basis of the detailed autopsy report he read to the coroner and jury.

The other evidence given to the inquest was to say the least conflicting. For one thing the old man's wife, Mary, said that Thomas Jones had sent his grand-daughter to Pantycerrig to deliver the invitation, while Jones said that when he arrived at Clunllydan Thomas Thomas 'didn't say he had any particular business, but his wife had sent him to see how he was.' The times of his arrival and departure as given by the Jones family were also at variance with those given by witnesses who had seen him walking towards Clunllydan, and one—Griffith Davies, a Carmarthen tinman—who had crossed the tree trunk 'bridge' at a time when he should have seen the body had the Joneses been right about the time they said he left, saw no body there.

Blacksmith Jones swore that Thomas Thomas was alive and in good health when he left his house late that afternoon and there was no one to contradict him. Were the injuries caused by Thomas Thomas slipping from the log and striking his head on a rock on the bed of the stream? Or had he been killed elsewhere and his body dumped in the stream? He certainly had not drowned and the whole locality was convinced he had been murdered. And if Thomas Thomas *was* murdered the answer must surely lie with the Jones family. His death was certainly fortuitous for the Jones boys, who, in consequence of the death of their prosecutor, could not now be tried for sheep stealing and at once came out of hiding!

The coroner's verdict was an open one. There was no evidence to warrant a criminal charge, he said, but so strong was the belief that the old man had been murdered that it persists in the area to this day—a hundred and forty years later—and Pantycerrig is said to be haunted.

One might ask what kind of investigation was made by the police into what, despite the coroner's verdict, was a highly suspicious death, but it has to be remembered that the newly formed Carmarthenshire Constabulary had only been in existence for about two months and had put its one officer—Sergeant W. H. Stanhope—in Brechfa only three weeks before. And he was proving as troublesome to his Chief Constable as many of the people he was supposed to keep in order. Within nine months he had been dismissed for 'Having been the worse for liquor on the evening of the 8th [of August 1844] and very drunk early in the morning of the 9th, and having made use of language subversive to the discipline of the force.' Furthermore, the Chief Constable declared that he could not allow Stanhope to leave the force 'without expressing his entire disapproval of his conduct in regard to a horse he obtained at Cross Inn . . . for which kindness he threatened if the party lending the horse required more than one shilling [5p] he would prosecute for a penalty of ten pounds.'[7] Not only was Chief Constable Scott labouring under the handicap of leading inexperienced, uneducated and largely ineffective men in those very early days, but he was also up against the hostility of the people towards the very idea of a regular, paid police force and often dogged by the drunkenness and indiscipline that went with having to recruit his constables and sergeants from the 'lower orders.' The men's superior officers were more often than not drawn from the army's officer class, appointed through previous association with Captain Scott, with the consequent lack of experience and skill to investigate properly old Thomas Thomas' death.

For some time yet, the magistrates would continue to be the mainstay of law and order in the countryside. They would continue to be the only investigators in a system that was just about on its last legs. The transition from the old to the new was occurring at a time of crisis and it was destined to be a long and difficult one for that very reason.

But even that was not the end of the Pantycerrig affair, for James and David Evans of Byrgwm farm came up at the next Carmarthenshire Assizes on the charge of assaulting the old man on the night of Rebecca's visit to Pantycerrig and of threatening to burn Tynyffordd farm on the same night. The evident willingness of the Evanses and all their witnesses to perjure themselves was too much even for their counsel, Edward Crompton Lloyd

[7]General Order Book of the Carmarthenshire Constabulary (in possession of the Chief Constable of Dyfed-Powys).

Capt. Richard Andrew Scott, the first Chief Constable of the Carmarthenshire Constabulary *(Dyfed-Powys Police Museum)*

Hall, and he withdrew from the case. A swift verdict of guilty brought each of them a sentence of twelve months hard labour.

And that was still not the end of it. The ghost of old Thomas Thomas still stalked Pantycerrig and Brechfa seeking vengeance, and just a year after his death a warrant was sworn out against one of the Jones boys—Benjamin—by Margaret Bowen, a servant at Pantycerrig at the time of the fire.[8] The case was sent for trial at the Assizes, which were held four months later, in March, 1845, in Carmarthen.

Margaret Bowen told a terrifying story of hearing gunfire, finding the house burning, with even her bedclothes in flames, and seeing Benjamin Jones bursting into the building. She had no doubt whatever that it was he, but she came under fierce attack in cross examination by Mr. Richards, counsel for the defence, who made much of the fact that she would stand to gain handsomely by way of reward in the event of Benjamin Jones being convicted, a point he put to other witnesses, including Thomas Thomas' widow. And when he opened the case for the defence, Mr. Richards suggested that it was time to forget Rebeccaism and that his client should not be on trial at all.

The jury found Benjamin Jones not guilty. But he remained in the dock to face a second charge—of cutting Margaret Bowen's throat 'with intent to do her harm.' The court heard that four or five minor wounds had been inflicted on her but she recounted a conversation with her attacker that had everyone on the edge of their seats: 'I said to him "Boy what are you doing there" [by the hedge] and he asked by way of reply where old Williams of Tynyffordd was. I asked what he wanted to do with him; whether he wanted to do with him as he had done by my master [Thomas Thomas]. He replied "Damn you, you old jade. I am not sorry for anything done to your old master *and I am sorry I did not kill him sooner*".'

The effect of this on the jury was electric, for the story of the 'murder' of Thomas Thomas was fresh in the mind of everyone in the district from which the jurors were drawn. At all events he

[8] In his *Rebecca Riots,* David Williams mistakenly connects this charge and a case of murder committed at Trecastle in Breconshire. This was probably due to the murderer's name being Thomas Thomas—the same name as the old man of Pantycerrig. By coincidence, though, that Thomas Thomas came from the same district, from the village of Abergorlech.

was found guilty of attempting to murder Margaret Bowen—and the judge's words in delivering the sentence of transportation for life seemed to show that he, too, had taken the point about Thomas Thomas: 'It appears that although you intended to take the life of the young woman, yet in point of fact no serious injury was done to her. I think that under the circumstances your life may be spared. But on terms which will, for the remainder of your life, deprive you of the liberty which you enjoyed and abused. You shall no longer be in a free country, but be assigned over to the discretion of a hard taskmaster, without a choice of labour or recompense for your daily toil, only with such sustenance as will enable you to attract life. You are yet a young man, strong and vigorous, but your years shall be lingered out in a hopeless exile away from friends and relations—away from those ties which render life elsewhere happy. If in the midst of that desolation you cast an eye back on your country and friends, it will be with unavailing regret, for you shall never see them more. I hope you will there repent of this crime, *and any other enormities which you might have committed but which have not been found out, and which may lay on your conscience.*'[9]

Perhaps the spirit of old Thomas Thomas, he who was so ready to resort to the law for the settlement of his many neighbourly quarrels, looked down and smiled at the irony of what he saw in that Carmarthen courtroom at what, to all intents and purposes, was the sentencing of a man for his murder. He would have smiled because *he* knew the secret. And a hundred and forty years after Benjamin Jones was transported for life, having, it was universally believed, paid at least a part of the price for murdering Thomas Thomas, we, too, can share the secret.

On the basis of the autopsy report prepared by Dr. Josuah Phillips for the Coroner's Inquest, one of Wales' leading present-day forensic pathologists[10] has delivered his verdict on its findings: the conclusion that 'the immediate cause of death was concussion of the brain' based upon 'connecting the outward bruise of the left of the forehead' is not acceptable to him. The injuries to the face and temple were, he says, consistent with

[9] *Carmarthen Journal,* 21 March, 1845. (Author's italics).

[10] Dr. Owen Glynn Williams, M.D., F.R.C.P., F.R.C.Path., Home Office Pathologist, who has worked with the author on many murder investigations and who became as interested as the author in this one.

a fall from the footbridge, a height of between seven and nine feet above the river bed. From the facts presented, death was due to a heart attack (from coronary atheroma) which occurred whilst crossing the footbridge. The relatively superficial head injuries were the result of falling into the stream. And his verdict? Death from natural causes!

Behold: Disastrous days have come!

For all the new diversity of Rebecca's targets, gate breaking still had its attractions, not the least of which was the fun of it all. Lampeter for example, had a further taste of it on the night of 1 August, when a huge crowd led by men on horseback and a band of music and carrying banners and flaming torches, marched noisily through the town, almost drowning the music with a barrage of gunfire and smashing the town's five gates as they marched. Before daylight they had cut down three more gates on the Aberystwyth road and a thoroughly good night had been enjoyed by all—without a sign of the soldiers who were supposed to be protecting the town. It was an event witnessed by another of Foster's informants, a Lampeter surgeon out on a late call who rode up to one of the gates and ran into the mob:

> One of them, a stranger to the neighbourhood armed with a double-barrelled gun, forced him into a house and compelled him to remain there until it was all over. While there, one of the party, evidently the leader, came past and my informant spoke to him. He was an Englishman and could not speak Welsh, and he was well dressed and well armed. He wore a handsome sword and had a pistol in his hand.[11]

Not only was a report like this a boon to the myth-making process already growing up around these disturbances, but it is also good evidence of the breadth of support they enjoyed and of the involvement of the high as well as the low in that rural society. Where else, for example, but from gentlemen could Rebecca have got her elegant carriages, her beautiful ball gowns, her jewellery and her black footmen's uniforms, with which to visit the erring fathers of bastard children and the hoarders of corn?

There was a curious irony about the sufferings of David Josuah, Carmarthen bookbinder and keeper of Glangwili gate.

[11] *The Times*, 22 August, 1843.

For David Josuah was a committed Chartist of the more rumbustious kind, a *Physical Force* man and a spirited orator, whose reputation owed much to his lively performance at the great torchlight meeting of January, 1839, which adopted lawyer Hugh Williams as Carmarthen's delegate to the great Chartist Convention in London. What happened to David Josuah makes a very interesting contribution to the debate on the possible connection between Chartism and Rebeccaism.

Chartist David Josuah may have been, but a supporter of Rebecca he was most certainly not and he lost no opportunity to say so. It was said, in fact, that the attack on the Water Street gate in June had been prompted by his prosecution of a non-payer of toll the previous week and that Rebecca had left a warning for him there. And other warnings had followed, until:

> About one o'clock in the morning of the 25th of August, the toll house of Glangwili gate near Carmarthen was surrounded by about two hundred Rebeccaites, who began shouting and yelling. They compelled the gate-man David Josuah to commence the work of destruction. The gate, being very strong, resisted their efforts for a considerable time, but ultimately the posts were sawn through and the gate smashed to pieces. They then attacked the toll house, which was speedily brought almost to the ground, the roof and walls being thrown in upon the furniture and stock-in-trade of David Josuah, who was a bookbinder.
>
> The house soon presented a ruinous appearance and the furniture and tools were buried beneath a heap of rubbish. Josuah was attacked by the Rebeccaites, struck several times with a hatchet and otherwise severely abused, while some country constables who were with him guarding (?) the gate took to their heels and made the best of their way towards the town.
>
> An express was sent to Carmarthen for the military and the dragoons were instantly called out and went off at a dashing pace for the scene of the riot. The sisters seemed to have taken measures very well, two of the party being placed as sentinels—one on the main road to Carmarthen and the other upon an elevated site from which he had a view of the road leading to Abergwili. When at some distance from the place of their destination, the dragoons heard the report of a gun, which was probably fired by one of Rebecca's sentinels as a signal of the approach of the military. When they arrived at the spot they found the gate and toll house destroyed, but no trace of Rebecca or her children.[12]

[12] *Carmarthen Journal,* 1 September, 1843.

David Josuah was determined to have justice and lost no time in finding a magistrate and naming four of his attackers—farmer David Thomas of Penlan farm, Llanllawddog, carpenter Benjamin Richards of Llynydd Styfle, Carmarthen, and two labourers, William Jones and Arthur Arthur of Abergwili. The reason why the constables could not find them to execute the warrants soon became apparent, for on the very next night, David Thomas of Penlan, Llanllawddog, led another expedition—the one which 'persuaded' Daniel Harries of Llanfihangel-ar-arth to defer to the other claimant under the disputed will.[13]

During the following day, David Josuah dug through the rubble of his toll house and pulled out the few things worth salvaging, but it was not easy to get someone to cart them into Carmarthen for him. Eventually he succeeded, and the cart set off with him on it for the two-mile drive to Cambrian Place, where he had rented a room in the Roundhouse Yard.[14] But word had gone ahead and when they arrived in Guildhall Square they were suddenly engulfed in a riot as the 'Carmarthen Mob' smashed every stick of furniture he had brought with him and scattered his precious collection of books to the four corners of the square. The horse was rearing and screaming in fright as the crowd cut into its traces, and Josuah was lying battered and bleeding on the ground, when Chief Constable Henry Westlake and his four-man borough police force came on the scene. It was as near a thing to Lynch Law as this tough town of Carmarthen had seen in a long time, but David Josuah was somehow extricated from the melée by Mr. Nott of Picton Terrace,[15] and taken to a place of safety, from where the sounds of riot were clearly heard by him for a whole hour more.

He was ruined—and he let the whole world know it. He published a handbill explaining his plight:

> *Behold!* Disastrous days have come; yea, days are these when men are traitors, hot-blooded and bombastic, loving to commit outrages during the dark hours of the night. Hardly a night passes without hearing of the destruction of toll-gates here—possessions fired there —and—what is much worse—treacherous attacks on the lives of

[13] See p. 220.

[14] The site of the original Roundhouse built in 1804, the first of the lock-ups and police stations that occupied the site until 1956.

[15] Brother of General Nott, whose statue stands in Nott Square.

those who venture a word of protest against the Rebecca movement. Among others who have been the object of sinful attacks by the thieving workmen of the night, I have become at last an object of visitation.

Between one and two o'clock on the morning of 25th August the destructive goblins descended on the toll gate of Glangwili and in a short time they completely destroyed everything; they stole from my house £9.19s.5d. [£9.97½p]; they burnt many of my valuable books in order to have light with which to carry out their thieving actions. Not only that, but when I escaped from their clutches one shouted 'Shoot him! Shoot him!' and another attempted to strike me with an axe.

Yours—rendered a pauper because of the above circumstances, D.W.J., Glangwili.[16]

Yet even after all this the indomitable David Josuah was determined to resume his tenancy of the Glangwili gate and even the burning of a temporary wooden shed there on 27 August could not deter him from doing so. Within a week he was back at the gate demanding tolls. And he was soon back in trouble, for a couple of days later he demonstrated once again his well known volatility when confronted by a refusal to pay toll: he dashed into his shed, brought out his shotgun, aimed it at the farmer and pulled the trigger three times. Three misfires brought his temper to absolute flash point and, throwing away the gun, he seized a sword and slashed the poor man several times on the head and arm before being restrained and arrested. His committal for trial at the Assizes for 'cutting and maiming' put an end to his antics in Carmarthenshire, and after serving two years in prison he seems to have left the district and, so it is said, ended his days in Aberdare.

Rebecca did only one more service to the Abergwili district after seeing off David Josuah. And it was a unique one, performed in broad daylight during the course of the sale of 'a great number of horned cattle and horses' at Abergwili fair on Monday 2 October. All Welsh country fairs represented something of a bonanza for the brewing trade, and Abergwili fair—held on the edge of Carmarthen, perhaps the most noted drinking town of west Wales—was no exception. On this occasion, though, Rebecca resolved to protect the interests of the local

[16] H. Tobit Evans, op. cit.

brewers against those in Carmarthen, and gave due notice of her intention to do so:

> . . . according to the Rebecca notices previously issued, not a single person from Carmarthen and other places adjacent was to be allowed to convey ale there for sale in the morning. A number of men stood as guard across the road by the gate and compelled them to return, and one man through his obstinacy had his casks stove in and his ale spilled on the road.
>
> The people of Abergwili take great credit to themselves for this act of restriction and say that as they never send ale to the Carmarthen fair they could see no reason why the publicans of Carmarthen should send ale to Abergwili, especially as they brew purposely for these fairs.[17]
>
> No person in authority interfered with the parties and the whole thing passed off very quietly.[18]

No wonder Rebecca had so many friends in the countryside!

It is not by timid submission . . .

Out in the west the behaviour of the notorious Fishguard Trust still rankled with the people of north Pembrokeshire. So blatant was its maladministration that George Ellis, down in west Wales to make a hurried preliminary enquiry into the causes of the disturbances, made a special point of visiting the trustees and explaining their wrong-doings to them. He even managed to persuade them to remove their Prendergast gate from its illegal site within the Haverfordwest town boundary to one outside it. But not before it had received another visit from Rebecca's daughters—who somewhow managed to lose their 'mother' on the way!

The enterprise began early in the evening of Friday 25 August, with the gathering of about three hundred men from the villages and farms around Wolfscastle and Little Newcastle, halfway between Haverfordwest and Fishguard, outside a tiny public house called the Three Corner Piece,[19] on a fork in the main road. And it was a long gathering, during which the Rebeccaites drank the landlord's ale in sufficient quantity to 'screw their courage to the sticking place' before setting off down

[17] In those days most beer was brewed by publicans on their own premises.

[18] *Carmarthen Journal,* 6 October, 1843.

[19] Now known as the *Corner Piece,* this pub is still open for business. The original building, a tiny adjunct to a later extension, stands on a triangular piece of ground in the fork of the road—hence its name.

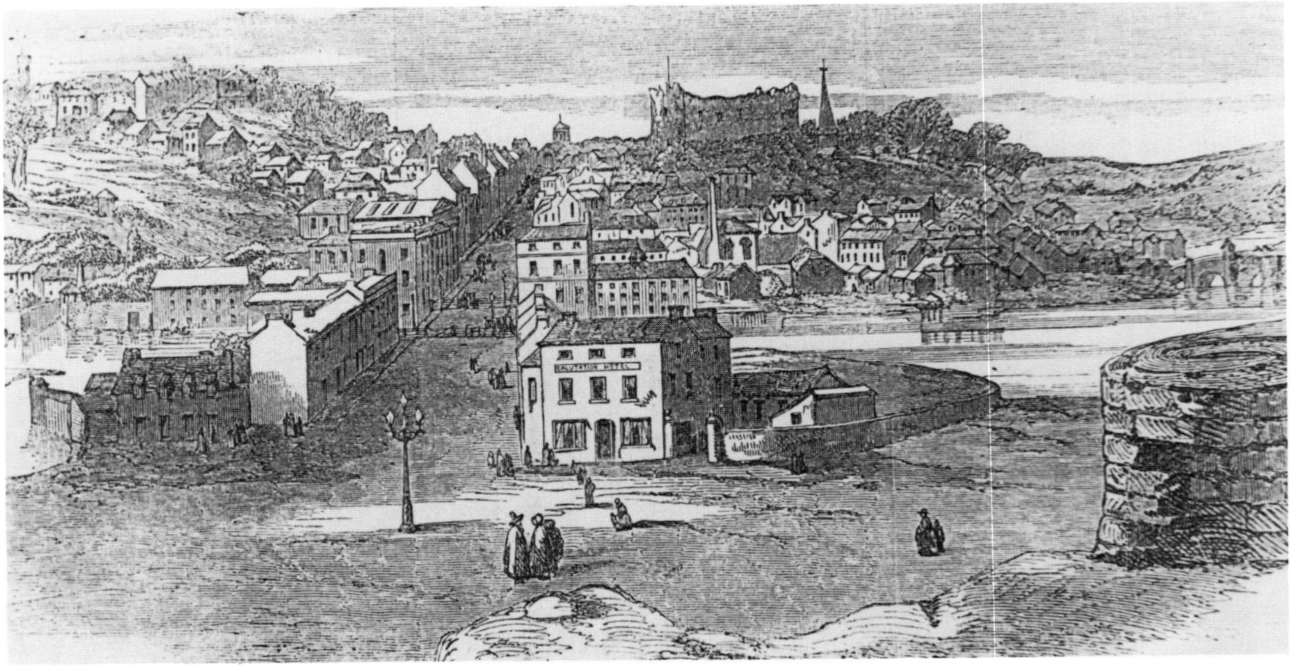

Haverfordwest, showing the toll gates on the bridge over the River Cleddau *(Haverfordwest Library)*

The toll gate on Haverfordwest Bridge later in the century
(Haverfordwest Library)

the road to Haverfordwest. That it would end in fiasco was assured by two things that happened at the Three Corner Piece. The first was that Rebecca—a gamekeeper named Thomas from Ford Bridge—decided to do a one-man reconnaissance and before setting off handed his double-barrelled shotgun to a youngster of the party named Davies for safekeeping, while ordering his three hundred daughters to await his return. The second was that during the long carousal at the pub, a spy among them slipped away and informed the authorities.

By the time the cellar had been drunk dry, the merry band was in the mood for action and it took only the urging of young Davies, waving Rebecca's gun in the air, for them to forget their leader's absence and march without him on Prendergast gate, where a reception party of parish and special constables was being posted by the Mayor. Unfortunately for young Davies, his zeal outstripped his support and on the four mile ride he left his companions farther and farther behind him—so far behind that he was all on his own when he ran into the ambush around the toll gate. A parish constable named Williams leaped at the boy, grabbed the barrel of the gun and struggled to wrest it from him and dismount him. As the other riders came up, to be challenged by the other constables, Davies' gun went off, miraculously missed the constable and killed one of Rebecca's horses. In the confusion of the fight that followed the constables secured only two twenty-year olds, while the rest, including the would-be young Rebecca, Davies, fled into the darkness. And there stood the prisoners, blinking in the light of the dozen lanterns that shone on their black faces, their gowns and their bonnets—young William Walters and David Vaughan from Little Newcastle—two frightened young boys who would be the only ones out of the whole bunch to face Her Majesty's Judge of Assize when he held court in Haverfordwest seven months later.

It was in mid-September that the Fishguard Trust sustained its final assault, when the unprotected harbour town of Fishguard was literally invaded and occupied for the attack on the Fishguard town and Parcymorfa gates. It provided another classic example of the audacity of Rebecca and the difficulties faced by the authorities both in combatting the disturbances and in bringing the perpetrators to justice.

The Fishguard gate keepers, braving the blows and curses of angry farmers and townspeople, had worked manfully at their task of collecting tolls and many were the warnings from Rebecca which they ignored. But they ignored one too many. At about midnight on Friday 8 September—the day on which many Fishguard people had paid toll to take their produce to Cardigan fair—Rebecca and her daughters came and smashed the town gates, leaving their keepers with the warning that they would be back on Monday to pull down their houses too if they continued to take tolls, and that they would do well to have their furniture and belongings out of them.

True to her word, Rebecca returned and entered the town with around six hundred followers, with all the gun-firing, horn-blowing bravado she could muster. But of magistrates or constables there was no sign, despite the three days warning the authorities had been given. Watched by a large crowd of enthusiastic supporters, Rebecca ordered the shaken gate keepers to empty their belongings from their toll houses and her daughters thereupon reduced the buildings to piles of rubble. Had there been a resident magistrate in Fishguard (an omission which was to incur the wrath of the Home Secretary) his life and limb would not have been worth much during the three hours in which the mob roamed the streets searching for further victims. One who had given some offence or other, Henry Collins, found his house the target of several volleys of gunfire, while the Fishguard Trust's road surveyor, John McKenna, had his garden wall levelled to the ground, and the curiosity of a bystander, a surgeon named Mortimer, was rewarded by the firing of a pistol in his face. Fortunately for him it was not loaded with shot, so he suffered only powder burns and a very severe shock to the system.

By the time the Rebeccaites marched off, the little town square of Fishguard, in which stood the thatched Royal Oak Inn, scene of the signing of the French surrender in the last ever invasion of Britain just over forty years previously,[20] was packed with as many as three thousand of the inhabitants—just about its entire population. Yet not one of the Rebeccaites was identified to the authorities until three months afterwards.

In the meantime, Colonel Hugh Owen, of Landshipping in south Pembrokeshire, the Vice-Lieutenant of the county, wrote to the Home Secretary asking for troops to be stationed in Fishguard because of 'the dread of the magistrates of drawing down the vengeance of the population by any act of interference against them.'[21] The Home Secretary's reply was a devastating broadside against the west Wales magistracy, summing up all the weaknesses in the maintenance of law and order that lay behind this desperate state of affairs:

> I am directed [by the Secretary of State] to acquaint you that the assistance of the military to quell tumult or to protect property can only be required by the civil authorities in cases where notwithstanding the most active exertions on their part the civil force has failed to restore order or is likely to be overpowered by the violence of the mob, *but that assistance cannot be afforded for the purpose of relieving magistrates from the responsibility of performing with energy, boldness and zeal the duties of their station, or as a substitute for the civil force which the*

[20] The Royal Oak is still open for business. The table on which General Tate (the French Commander) and Lord Cawdor (the Commander of the local volunteers) are said to have signed the Treaty of Surrender is on display there, together with other relics of the time.

[21] Letter dated 22 September, 1843, Col. Hugh Owen to Home Office: Public Record Office, File HO 41/18.

magistrates, by using every exertion, are bound to render as efficient as possible for the suppression of disorder and for the enforcement of the law.

It is with deep concern that the Secretary of State has learned from you that the magistrates existing in the vicinity of Fishguard shrink from the performance of their duty in the dread of exciting the vengeance of the mob. If Gentlemen high in station and in the Commission of the Peace hesitate to perform the duty they owe to the Crown and to the public it cannot be a matter of surprise that persons in a humble station, who look to the magistracy and gentry for an example, should display fear and should shrink from giving their active assistance in support of lawful authority [by enrolling as special constables].

It is not by timid submission to the demands of a mob, nor by the display of hesitation or supineness by magistrates that respect for the law can be maintained in the minds of the people. Neither is it by reliance on the military force to the exclusion of any other effort that tranquility can be restored and the supreme power of civil authority be established.

Vigour of activity on the part of the magistrates and of those who are disposed to obey the law are urgently required, and I am to request that you will inform the Secretary of State of any case in which you do not receive from the magistrates of your County that cordial co-operation and assistance in your exertion to restore tranquility and to punish crime which it is their bounden duty to afford.

Magistrates who do their duty may rely on the cordial support of the government. Those who are remiss will incur the displeasure of Her Majesty, and the Secretary of State expects that you as Her Majesty's Vice Lieutenant will notify to him any neglect of duty which may come to your knowledge.[22]

It is to be assumed that Sir James Graham's broadside found its target, because nothing more of the kind was heard from Pembrokeshire.

In a sequel to the affair two months later, one of the men involved in the destruction of the Fishguard toll houses—Thomas Williams—decided to bid for the reward and the promise of immunity from prosecution promised by Queen Victoria's Proclamation, and he swore a statement naming thirty-three others as members of Rebecca's band. And *on his entirely unsupported testimony* all thirty-three, including William Owen, the alleged leader, were arrested. There was pandemonium in Fishguard as thirty-three prisoners were crowded into the town's market hall,

[22] Letter dated 26 September, 1843, Home Office to Col. Hugh Owen: Public Record Office, File HO 41/18. (Author's italics).

which was ringed by three ranks of Royal Marines with fixed bayonets to keep the angry crowds at bay. The magistrates sitting in the market hall discharged seven of the prisoners but committed the rest, on bail, to stand trial at the next Assizes. But at the end of it all, with the inevitability that continued to dog the efforts of the authorities to get convictions for gate-breaking, the Crown offered no evidence and they were all freed, while Thomas Williams and his wife, who had to be locked in Haverfordwest Gaol for their own protection, were obliged to flee for their lives from the Fishguard area, on a Home Office grant of £20. They were last heard of in Aberystwyth, fifty six miles away.

Chapter Ten

MEET NO MORE BY NIGHT

Edward Crompton Lloyd Hall may not have been strictly correct when he told the Home Secretary that 'Ye offer of a reward, however great, has I believe never been known to produce any effect in this country',[1] but he certainly caught the spirit of the times. True, pig dealer Lewis Griffiths had taken up the offer by informing on Thomas and David Howells after the attack at Trevaughan and Thomas Williams had instigated the thirty-three equally abortive arrests at Fishguard, while John Jones had been similarly responsible for the arrests of Daniel Lewis and the others for the Bolgoed affair, which had still to be judged. A handful of others had also informed, while gatekeepers here and there had recognised—or claimed to have recognised—some of the rioters at their gates. But the significant thing about all the informings up to the month of August, 1843, was that they had occurred *after* the event, and in every case too the arrests had been made solely on the unsupported word of single informers, so that such few cases as had gone before the courts had been lost through the failure of witnesses to give evidence or through the discrediting of the informers themselves. Those cases still pending—such as the Bolgoed case—carried the same potential for failure.

Rebecca's nightly meetings, held all over the three western counties, were the talk of the markets and fairs, but the loyalty of her daughters was total, partly of course through fear of Rebecca's vengeance, but largely through the genuine support which her cause enjoyed among the mass of the people. And not all the meetings were councils of war. Most were for the discussion of grievances and of the means whereby the authorities might be persuaded by argument rather than violence to redress them. Not an easy matter in a situation where ordinary people had no say in parliament, no confidence in their local administrative

[1] Letter dated 15 June, 1843, to Home Secretary: Public Record Office, File HO 45/454.

institutions and a well-founded fear that their attempts to organise themselves might be regarded as seditious or otherwise unlawful. Hence the resort to night meetings.

Colonel Love would have given his right arm to get someone into one of those night meetings, yet all the efforts of his disguised London policemen had come to nought. But Thomas Campbell Foster did it. He attended and reported on a night meeting for *The Times,* in a scoop of which any modern investigative journalist would have been proud. He wrote his story in Llandovery on 4 August:

> *Meeting of the Rebeccaites:* Having heard that there was to be another meeting of the Rebeccaites at Penlan, a small village in the hills at the roadside between Llangadog and Llandeilo, and not far from Cwm Ifor where the Rebeccaites held a meeting a fortnight ago, I last night proceeded [from Carmarthen] to Llandeilo, determined if possible to be present. I learned that the meeting was to take place at a solitary farmhouse in the barn at nine o'clock.
>
> The night was windy and stormy, with occasional heavy showers of rain, and its uninviting aspect was calculated to keep all indoors whose business or necessity did not compel to go out. The country around the place of the meeting is among the most romantic and beautiful in Carmarthenshire. On all sides are lofty hills, verdant and clothed with woods to their summits, with deep and luxuriant valleys between them. From the smallness of the farms—and they rarely exceed fifty to eighty acres—the whole landscape is dotted over with the whitewashed cottages of the farmers, and the country, for an agricultural district, very thickly populated.
>
> My Welsh guide and I made our way about a mile along some lanes and then struck into a path across the fields and in a short time arrived at the place of meeting, a solitary farmhouse in a sequestered dell, not visible till within a field's distance from it. All was silent save the rushing noise of the occasional blast through the trees. The dark clouds intercepted by the hill tops hung upon them and rolled down their sides like curling smoke.
>
> To this centre the farmers from the surrounding farmhouses kept coming by different pathways. I addressed one or two who appeared to be leaders amongst them and shortly explained my object. It was evidently viewed with caution and distrust. My young guide, who appeared known to most of them, was called on one side and questioned about me. At length, after much whispering and consultation, one who appeared a leader amongst them again approached me and to him I produced one of *The Times* printed Parliamentary circulars

to its reporters which I happened to have in my pocket. This served as a sufficient credential and I was then told that I might be present at their meeting. The farmer led the way and I followed him into the barn.

In the centre was one small round table with one small candle burning upon it, throwing a feeble light on the figures of about seventy men, all seated around on chairs and benches or on the straw, whilst numbers whom I could not see were laid about in every corner among the bundles of straw. Most of those present were evidently respectable farmers.

On my entering and seating myself on a chair a dead silence prevailed, which continued for some minutes, and then one appeared disposed to speak. Thinking that my presence might have caused this I briefly addressed them and told them my object in coming amongst them—that as your reporter I sought only to ascertain the truth and to make it known to the public, and with that simple object and honesty of purpose I trusted myself fearlessly amongst them; that I did not wish to, nor would I, name or make any of them known, but merely give an account of what they said.

My Welsh companion was asked to repeat in Welsh what I said, which he did, and they appeared more satisfied. Having requested my interpreter to repeat to me in English what was spoken, I now proceed to give you a report of the proceedings.

Foster went on to explain that the meeting had been called for the purpose of forming a farmers' union, and he noted the careful attention that was paid to the rules of committee procedure, a reflection perhaps of the influence of the chapels, which would be commented upon a few years later in the Reports on Education in Wales. The meeting began with an announcement by the chairman, who:

. . . wished to make known a circumstance which might not be known to all—that the government had sent down Commissioners[2] to look at the way in which the trustees managed their accounts and to ascertain where the fault lay and what the trustees had done with the money, so that the country might know how the accounts stood.

Said a farmer of this development:

It is one of the best things that ever came into this country to see persons well off in the world come and try to take off the grievances of the poor. When we elect members of parliament they do just as they please. We have no voice.

[2] T. J. Hall and G. H. Ellis, already mentioned.

There then followed a long discussion on the need for the farmers to organise themselves, on the aims and objects of the proposed farmers' union and on the fact that upwards of two hundred farmers had already subscribed to the proposition, and when the meeting closed Foster left the glow of that single candle, went out into the black and rainy night and:

> . . . scrambled my way back across the miry fields in the dark till I reached the lane. I stopped a moment to listen, but there was not a sound to indicate that nearly a hundred men were dispersing themselves in all directions within two hundred yards from me. All was darkness and silence. I reached the roadside inn in about ten minutes and found it to be past eleven o'clock. The landlady said the dragoons from Llandeilo were expected every minute to patrol past. I ask of what use in such a country and with a people like this are dragoons?[3]

Of what use indeed? The next day, Foster added a postscript to this report which spoke volumes on the relationship between Rebeccaism and Chartism, which so troubled the authorities:

> I should have mentioned that one of Feargus O'Connor's representatives from the *Northern Star* attended. He [a Physical Force Chartist] appeared sadly frightened, for the farmers would have nothing to do with him.[4]

Foster could now write with a good deal of conviction that:

> It is difficult to stuff the head of a Welsh farmer, who speaks and reads only Welsh, with the political crotchets of Chartism. All he knows and grumbles at is that he cannot live and pay the sum he is rented at; that tithes are increased in amount from 20 to 50 per cent and that he is now compelled to support the poor of his Parish at a distant union workhouse without the chance of getting one iota of their labour in return. I do not think, therefore, that Mr. O'Connor is likely to make any proselytes here.[5]

The government, though, took a rather different view, and was particularly interested in the activities of the Carmarthen-based Chartist lawyer, Hugh Williams. He was now making a name for himself as an authority on the turnpike laws and court

[3] *The Times,* 7 August, 1843.

[4] *The Times,* 8 August, 1843. The *Northern Star* was the organ of the Chartist movement. See page 9 for more on Feargus O'Connor and the *Physical Force* aspect of Chartism.

[5] *The Times,* 18th August, 1843.

defender of those summoned for non-payment of tolls, so much so that the Home Secretary, suspecting him of being behind the destruction of the toll gates, issued warrants for the interception of his mail.

Thomas Campbell Foster first met Hugh Williams on 16 August, at another meeting of farmers, this time in the Blue Bell Inn in Cynwyl Elfed, six miles north of Carmarthen.[6] There were about a hundred farmers present and Hugh Williams was elected to the chair, where he immediately announced himself 'the advocate of the farmers.' With one eye on Foster and his reporter's notebook he went on to state their grievances: 'The trustees do just what they please,' he said. 'They impose what burdens they like and the farmers have no remedy. By inserting a notice in a local newspaper—not always read by the farmers—and by fixing up a notice at the different gates of the trusts, a fresh gate is stuck up anywhere.' And so on, through the Poor Law, the tithes, rents, rates and magistrates, until Foster, wishing to hear the view of the farmers from their own mouths and determined that their 'advocate' should not monopolise the proceedings, politely interrupted, thanked Hugh Williams for his lucid exposition of the problem and suggested that each farmer should now be allowed to make his own speech 'without any prompting or leading questions whatever.'

Hugh Williams gracefully sat down and took no further part, leaving it to Foster to probe the feelings of the audience. Asked if troops or police would be needed if the farmers could get justice, one of them stood up and answered, in English:

> My opinion is if we could only get justice it would be perfectly unnecessary to have either soldiers or policemen. The people are peaceably disposed and so averse to any kind of injustice and so attached to their superiors and to each other that if proper means of redress were afforded there would be no disturbances in Wales. If the magistrates now would only take proper means to satisfy the country by doing simple justice they may take away the soldiers whenever they please.

Echoing the distorted version of it in the Rev. Rees' *Y Diwygiwr,*[7] another farmer referred to the speech of the Vice-

[6] The Blue Bell Inn is still open for business in Cynwyl Elfed, on the Cardigan road out of Carmarthen.

[7] See page 163.

Lieutenant of the county at his meeting with the Newcastle Emlyn farmers on 23 June:

> The farmers were told by Colonel Rice Trevor that he knew how to pacify the country. He said he would kill the people one by one and that he would have all the husbands taken away from their wives if they were not quiet.

And others followed in quick succession, anxious that Foster should put their views and actions before his readership in their proper perspective:

> The Carmarthenshire magistrates look upon the people as if they were beasts and not human beings and treat us with the greatest indignity.
>
> Scores of people cannot seek justice because the law is so very dear; the country people can have no justice because the law costs so much and they are so poor.
>
> The people have been so goaded that they do not know what to do. They are so oppressed that they don't care if they were to be slaughtered, and some of them talk that it would be as well for them to be so, working hard as they do and not able to get the necessaries of life.

Foster's final question brought the meeting to an excited and noisy close: 'Have the farmers any *political* grievances?' he asked. 'If you were well off and contented that justice was done to you would there be anything like the disturbances that now exist?' To which 'the whole meeting came to its feet, raising hands, shouting "*No, No, that is the truth*".'[8]

The message could not have been plainer to Foster. There was no political disaffection among the people; merely a desire for justice and an explosive feeling of frustration. As to politics, he had seen a Chartist *Physical Force* man frozen out of the Cwm Ifor meeting, and now the renowned local Chartist, Hugh Williams, was being told in the clearest terms that he could expect no political mileage out of his association with Rebecca and the farmers' cause. Even so, it was too good a bandwagon for a man of Williams' political leanings to allow to pass him by, and he was now firmly aboard. And at least the farmers' meetings were beginning to come out into the light of day, thanks not only to Hugh Williams' encouragement but also to the fact that the

[8] *The Times,* 19 August, 1843.

government seemed to be stirring out of its apathy towards the affairs of west Wales and to have provided already a forum of a kind for the expression of the farmers' grievances.

Don't shoot the horse

The Home Secretary, stirred by the reports of Colonel Love and the Vice-Lieutenant—and by the articles in *The Times*—on conditions in the area, had sent two men to west Wales in the last week of July to make preliminary investigations and report to him as a matter of urgency. T. J. Hall, a London Stipendiary Magistrate (a barrister and paid, professional magistrate) came down to west Wales with George Ellis, a London solicitor with a special knowledge of the turnpike laws, and their investigations were completed within a fortnight. True there was some criticism of the rapidity of their progress through the area and the lack of due notice of their hearings, which led many to believe that they were not getting as full a picture as they might. The choice of a stipendiary magistrate also aroused suspicion as to the true intention of the government, the suspicion that Hall might be more interested in identifying the rioters than the *causes* of the riots. There is no evidence of this, nor is there any evidence to substantiate the claim that their progress through the countryside was deliberately kept secret, a claim which ignores the numbers of people of all ranks who came before them in the towns they visited to air their grievances.

Thomas Campbell Foster met Hall and Ellis at the first of their hearings, in the Black Lion Hotel in Cardigan, on Monday 31 July, where Ellis was collecting evidence relating to the administration of the turnpike trusts and Hall was dealing with all the other grievances behind the troubles. As Foster told his readers in the dispatch he wrote at the hotel:

> Numbers of farmers are here from the surrounding districts who, having heard of Mr. Hall's arrival, are anxious to tell their tale of oppression and much-enduring poverty before him. I had not been an hour in the hotel before it was generally known amongst the attending farmers through the usual channels of intelligence—the coach guard, the boot boy and the landlord—that I had arrived for the purpose of ascertaining the truth through personal enquiry and investigation, and on my return to the hotel from calling on one or two of the magistrates of the town I found several of the farmers and

Fishguard Harbour (Lower Town): the Parcymorfa gate lay behind the hill, centre right *(Haverfordwest Library)*

A Cardiganshire toll house: the South gate at Penparciau, Aberystwyth
(Haverfordwest Library)

> others who had been before Mr. Hall anxious also to come and state their grievances before me.[9]

Through such well-attended hearings as this, which they held at Newcastle Emlyn, Haverfordwest and Carmarthen, Hall and Ellis collected sufficient evidence to persuade the government that a full public enquiry was necessary, while at the same time demonstrating to a suspicious population the government's willingness at least to listen. For his part, Ellis produced some immediate results by demonstrating to some of the trusts the folly of their policies and their deviations from the letter of the law, and persuading them to mend their ways. Gates were removed, others were relocated, and payments at certain gates were regarded as clearing others. Not that any of this stopped Rebecca, who, sensing victory, continued to pile on the pressure, but it did at least bring the debate into the open, and the meetings in the countryside now began to take place not only

[9] *The Times,* 3 August, 1843.

Aberystwyth: the North gate is at the road junction at the right of the picture *(Ceredigion Museum, Aberystwyth)*

Aberystwyth North gate later in the century: Jac y Gât (John the Gate) is standing by the right hand gate, on the Llanbadarn road

(Ceredigion Museum, Aberystwyth)

more frequently but also more and more openly, attracting larger and larger attendances.

At one such meeting in Llanon near Llanelli, Foster heard a farmer deliver a parable which set a rural problem in simple rural terms and summed up exactly how he and his fellow farmers felt about it:

> There was a gentleman who had a very fine horse which he rode for years and which carried him in ease, in comfort and in safety, and in coming home one night he was much surprised that the horse, instead of being quiet as usual, attempted to throw him over the hedge all the way home, and when he came near home the horse did throw him over the hedge.
>
> He walked to his home, called all the servants and gave orders for the horse to be shot. An old woman of the household came to him and said 'Don't shoot the horse. Perhaps there is something wrong with the saddle, for if there is not why should he carry you for so many years in comfort and in safety without throwing you?' They examined the saddle and found that some protruding nails had worn a severe wound in the horse's back. The saddle was repaired, the horse's wound healed, and it never threw the farmer again.
>
> Rebecca has suffered until her flesh has been torn to the bone, and at last she throws down the gentleman. But we beg them to join

together to heal her wounds, to set things to rights and to mend the saddle, that neither she nor they might suffer any more.[10]

Llanon, where these words were spoken, was in the middle of an area which was about to see some of Rebecca's most violent acts, the area bounded on the west by the Gwendraeth Valley, on the north by the Carmarthen to Swansea road and on the east by the Loughor River, the boundary between Carmarthenshire and Glamorganshire. It was a place of coal mines and iron works, of depressed mining villages and of restless coal miners and iron workers driven to desperation by unemployment or reduced wages and the iron grip of the factory shop system which squeezed high prices from them in the form of charges for continuing and inescapable debt. Reporting on the conditions of the colliers there, Foster took as his example those in the Cwm-mawr district near Tumble, whom he estimated at about a thousand in number:

> So far as I can ascertain they are all in work, but on a reduced scale of wages. The general wages now being paid are nine shillings [45p] a week to men and 3s.6d. [17½p] to boys. Now that wages have fallen, for the slackness of the demand for coal, the people are dissatisfied. I learn too that the abominable system of tally shops[11] attached to the different collieries is in full work. Though generally owned by the proprietors of the collieries, these shops are, to evade the law, kept in different names. The system is to pay the men once a month. They are thus compelled to purchase on credit at these shops and are made to pay considerably above the market price for everything. Every article of food and clothing they are obliged to get at these shops is at an addition of about 20% of its value. In some instances the colliers have been so exasperated that they have threatened to pull down the shops, but the screw has been applied, the shops have been closed for a while, the monthly system of pay has still been continued, and the colliers have been fairly starved into begging for them to be open again.[12]

And it was difficult farming country, where, as Foster put it:

> The poor farmer, who is in reality nothing more than a farm labourer, having no money to purchase food, much less to procure

[10] *The Times,* 25 August, 1843.

[11] A shop dealing only in credit. The Truck Act of 1831 had made illegal the payment of wages in goods instead of money, and the tally shop was a device to get around the law; hence the concealment of the true ownership of a colliery-owned tally shop.

[12] *The Times,* 31 July, 1843.

manures and in sufficient quantity, his land becomes more and more impoverished, his rent and rates and tolls absorb all, and at last a bad season comes and having no capital to fall back on he is utterly ruined.[13]

It was in the heart of that area—a veritable tinder box—that the greatest of all the meetings was held, high above the Gwendraeth Valley on the broad, open summit of Mynydd Sylen.

The people's advocate

On Thursday 24 August, 1843, the day before the great meeting, lawyer Hugh Williams was entertaining a visitor in Carmarthen. It was his old friend and fellow political radical, the lithographer William James Linton.[14] Over dinner that evening they talked as they had talked many times before of the Charter and its ideals, of the movement's progress and of the obstacles it faced. And they talked of Rebecca and what Hugh Williams saw as the common cause of the Rebeccaites and the Chartists. He sensed that a climax was coming, that his own moment was at hand, and that he would be the one to bring the two movements together. Tomorrow was to be his day. Thousands would see him take his place as the principal speaker in a meeting the like of which had never been seen before in west Wales.

Hugh Williams' feeling that history beckoned to him impressed Linton so deeply that fifty years later, many years after the death of his friend, he would write this of him:

> Hugh Williams, the Carmarthen Lawyer, a man of large business till he lost favour by his defence of poor men, was the instigator and undiscovered leader of the 'Rebecca Movement', the one successful uprising in England [sic] since the Great Rebellion.[15]
>
> Soldiers were sent into the district, but their interference was rendered of no avail by the universal sympathy with the movement and the clannishness of the Welsh peasantry. 'Going to catch Becky?' would be tauntingly sung out by the boys at the soldiers.
>
> I dined with him one evening and he sent me off to Pontyberem,

[13] *The Times,* 21 September, 1843.

[14] Born in London in 1812, Linton was regarded as the best wood engraver of his day, and in his younger days was active in politics and an advocate of republicanism. He was widely acclaimed for his artistic work and, to a lesser degree, for his poetry, and in 1866 went to America, where he became the head of a large engraving establishment. He died there in 1898.

[15] A reference to the civil war of the 1640s.

> where next day was to be a gathering in favour of universal suffrage, a step beyond the toll gate movement, which Williams from the first had meant as a preparation for farther political action.[16]

A large claim indeed. If true, it meant that Hugh Williams was the most wanted man in Wales!

Friday 25 August, 1843. On that damp August morning, above the mist-filled valley of the Gwendraeth Fawr river, wisps of cloud clung to Mynydd Sylen and its adjacent hills, while the slow brightening of the sky after the night's rain held out the firm promise of a fine day. As early as seven o'clock the narrow twisting lanes from Llanon, Tumble, Cwm-mawr, Pontyberem, Pontyates, Five Roads and Llanelli were filling, as small knots of labourers and colliers on foot and of farmers, preachers and gentlemen on horseback, mingling with the occasional carriage, swelled to a steady stream moving upwards through the thin cloud to the mountain top, nearly a thousand feet above the sea, which was still hidden beyond the valley mist.

By noon the grassy summit of Mynydd Sylen held eight thousand people and the bright hot sun had banished the mists and revealed the full grandeur of the setting—Carmarthen Bay sparkling below, the Presely hills a hazy blue beyond, and the surface gear and waste tips of a hundred collieries dotted among the villages and the white farm cottages in the valleys around.

The *Carmarthen Journal*'s local correspondent was there and it struck him that '. . . when it is considered that this is a season of the year when the labours of the husbandmen are most in demand, it must be conceded that the causes which operate upon the minds of the "greycoats"[17] of Carmarthenshire so as to induce them to forego the advantage of a day's labour in harvest time must be weighty and powerful.'[18] They were indeed.

In the centre of that vast assembly, the principal speakers gathered around the large open carriage which did duty as a platform, and the meeting began with the election as chairman of Mr. William Chambers, Junior, the Llanelli magistrate, on the motion of Hugh Williams, seconded by Mr. Rees of Cilmaenllwyd, to an enthusiastic welcome from the crowd. Mr.

[16] *Memories* by William James Linton, published by Lawrence and Bullen, London, 1895.
[17] A term applied to tithe-paying farmers.
[18] *Carmarthen Journal,* 1 September, 1843.

The great meeting at Mynydd Sylen *(Illus. London News)*

Chambers was destined to be somewhat less popular in the light of later events, but for now the people were delighted by the respectability bestowed on the meeting by his very presence, for which he in his turn would come under the lash of the Vice-Lieutenant of his county.

As for other such gatherings, Hugh Williams had been asked to prepare a petition to the Queen, and he read it out to the crowd. It set out the people's grievances, pointed out the apparent unwillingness of the government to remedy them, and called for its removal from office if it failed to pay heed to the people's demands for justice. But for all its demands it was a petition couched in the most respectful terms of supplication to the Queen, and with a neat touch of irony it fell to farmer Stephen Evans of Cilcarw to read it out in Welsh and to move its adoption. Stephen Evans, whom many present knew to be an active night-riding Rebecca leader!

There followed a lengthy discussion involving a number of amendments before the assembly signified its approval of the final draft, and there were many eloquent speeches. Hugh Williams, a fine judge of timing and of the temper of a mass meeting, saved his speech until last, and it was punctuated by

Stephen Evans of Cilcarw Uchaf (centre), an active night-riding Rebecca
(Mr. A. D. G. Williams, Gwendraeth Valley Historical Society)

loud cheering. He was indeed the people's advocate, but whatever clandestine connections he might have had with Rebeccaism, under the sunshine on the summit of Mynydd Sylen he condemned violence and advocated the constitutional approach for all he was worth:

> I have no confidence in the present parliament doing enough. The people want a House of Commons who will compel the government to move forward rather than to obstruct their progress, something that will happen only when all men have the vote. I am not desirous of removing the present ministry from office provided they are able and have the inclination to redress the people's grievances. What the country wants is good government—a paternal government, a government powerful enough to protect the people from petty tyranny and from local oppression such as has driven the hitherto peaceful population of South Wales into a state of incipient insurrection against the authorities of the country.[19]

He went on to draw attention to the presence of Thomas Campbell Foster of *The Times,* to whom he proclaimed the indebtedness of the people 'for the faithful reports of the various proceedings so fully given in his columns and the complete exposure of the grievances which had thus been laid before the world.'[20] Hugh Williams proposed a vote of thanks to the editor of *The Times,* to which the whole gathering responded with three cheers. Returning finally to the petition, he said it '. . . contained nothing that a Christian, a Welshman or any honest man could object to' and proposed the thanks of the meeting to the chairman, Mr. William Chambers Junior. Seconded again by Mr. Rees of Cilmaenllwyd, the motion was greeted with three more cheers, followed by yet another three, for Hugh Williams, and finally three for Her Majesty the Queen, 'which were given in a style worthy of Welshmen.'[21]

And then, with the echoes of the cheering ringing in their ears, the eight thousand departed, filling the lanes as they wended their ways back to farms, mansions, labourers' cottages and hay-loft lodgings. Hugh Williams, elated by his reception, drove his friend Linton the ten miles directly back to Carmarthen, but for most the first stop was the ale-house, and great was the con-

[19] *Carmarthen Journal,* 1 September, 1843.
[20] *The Times,* 29 August, 1843.
[21] *Carmarthen Journal,* 1 September, 1843.

sumption of beer and grog that afternoon and evening in the wayside inns, the village alehouses and colliers' drinking dens over the sixty square mile area from which the people had flocked to Mynydd Sylen.

By God, I am Rebecca!

It was at about nine o'clock that night, outside Powell's shop in Pontyberem, two miles from Mynydd Sylen, that John Levi saw something that nearly frightened the life out of him—a huge bearded man wearing a tartan cloak over a dirty white gown, and with a straw bonnet on his head tied with a cloth under his chin. He was roaring drunk and waving a shot gun in the air. For some reason Levi asked who he was, at which the man rammed the muzzle of the gun into his ribs and cried 'Stand back!' Levi grabbed the barrel and turned the muzzle from his chest. The man kicked him and the gun went off with a blinding flash, whereupon Levi fled for his life. He ran to the New Inn, fifty yards down the road,[22] and hid in the kitchen, with the raging gunman in hot pursuit, bursting his way into the pub by charging the door with his shoulder.

Evan Jones, who lived only a few yards from the New Inn and had been alerted to trouble by the sounds of shouting and foul language outside Powell's shop, saw the gunman go into the New Inn, come out again and stagger to the kitchen window where he raised his gun as if to fire through the window, and pulled the trigger. There was a flash and a crack, but it was a misfire and he got down to his knees and refilled the firing pan. In the meantime, widow Mary Bowen, landlady of the New Inn for forty years, had heard the crash of her front door and came up the cellar steps, candle in hand. She asked a customer, Walter Rees of nearby Ponthenry, to close the door, by which time the huge drunk in the white nightgown and Scotch plaid shawl was standing outside again, his gun raised to his shoulder. As the door closed there was a roar and a flash, and a powerful charge of shot hit the door, blew a great hole in it and buried itself in the cellar door and the kitchen dresser, grazing the shoulder and cheek of Walter Rees and blowing off his hat. '*By God, I am Rebecca*,' roared the gunman, '*and I will have justice done!*'

[22] Where it is still open for business.

'Justice' at that moment meant that he wanted his ramrod back. It seems that when John Levi grabbed the barrel of the gun to remove its muzzle from his chest, he had withdrawn its ramrod and absent-mindedly taken it with him in his blind rush for cover in the New Inn, where he had dropped it on the kitchen floor. Widow Bowen picked it up and gave it to the gunman, who, somewhat molified by its retrieval, left, returning a few minutes later to pay for and drink a quart of ale. While he was drinking it, John Hughes the landlord of the Star in Pontyberem came in and persuaded him to go with him. At the Star the drunken gunman quaffed yet more beer and when the landlord expressed his surprise that he should behave that way after being on Mynydd Sylen in the forefront of the cheering for the idea of an end to violence, he slammed down his jug and roared 'By the devil I'm sorry I did not kill him as dead as a clod!' And, throwing off his Rebecca garb, he reloaded and stormed out of the door. The ever more distant sounds of shots marked his drunken progress towards the hay loft and the bed of straw which was home for the night to such as he.

Word of the shooting at the New Inn soon reached the ears of Sergeant Hall, one of the London policemen stationed in Pontyberem, but try as he might he could get none of the witnesses to speak a word about it, for the gunman's name was already a byword for violence and terror in the Gwendraeth Valley. He epitomised a new and frightening element of Rebeccaism—the freelance, who under the guise of Rebecca would burn anything, shoot at anyone and do any man's dirty work for him for half a crown. And his name was John Jones, a coal miner recently arrived in the west from Merthyr Tydfil. John Jones. Alias *Shoni 'Sgubor Fawr.*

Chapter Eleven

THE MOST DESPOTIC GOVERNOR

No part of Wales was so thickly planted with toll gates and toll bars as the area between Llanelli, Llanon and the Gwendraeth Valley. And in no part of Wales did Rebecca reap such a rich harvest.

Describing the impact of the riots on the Kidwelly Trust, which gated and barred many of the roads of that district, Thomas Campbell Foster wrote:

> The Kidwelly Trust extends over seventy four miles of roads and there were on those roads *thirty* turnpikes and bars, or a bar or gate for every two and a half miles of road throughout the Trust! That this was thought a grievance by the people is evidenced by the fact that only three of them have not been destroyed.[1]

It was in that corner of Carmarthenshire, in July, that Foster had ridden alongside Colonel Love with Major Parlby and his Light Dragoons on their futile patrol through Porthyrhyd, Tumble, Cwm-mawr and Drefach, under the glare of hill top signal fires and soaring skyrockets; a patrol in whose wake gates and toll bars fell like ninepins—a pattern repeated so often as to put the Gwendraeth Valley almost beyond the reach of the law. The London policemen deployed with small detachments of infantrymen in Pontyberem, Trimsaran and Llanon did their level best to cultivate informers, infiltrate meetings and lay ambushes at and between the gates, but the hostility of the populace and the wall of secrecy surrounding the activities of Rebecca and her daughters, who ranged across the whole ten mile breadth of the area, brought all their efforts to nothing.

Foster, travelling on horseback the eighteen miles from Llanelli to Carmarthen three weeks later, passed 'no fewer than nine or ten gates which had been destroyed, in some instances with the toll house, and one toll house near Llanon which had been burnt down. At these gates,' he wrote, 'no tolls are now asked and

[1] *The Times,* 18 September, 1843.

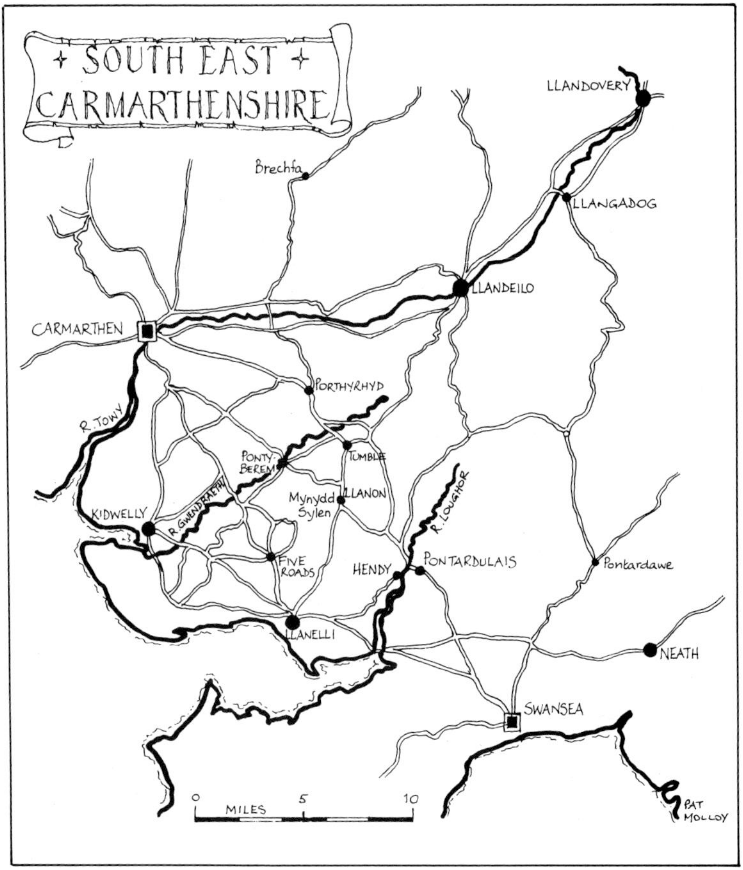

I am informed that persons cannot be found who will undertake to collect them.'[2] And no wonder, if the experience of Richard Williams (known as *Dick Morganwg* on account of his being from Glamorgan) was anything to go by.

Dick Morganwg's gate at Porthyrhyd (seven miles from Carmarthen on the Swansea road) was destroyed at least nine times in eight weeks between July and September and his house unroofed or pulled down as fast as it could be repaired or rebuilt. And it was the very fact of Dick's stubbornness in defying every threat and bouncing back after every attack that made him such

[2] *The Times,* 18 August, 1843.

Pontyberem gate destroyed *(Illus. London News; from Mr. A. D. G. Williams)*

a favourite target, a situation hardly helped by the antics of Porthyrhyd's parish constable, Llewellyn Evans. His daylight boastfulness and night-time reticence had earned him the nick-name of *Llew Porthyrhyd*—the Lion of Porthyrhyd—and the Rebeccaites came from as far as Trimsaran, Pontyberem and Llanarthne to have sport with him. Three times in one week they came, and even the *Carmarthen Journal*—a conservative, anti-Rebecca paper if ever there was one—began to see the humorous side of it:

> Why this poor devoted gate should have become the especial object of Rebecca's wrath we are at a loss to divine, guarded as it is by a *Lion,* and one would have imagined that a parcel of disorderly curs would have shunned the spot. But the contrary seems to be the state of the case, for no sooner is the gate replaced than down it comes again, in spite of the *Lion* and his claws.
>
> We have now to relate a third attack which was made since our last publication. On Thursday [17th August] some of Rebecca's scouts were sent to reconnoitre. Finding that workmen had been employed in repairing the gate and re-erecting the toll house they, according to ancient custom, 'smote upon their thighs', vowed by

their mistress's shoe tie that toll should no longer be collected there and cautioned *Dick Morganwg,* the toll collector, to be aware of them, for if he continued to take toll dire vengeance would assuredly be taken and he would be made to repent his contumacy. The deceitful rogue promised compliance but, apparently having perfect confidence in his 'light heels' which had so well served him on former occasions, he remained at his post and exacted toll as usual.

Of course the audacity of this subordinate of the lessee could not be borne. The majesty of Rebecca's mandates were not thus to be insulted. Accordingly, on Saturday morning last at a very early hour a strong party of 'greycoats' made their appearance at the spot, seized the Constable—an official rather unpopular with those gate-levellers—in his bed, compelled him to turn out in his shirt, take a pick in his hand and march before them to the gate and begin the work of destruction with his own hands, which they soon completed.

Thus was the gate a third time destroyed. The poor Constable, alias *The Lion of Porthyrhyd,* was kept in custody for some time longer by the party and made to swear upon his knees that he would never more, directly or indirectly, meddle with or interrupt Rebecca and her daughters. The party of destructives soon after fired off their guns, huzzahed and disappeared.[3]

Four nights later, hearing that Dick Morganwg was back in business and that the *Lion* had gone back on his oath, they returned. Dick himself immediately disappeared, but they found the *Lion* hiding in a nearby cowshed, from where he was brought to the toll house and put on trial before a court of white-robed, straw-bonneted, black-faced Rebeccaites under the flickering glare of a hundred flaming torches. Defying Rebecca's Law was the charge, and sixty lashes was the sentence, which was administered by stinging horsewhips as the wretched constable was forced to crawl on his hands and knees around the toll house. But even the worm turns, and suddenly the *Lion* had had enough:

The sixtieth lash succeeded at last in putting the Welshman's blood up. The constable, starting to his feet, swore he would stand it no longer and furiously began laying about him and hurling the stones of the demolished toll house at his tormentors, who thereupon in their turn became passive and took to their heels.[4]

[3] *Carmarthen Journal,* 25 August, 1843.
[4] *The Times,* 26 August, 1843.

On another visit to Porthyrhyd the Rebeccaites went straight to the parish constable's house and on finding he had escaped fired several shotgun volleys through the windows, filling the house with smoke and injuring the *Lion*'s ten month old child while it was held to the breast of its screaming mother. Then down went the Porthyrhyd gate for the eighth time.

Out of about a hundred men, the constable's wife said she recognised one—a farmer named Thomas Thomas of Llwyn-ypiod farm near Pontyberem, who was arrested a few days later and bailed to take his trial at Carmarthen Assizes. Not much to show for such a concentrated series of attacks, which had taken on the added element of personal violence and terror by gunfire when Shoni 'Sgubor Fawr had taken up the reins on 18 August and sentenced the *Lion* to his whipping.

And where were the military? Foster described the problem they were facing when he commented on the burning of hayricks by a band of armed men at nearby Middleton Hall, the home of Edward Adams, 'an English gentleman of large property', who was also the well-liked employer of some three hundred local people . . . who found themselves thrown out of work when these arson attacks finally drove him away.[5]

> This town [Carmarthen] is in a strange state of excitement. Troops have been marched to Middleton Hall now the mischief is done. Different bodies of dragoons are going off in various directions and the streets are full of people.
>
> To show the way in which we manage things here, two old stage coaches were run out into the open street at two o'clock and dusted and rubbed down with a vast fuss. The Welsh are naturally inquisitive and many wanted to know where they were going. An air of profound mystery was thrown about the matter. Two men were busy putting clean faces on two old stage coaches and 'nobody could not tell nothing' about them. In two hours *everybody* in Carmarthen knew that the two stage coaches were going somewhere. In two hours more *everybody* knew that they were going to be filled with soldiers to go on a *Secret* expedition that night to outwit the Rebeccaites. At half past six o'clock (broad day) they started, crammed with soldiers, with a crowd of two hundred people looking at them.
>
> I may venture safely to say that they will not pass over a single

[5] Edward Adams later changed his surname to Abadam, a name preserved by the Abadam Arms public house in Porthyrhyd. Middleton Hall no longer exists.

> mile of road where two hours previous notice of their approach has not been given.[6]

And from Llanelli at about the same time Foster reported on the effect all this was having on the morale of the troops:

> Fine bodies of soldiers have been trailed about night after night to no purpose, till the poor fellows are thoroughly sick of it. It is an interesting spectacle, for instance, to see John Jones [the name by which Foster referred to what he saw as the typical west Wales magistrate] with twenty gallant soldiers at his back, march out of Carmarthen town at night, and the little boys following shouting 'Hurrah Becca. Going to catch Becca?' It is equally imposing to hear the clatter of a dozen horses' hooves galloping over the stone pavement at midnight to one rendezvous and to see a score of night-capped heads thrust out of bedroom windows in alarm and peeping from every house at the passing 'Long sword, saddle and bridle.'
>
> With what dignity John Jones lights his cigar and mounts! The word 'March' is given; the sabres clatter and the horses march away. How should Rebecca know anything about their coming?[7]

Foster's most scathing commentary on what he saw as the arrogance of the magistrates towards the 'lower orders' was contained in a dispatch he wrote on 29 August after attending a magistrates' meeting:

> I was rather curious to observe the demeanour of the magistrates to their poorer neighbours, about which pretty loud complaints have been made. I must say that the mode of intercourse and demeanour of the generality of these magistrates with their poorer neighbours and dependents would, if pursued in England, very quickly raise the bristles on the back of John Bull's neck.
>
> Generally dressed in some sort of light shooting coat, with the stock of a hunting whip in their hands, an aspect, a tone of voice and a 'bumptious' mannerism seems to say when addressing you 'I am John Jones, and my father was John Jones, and my grandfather and all my ancestors have been John Joneses of Llanfairpwllgwyn Hall. Who are you?'
>
> This may be very awe-inspiring to the natives, who have an hereditary reverence for the very pigs that grunt at Llanfair-pwllgwyn Hall, but for an English stranger this demeanour, when the first surprise subsides, excites a considerable merriment.
>
> The exhibition is unique. It cannot be witnessed for love or

[6] *The Times,* 16 September, 1843

[7] *The Times,* 12 September, 1843.

money in England, and from what I have seen of the patient endurance of the Welsh people and how much they will bear putting upon without complaint, this sort of thing must have proceeded to a considerable extent before it was grumbled at.[8]

It was plain to *The Times* reporter that things could only get worse in a situation where virtually the whole burden of peace-keeping had to be borne by soldiers, and his dispatches highlighted the tell-tale signs. In Swansea, for example, Colonel Love was having great difficulty in getting proper accommodation in the form of a barracks for his troops and was threatening to withdraw them altogether if it was not provided. Indeed the building of barracks throughout south and west Wales was a recurring theme in Love's correspondence with the Home Office and he even suggested that it would be one way of absorbing some of the increasing numbers of unemployed. In Swansea, as in most other places, the inns and alehouses were the only available billets, with the inevitable disciplinary consequences, the worst example of which occurred on the night of 12 September when a riot took place between the troops and the Swansea Borough Police. 'One of the Dragoons having taken offence at a policeman for some real or supposed insult, seeing the policeman, insisted on him going on his knees to beg his pardon,' wrote Foster, who went on to describe how the ensuing affray drew in other policemen, cavalrymen and foot soldiers.[9] Having seen at first hand all the frustrations and morale problems of the soldiery and the hostility of the populace towards them, Foster was appalled at the prospect which was now on everyone's lips: the logical end to it all—the imposition of martial law:

Nothing can exceed the exasperation experienced by all classes of the people as this idea gains ground. 'Are the government mad enough' they say 'instead of boldly redressing the grievances, to seek to proclaim Martial Law and hang up Welshmen at the behest or on the evidence of a soldier or so? If they do they will have the whole country in a flame and must proclaim Martial Law everywhere'.[10]

[8] *The Times,* 31 August, 1843.
[9] *The Times,* 16 September, 1843.
[10] *The Times,* 21 September, 1843.

Mr. McKiernan's amenity of manners

On the southern edge of the troubled south eastern corner of Carmarthenshire, at the junction of five turnpike roads, lay the seaport town of Llanelli, a town tightly ringed by a dozen gates and bars, and the night of 2 August saw the first of a number of attacks on them; the gate at Sandy Bridge, on the road to Kidwelly and Carmarthen, being the first to go.

Catherine Hugh, the toll collector, went to bed at about one in the morning, leaving her husband Jenkin asleep on a settle. She was still awake three quarters of an hour later when she heard a crash outside and a hammering on the toll house windows. She needed no telling what was happening and ran to awaken her husband, who 'went on his knees on top of the table to look over the shutters at the people breaking the gate.' As he did so two blasts of gun shot shattered the window panes and only the thickness of the wooden shutter inside saved him from injury. In the same instant the door came crashing in and several black-faced and white-gowned men burst into the house, setting the woman and her children screaming with terror as they ran into the back room. Jenkin Hugh asked the men to allow him to take his family and furniture out of the house but he was ordered to leave the house or die. He left, and went among the rampaging crowd outside, where the flickering glare of the flaming torches illuminated the wreckage of the gate and flying fragments of roof timbers and slates. He went down on his knees and begged them not to pull down the house on top of his family, but as the roof tiles began raining down inside the building, mother and children escaped through the back window—to be greeted by the flashes and bangs of shotgun fire and the whistle of shot passing over their heads.

Terror gripped the whole family, and yet, in one of those irrational acts which often occur in moments of panic, Jenkin Hugh ran back through a hail of Caernarfon slate and gunshot to rescue, of all things, his old clock! With a few other damaged articles that clock was just about all he was able to salvage from his ruined home.

And off went the mob, cheering and firing—not directly back to town but up the side road to the Furnace gate, their next target, half a mile away. The same scene was enacted there, but with an even greater element of physical violence, on gatekeeper

Llanelli

(Dyfed Archive Services, Carmarthen)

Sandy gate, Llanelli *(Nat. Library of Wales)*

Williams, who was severely beaten and took a charge of powder and wad full in the face.

Next morning, Jenkin Hugh, his arm in a sling through a blow from a gun butt, walked with his wife into Llanelli and found a magistrate to whom he named three men as leaders of the attack on Sandy gate—Francis McKiernan, innkeeper and mail coach operator, George Laing, publican and haulier, and John Phillips, all of Llanelli town. The magistrates' clerk, Thomas Atwood, wrote their sworn statements and the magistrate issued warrants of arrest.

There was consternation and something approaching a riot in the town as the word spread that 'two individuals of great respectability' (McKiernan and Laing) were being brought before the magistrates, and soldiers of the 73rd Regiment stood guard around the workhouse where the magistrates were holding court. As the Llanelli correspondent of the *Carmarthen Journal* reported, 'The town of Llanelli was full of excitement as Mr. McKiernan's amenity of manners upon all occasions had rendered him very generally beloved and most people heard of his position with regret.'

Magistrate William Chambers Junior banged his gavel impatiently and kept order only with great difficulty while

Jenkin Hugh, his wife, and a neighbour, Edward Chalinder, a Llanelli tide-waiter,[11] took the oath and gave evidence. On the day before the attack, said Jenkin Hugh, he had met the Llanelli letter carrier who had a letter for him. It was like several letters he had already received—a warning signed 'Becca'—but this one had the feel of genuineness about it and it worried him. Calling at McKiernan's inn, he drank three pints of beer with him and showed him the letter. 'What do you think of it?' he asked him. McKiernan dismissed it as probably coming 'from one of the teetotals', but Jenkin Hugh still asked if he thought he should take his wife and children away from the house just in case. 'Never mind, Jenkin,' said McKiernan significantly, 'if the gate will be broken I will take care that neither your wife or children shall be hurt.'

The gatekeeper went home and, sure enough, Rebecca and her daughters came to Sandy gate that night. When he went outside, he told the magistrates, he saw McKiernan 'and asked him to make them let him have his wife and children and furniture out' before they pulled down his house. McKiernan gave the order, but Laing jumped into the middle of the road and said 'Take it down; don't stop. Take it down. To the devil with them!' It was at that point that Jenkin Hugh braved the gunfire and falling slates to go to the rescue of his clock.

The solicitor for the defence, Mr. Gardiner, pressed him hard under cross-examination, even alleging that he was drunk when he made his statement to the magistrates, but he could not shake Hugh's story. Nor did he fare any better with Catherine Hugh or Edward Chalinder, though neither of them identified any of the prisoners as being among the rioters. Catherine Hugh told the court that her husband had named McKiernan and Laing to her immediately after the mob had left and that she had pleaded vainly with him not to risk his life by informing on them.

On that evidence the magistrates sent the three men for trial at the Assizes, allowing them bail on account of their good character. As for Jenkin and Catherine Hugh, it took a strong guard of policemen and soldiers to get them safely through the hostile crowd around the courthouse and back to Sandy Bridge. But their escort left them there, and they were alone when

[11] A man employed by H.M. Customs to watch the unloading of ships and identify dutiable goods.

Rebecca's messenger paid them a visit late that night. It was a message that sent Jenkin Hugh scurrying back to the magistrates' clerk's office first thing next morning. He *was* drunk when he made his statement, he said. He had *not* seen McKiernan, Laing or Phillips among the mob at Sandy gate, *and he had lied on oath at the committal proceedings!*

It was an extraordinary—but perhaps understandable—about face, and magistrate William Chambers, Junior was furious. He knew that McKiernan and Laing, as carriers of passengers and goods, had more reason than most to dislike toll gates and those two in particular, and he knew that Jenkin Hugh had *not* been drunk when he named them to the magistrates. Someone must have got at him and deprived the authorities of the only witness against them. Even so, his decision to have the unfortunate gatekeeper charged with perjury was hardly a rational one, since there was no way of proving that he had lied. In fact, with a withdrawal of that nature no-one would ever know where the truth lay. But charge him he did, and left the next Carmarthenshire Assizes to sort out the mess. In the event all the prosecutions were dropped. And Rebecca had scored yet again.

A formidable combination

In the aptly-named hamlet of Five Roads, five miles north west of Llanelli, carpenter William Walters kept the Stag and Pheasant Inn[12] at the junction of the five roads leading to Carmarthen (via Pontyates), Llanelli, Trimsaran, Pontyberem and Mynydd Sylen. In August, 1843, his house was not only the meeting place for Rebeccaites of the immediate neighbourhood, but it was often the centre for co-ordination of the activities of several Rebecca parties whose areas of operations covered the whole of that south eastern corner of Carmarthenshire. It could be a formidable combination, and some formidable leaders gathered there: farmer Stephen Evans of Cilcarw Uchaf, miller John Phillip, the Pontyates Rebecca, farmer Thomas Phillips of Topsail Farm on Pembrey Mountain, Thomas Morris of Five Roads, and the effervescent chapel minister the Rev. David Jones, who fortified his flock with beer and scripture in the Stag and Pheasant as they prepared for their night's work.

[12] Now called the Five Roads, and still open for business.

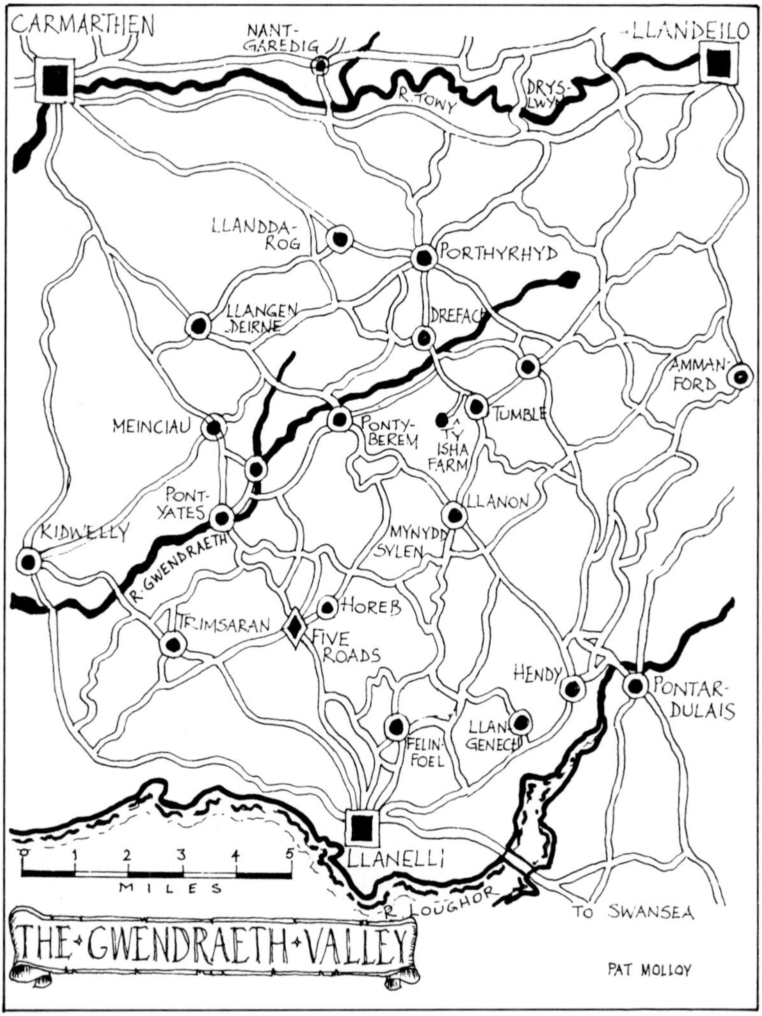

But the Stag's most notorious customers were colliers John Jones (alias *Shoni 'Sgubor Fawr*) and David Davies (alias *Dai'r Cantwr*), for whose services the farmers were at first prepared to pay generously, but who so terrorised and blackmailed those same farmers as to create their own reign of terror and bring ruin to them. As magistrate and Gwendraeth Valley landowner William Chambers, Junior said of Shoni:

> I know in my own district almost every man that was at the breaking of the gates, but you cannot get them to give evidence. There is no doubt that they had a great deal to complain of in the erection of those gates, but the influence of such men as that John Jones, or Scybor Fawr, got over the minds of the farmers arose from his having been employed by them in that way and being rather a sharp fellow the others all felt that they were in his power, and then he ran riot over that part of the country. He went to a farmer's house, lived there as long as he pleased, paid nothing for it and then to the next house, and not a soul ventured to oppose him. I knew a man that he went to—a farmer—and because he would not go out at night he went to him and cocked his gun at him and said 'Now if you do not go out this night I will shoot you', but the man did not go. He threatened to shoot at this man and he did shoot another man because he offended him. *He was the most despotic governor they ever had.*[13]

For John Jones it is not easy to argue (as has been argued) that men such as he were forced out of employment into poverty and thereby into crime. For every one like him there were hundreds who bore their misfortunes philosophically and with resignation, as part of life's natural burden on the poor. Shoni was not a product of the grievances which led to the Rebecca Riots, nor even of the industrial recession in Merthyr from where he had worked his way westward to the Gwendraeth Valley coalfield. He was, though, a product of the dehumanising squalor and drink-sodden brutality of the dark heap of humanity which the industrial revolution had pressed into the Glamorgan and Monmouthshire valleys, where, for example, 'in rooms of not more than twelve feet square, sometimes sleep four and twenty men, women and children, naked on straw, their clothes being detained for security of rent.'

The top of that heap was occupied by gangs of thugs, led by huge bullies of massive strength, who held their leadership by virtue only of their prowess at fighting and drinking. Such a man was Shoni 'Sgubor Fawr, who claimed to be the best fist-fighter in Wales and who had many bloody victories behind him to prove it. But he was also known to the authorities as one prepared to inform on others, as he did on the 'Scotch Cattle' who terrorised the Monmouthshire mining and iron districts in the

[13] *Report of the Commission of Inquiry for South Wales*: evidence of William Chambers Jnr., J.P. (Author's italics).

early 1830s, when Shoni was a private in the 98th Regiment of Foot which was stationed there at the time. He ruled Merthyr with an iron fist . . . until one day in 1842 when he met Police Sergeant Davies of the Glamorganshire Constabulary. Disdaining to use his truncheon, Sergeant Davies took on Shoni single-handed and beat him into bloody submission after a furious twenty-minute battle. And it was then, toppled from his pinnacle of power among the hardest of a race of hard men, that Shoni left Merthyr Tydfil and worked his way west, picking up several more convictions for drunkenness and violence on the way. He found an easier heap to climb there, among the miners and farmers of the Gwendraeth Valley.[14]

While Shoni has been seen by some as a victim of the oppression of the early nineteenth century industrial system and therefore something of a working-class martyr, his partner Dai'r Cantwr (David the Singer) achieved a different kind of immortality—as a 'finer type' of man than Shoni,[15] 'a man of considerable ability',[16] whose outpourings of song and ballad have been seen as expressing all the suffering of the oppressed people of Wales. Indeed something of a Dai'r Cantwr ballad 'industry' flourished in the 1840s and 1850s and his image of cultured sensitivity was enhanced accordingly.

A native of Llancarfan, Glamorgan, David Davies had worked on farms, in quarries and in the mines and ironworks of Monmouthshire and had been a Wesleyan preacher. There is no doubt that he had a talent for verse and song and it has even been said that 'he may have been the person of his name who won the harp at the Abergavenny Eisteddfod in 1838.'[17] And so he may. But such is the power of the mythology with which the history of the Rebecca Riots is so richly endowed that this image of Dai'r Cantwr has all but smothered his record of riot, assault and armed robbery. As will be seen.

A feather thrown before the wind

The lawless state of the south eastern corner of Carmarthen-

[14] *Thoughts from a Police Museum,* an article in the *Police Review* of 17 September, 1982, by Ron Baker, OBE, QPM, LL.B., Curator of the South Wales Police Museum, Bridgend.

[15] David Williams, op. cit.

[16] H. Tobit Evans, op. cit.

[17] David Williams, op. cit., referring to the *Western Mail* of 10 July, 1933.

shire was most strikingly demonstrated by the great gathering of several bands of Rebeccaites in the village of Llanon—a place supposedly garrisoned by troops and police—in the early hours of Wednesday 23 August, when over five hundred came from Cross Hands, the Gwendraeth Valley and the neighbourhood of Llanon itself. And a spectacular gathering it was as a white-gowned Rebecca on a large bay horse led her black-faced daughters along the narrow road through the village, while literally hundreds of shotguns created a deafening and continuous flash and bang of gunfire, rockets soared into the night air and burst into cascades of light, horns blared and the bright lanterns of a carriage which followed Rebecca 'shed a lustre over the crowd and lighted the apartments of many of the inhabitants, who were afraid to leave their bedrooms, and enabled them to take a better view of the procession.'[18] It is to be assumed that the police and soldiers were elsewhere at the time, or, perhaps overawed by the immensity of the number they would have had to contend with, mere spectators of their passage through the village.

At the southern end of Llanon the road divides, to the left the Pontardulais road, and straight on that to Llanelli. To Rebecca's cry of 'Halt' the shooting ceased, the sound of horns died away and the whole procession stopped, almost as if the leader were unsure of the intended destination, but more likely to marshal the huge procession and allow the tail end to catch up. At all events it was the Llanelli road that was taken, but another halt was called less than a mile further on, on the Morlais River bridge. For an hour and a half they remained there, an immense torchlight procession, guns firing, horns sounding and rockets streaming into the blackness of the sky, until they were joined by another large body from the direction of Llanedy and by one from the area around Mynydd Sylen. Thus swollen to seven or eight hundred and leaving their carriage on Morlais Bridge the Rebeccaites marched noisily to the farm of Gelliwernen, a mile further on, and the feelings of the occupants of that house may be imagined as the cacophony of gunfire, horns and shouts drew near. They could not have doubted where the mob was heading, for John Edwards, the head of the family, was the agent for Rees

[18] *Carmarthen Journal,* 1 September, 1843.

Goring Thomas, the 'lay-improprietor' of the parish,[19] the man to whom the farmers paid their ever-increasing tithes as a proportion of their rents. What was more, he was inclined to be overbearing and insensitive in the collection of rents and debts and intensely disliked on that account.

Seven or eight hundred bizarrely-dressed men carrying flaming torches and firing guns surrounded the house, baying loudly for Edwards' blood, but he was ill in bed and his wife Elizabeth went to the window of the bedroom where he lay to tell them so. Fortunately for her she stood to one side of the window, for a charge of gunshot crashed through the panes and buried itself in the door and wall opposite. Again she went to the window and again she was shot at. She backed away and cowered with her daughter out of the line of fire, while the guns roared and blasts of shot whistled into the room, some of it lodging within eighteen inches of John Edwards' sick bed. Four other windows were shot through as the fusillade continued, and yet Edwards' twenty three year old daughter, Hannah, went downstairs and out through the door into the glass-covered front porch. There she was showered by broken glass from a volley of stones thrown from the crowd, while someone called out that neither she nor her mother had anything to fear but that 'they would not set a greater value on her father's life than a feather thrown before the wind, and they would have their tithes lowered.' But still she stood her ground and upbraided them on their inhumanity in so upsetting her father who, she said, was exceedingly ill.

Somewhat abashed at the young woman's courage, they fired a few more token shots at the windows and wandered uncertainly away, venting their frustrated anger by trampling through the garden, uprooting plants and vegetables, chopping and cutting the fruit trees and breaking all the glass in the extensive greenhouses. Finally they attacked the gamekeeper's cottage. He fled, leaving his wife and young children to the mercy of the mob, who fired a charge of powder into her face, nearly blinding her and injuring the baby she clasped in her arms, before rampaging through the cottage, ransacking and smashing everything they could lay their hands on.

Back towards Llanon went the sounds of horns and gunfire.

[19]The layman of the parish whose duty it was to apply the income of the parish for the upkeep of its church and its incumbent.

The Edwards' grandfather clock, pitted with shotgun pellets (still embedded in the door) in the attack on Gelliwernen

(Courtesy of Mr. J. A. Davies, Five Roads)

Back to their villages and hamlets went the colliers and farmers, with little to show for their night's exertions but the feeling of satisfaction that their message would be delivered to Rees Goring Thomas. One cannot but wonder how much of the shine was taken off that feeling by the memory of a young woman braving a rain of broken glass and gunshot and lecturing seven or eight hundred armed men on the quality of humanity.

By the Lord God, you will be a dead man

It was not the Stag and Pheasant but the nearby Farmers Arms that was crowded and hazy with pipe smoke on Thursday night 5 September when William Richards and another sou'westered Llanelli harbour pilot came to Five Roads to put a price on John Pasley Luckcraft's head.

William Walters, the landlord of the Stag and Pheasant had heard about the offer and was down at the Farmers Arms when his apprentice William Davies came looking for him at the behest of his wife. Shoni 'Sgubor Fawr was there, and so was Dai'r Cantwr. Half a crown (12½p) each was the price the two pilots offered the men for terrorising John Luckcraft, with whom they were in dispute over the pilotage rates at Llanelli. Half a crown for putting such a fear into him as would drive him for ever from the town. And they could not have come to a better place, for there were plenty of takers. Shoni and Dai, of course—the former carrying a shotgun and wearing a gown and bonnet, the latter unarmed and also disguised. And the rest were nearly all armed and disguised: Thomas Morris and William James of Five Roads, Charles Edmunds of Crosnant farm, Evan Jenkins of Gellihir farm, David Thomas of Cilferi Uchaf, Evan Hugh of Cilferi Isaf, and the landlord of the Farmers Arms, William Jenkins, to whom the Llanelli pilots had first put their proposition.

They set out from the Farmers Arms—Shoni alone on horseback—and went down through Furnace and around the edge of Llanelli town to Seaside and the harbour, where they arrived outside the harbourmaster's house at about one in the morning. John Pasley Luckcraft, the object of their attention, takes up the story:

> . . . I was awakened by a knocking at the front door of my house. I supposed it to be one of the harbour men calling me and I tapped the

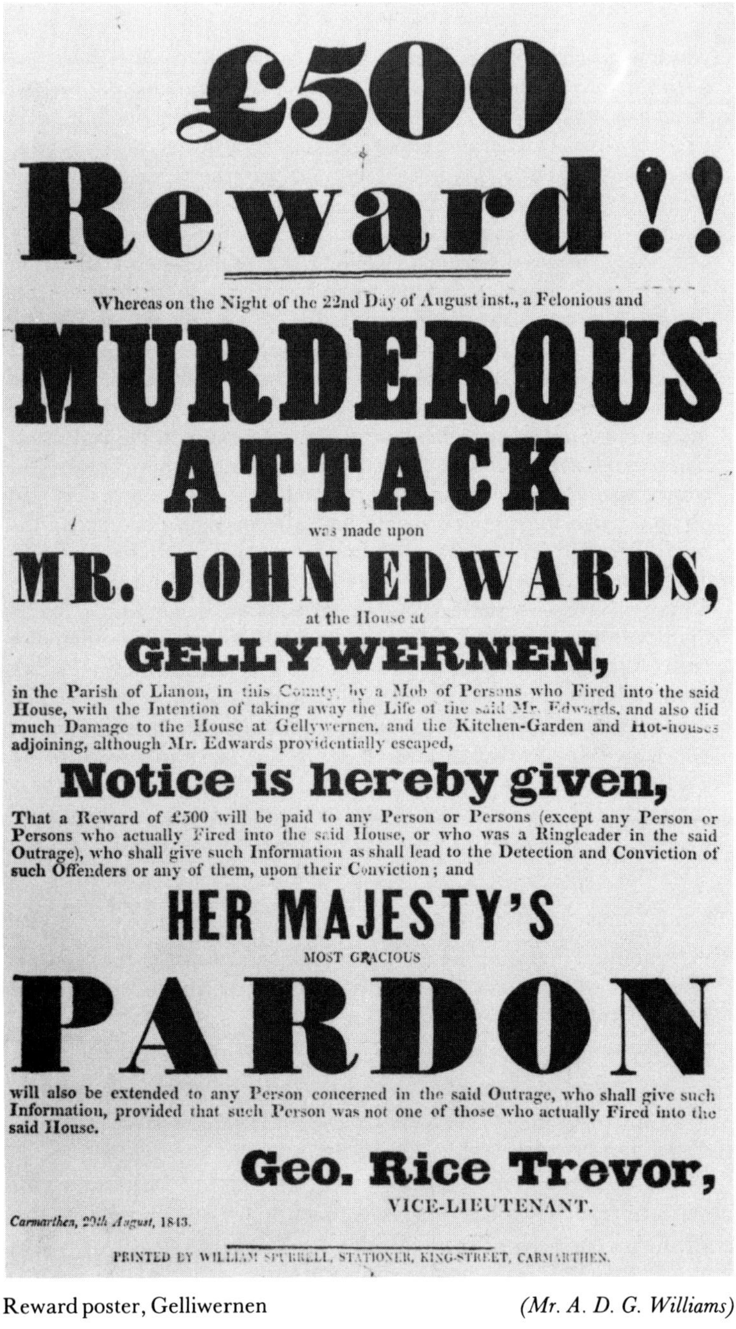

£500

Reward!!

Whereas on the Night of the 22nd Day of August inst., a Felonious and

MURDEROUS

ATTACK

was made upon

MR. JOHN EDWARDS,

at the House at

GELLYWERNEN,

in the Parish of Llanon, in this County, by a Mob of Persons who Fired into the said House, with the Intention of taking away the Life of the said Mr. Edwards, and also did much Damage to the House at Gellywernen, and the Kitchen-Garden and Hot-houses adjoining, although Mr. Edwards providentially escaped,

Notice is hereby given,

That a Reward of £500 will be paid to any Person or Persons (except any Person or Persons who actually Fired into the said House, or who was a Ringleader in the said Outrage), who shall give such Information as shall lead to the Detection and Conviction of such Offenders or any of them, upon their Conviction; and

HER MAJESTY'S

MOST GRACIOUS

PARDON

will also be extended to any Person concerned in the said Outrage, who shall give such Information, provided that such Person was not one of those who actually Fired into the said House.

Geo. Rice Trevor,

VICE-LIEUTENANT.

Carmarthen, 29th August, 1843.

PRINTED BY WILLIAM SPURRELL, STATIONER, KING-STREET, CARMARTHEN.

Reward poster, Gelliwernen *(Mr. A. D. G. Williams)*

window to show I was awake. A voice cried out 'Is it here the harbour master lives?' I replied 'Yes.' The same voice answered 'Come down here, we want to speak to you.' I dressed and prepared to go down and several voices called out in a threatening manner that if I did not come directly they would burn the house about me. I went out and saw in front of my house from twelve to twenty men all disguised, one on horseback. One person stood on my right as I came out. He was disguised in a light garment like a petticoat on the lower part of his person and had a handkerchief or something tied on like a turban on his head. He was a tall man and appeared to take the most active part. The man on horseback [Shoni 'Sgubor Fawr] spoke first: 'We have come respecting those poor people you are sending to our workhouse and you must go away.' I said 'Do you mean that I must leave this house?' and the man on the right said 'No, we mean that you must leave this place altogether. Before you came those men were getting forty pounds a year. Now they are obliged to go to the parish.' He had a woodman's hatchet in his hand. I replied that as I was in their power I must do as they desired. The man lifted the hatchet in a threatening manner and said 'If you do not promise, by the Lord God you will be a dead man.' I saw a man pointing a gun at me and I asked the man with the hatchet 'What is that man about with the gun?' The man with the hatchet ordered him to put the gun up, which he did and shrunk back. The man with the hatchet said that he would stand between me and harm and added 'You must promise to leave this place in a week or by God Almighty you are a dead man, and don't you think the soldiers can protect you, for they can't, and that they know—and they know that we are here now.' I said 'Do no violence and I make you the promise.'

The man on horseback turned towards the new dock and all the rest turned to go away. The man on the horse said something and a man pointed a gun at me and discharged it, but it hit the window three feet to my right. Three discharges were made towards the upper windows.[20]

By four o'clock that morning, as daylight streaked the eastern sky, they were back at the Farmers Arms collecting their half crowns and drinking William Jenkins' beer. Within a week, Llanelli had a vacancy for a harbour master.

Thus had freelancers Shoni and Dai carried out their half crown contract. But there was something much bigger in the wind, for in the Gwendraeth Valley the final touches were being

[20] The Chambers Papers (*Carmarthen Antiquary,* Vol. I).

put to a plan which would at last bring the much-dreaded confrontation and pitched battle between Rebecca and the forces of law and order that the present escalation of violence in that south eastern corner of Carmarthenshire had made inevitable.

Chapter Twelve

PONTARDULAIS

The Gwendraeth Valley was alive with rumour. The march through Llanon had ended in the anti-climax of Gelliwernen, from which Rebecca's shield had emerged somewhat tarnished. And there was a feeling that the Rebeccaites were looking for a spectacular demonstration to remove that tarnish and at the same time force the pace set by their earlier successes and by the great open-air meetings.

Within their own area of operations the Gwendraeth Valley Rebeccaites held complete sway. They were accustomed to riding unimpeded across seventy square miles of a countryside supposedly protected by detachments of police and foot soldiers and patrolled by troops of dragoons, and they could point to the ruin of every gate and bar between Llanddarog and Llanelli and Llanon and Kidwelly for evidence. So they looked farther afield —eastwards, towards the main outlet for their agricultural produce, the County of Glamorgan. And word leaked out, which was not really surprising given the number of written summonses sent out to the farmers in the name of Rebecca, the wording of which left no room for doubting the consequences of failure to attend, fully disguised, well mounted, armed with gun, powder and shot, and provided with appropriate tools of destruction.

On Wednesday morning 6 September, a farmer named Davies of Cefnybryn farm told John Edwards of Gelliwernen (whose house and family had been attacked so violently a fortnight earlier) that Rebecca was going to march on the Hendy and Pontardulais gates that very night. And there can be little doubt that the whisper had been heard in the headquarters of Shoni 'Sgubor Fawr and Dai'r Cantwr, the Stag and Pheasant, only a few hundred yards up the road from Cefnybryn farm.

John Edwards' daughter Hannah immediately wrote a note to Llanelli magistrate William Chambers, Junior and sent a servant off with it at a fast gallop. Chambers lost no time either in

William Chambers, Jnr., Llanelli Magistrate *(Nat. Library of Wales)*

sending gallopers to Glamorganshire's Chief Constable, Captain Charles Frederick Napier (in whose jurisdiction the Pontardulais gate lay, on the Glamorgan side of the Loughor river) and to Carmarthen to call out Major Parlby's 4th Light Dragoons. He sent, too, for Captain Rochford Scott, Colonel Love's aide-de-camp and the officer commanding the garrison in Llanelli,[1] to make plans for the defence of the Hendy gate, on the Carmarthenshire side of the Loughor. A fellow magistrate,

[1] Not to be confused (as he has been) with Captain Richard Andrew Scott, also of the Staff Corps, who was the Chief Constable designate of the new Carmarthenshire Constabulary, which he would be forming over the next couple of months.

Pontardulais, showing the Old Post Office on the Glamorgan side of the Loughor Bridge *(Nat. Library of Wales)*

Mr. Payne, was also called in so that if there should be need to divide the two companies of the 76th Regiment of Foot (who were to lay the ambush) one magistrate could go with each party.

The village of Pontardulais was the point at which the Carmarthen to Swansea mail road crossed the River Loughor, on the Carmarthenshire side of which the road was joined by that from Llanelli. Half a mile on the Llanelli side of that junction lay the Gwili bridge, at the hamlet of Hendy, where a road from Llanon came in from the north. Pontardulais was, therefore, a bottleneck with no way around it for the farmers of south east Carmarthenshire to get their produce to the Glamorgan markets. And it was there that that notorious toll farmer Thomas Bullin—whose name was indelibly linked with Efail-wen—had one of his gates.

So far as secrecy was possible in the mustering of troops, it was observed. Their departure was delayed until after dark and they avoided the road by marching through fields. Surprise would be complete . . . in more senses than one as it turned out.

In Glamorganshire preparations to put a force of men in ambush at Pontardulais also went ahead under a cloak of secrecy. But whereas the Carmarthenshire party was to consist of some forty soldiers, that on the other side of the Loughor was destined to consist solely of men of the Glamorganshire Constabulary; Captain Frane's detachment of the 4th Light Dragoons, ordered from Swansea, would arrive only when it was all over. There were eight police officers: Captain Napier, Superintendent Henry James Peake, Sergeants Jenkins and George Jones, and Constables Thomas Jones, John Price, William Robertson Williams and Peter Wright. They, too, were accompanied by magistrates (as was required in those days to deal with a riot)—John Dillwyn Llewellyn, his brother Lewis Llewellyn Dillwyn and Matthew Moggridge. All carried pistols, two brace each in the case of the magistrates so that they could fire four shots before having to reload. The police also carried cutlasses which, like the pistols, were issued only when an armed confrontation was anticipated. The soldiers from Llanelli were, of course, armed with muskets and bayonets and the dragoons from Carmarthen, who had a good two and a half hour ride ahead of them before reaching the scene of action, carried carbines and sabres.

Captain Napier's intention, with which his magistrates concurred, was to capture as many of the Rebeccaites—preferably the leaders—as he could, for which purpose he planned to allow them to begin breaking the gate and tollhouse and pounce on them while they were so occupied. On the other side of the river, William Chambers' intention was to protect the Hendy gate which he thought would be reached first by the men coming down from Llanon, though there was an alternative road directly from there to Pontardulais.

Anyone who has had command on the ground of policemen or soldiers in night operations appreciates the confusion that can arise from the most carefully laid plans, even with the benefit of radio communications and other modern technology, but confusion was made all the more inevitable on that night by the fact that there was no communication or co-ordination whatever between the two parties. Clausewitz's dictum that 'No plan survives contact with the enemy'[2] is probably as true to-day as it was when it was published in 1833, only ten years before Rebecca, and so it proved at Pontardulais and Hendy when a

[2] *Vom Kriege (On War)* by Karl von Clausewitz (1780-1831), the Prussian soldier and military writer, upon whose writings rested the creation of the Prussian, and later the German, army, and indeed most of nineteenth century military theory.

Magistrate John Dillwyn Llewellyn of Penllergaer
(University College of Swansea)

Magistrate Lewis Llewellyn Dillwyn of Penllergaer
(University College of Swansea)

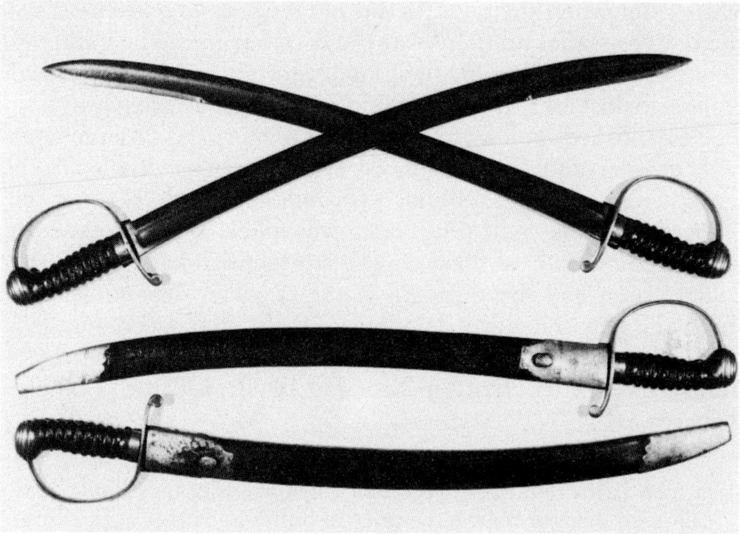

Police cutlasses issued at the time of the Rebecca Riots
(Dyfed-Powys Police Museum)

hundred and fifty Rebeccaites rode down from Llanon on that September night. For those on the Carmarthenshire side of the River Loughor were totally ignorant of the intentions or movements of those on the Glamorgan side. And vice versa!

Jac Tŷ Isha

John Hughes was the twenty four years old son of farmer Morgan Hughes of Tŷ Isha farm near the mining village of Tumble. His two brothers and five sisters were aged between five and fifteen and the family was one of the most respected of the district. It was no secret among his neighbours, though, that this strong and intelligent young man was very active in the Rebecca movement, for who was not among the struggling farmers of the Gwendraeth Valley? And he took it seriously, even to the extent of training his horse to remain steady under fire, with the enthusiastic help of his mother Mary, who held the bridle while John fired his shotgun. Morgan Hughes, on the other hand, was rather less happy about his son's involvement.

Riot by proxy was by now well established in the Gwendraeth

Valley, for when the farmers did not wish to go gate-breaking themselves—after all there was the corn harvest to be gathered now—they would employ their labourers and servants and local colliers to do it for them. The going rate for riot by proxy was also well established: half a crown (12½p) a man, and provide your own powder and shot. At more than a quarter of a collier's weekly pay of nine shillings (45p), a few night's work for Rebecca could be quite profitable, even allowing for the expense of powder and shot, so there was no shortage of takers. In fact the colliers soon had the measure of the farmers' dependence on them and began making demands of their own. At one of their night meetings for instance (at Llangyndeyrn, two or three miles from Pontyberem) on Monday 14 August, the 'Colliery Rebeccaites':

> . . . came to resolutions that inasmuch as they had assisted the farmers in the reduction of rents and turnpike tolls, they should now call upon them to reduce the price of butter and other agricultural produce and insist upon the publicans reducing the price of beer.[3]

But for the night of Wednesday 6 September it was a farmers' Rebecca, John Hughes (or Jac Tŷ Isha as he was better known) who donned his mother's copious nightgown and straw bonnet, blacked his face, loaded his brace of pistols and, at about ten o'clock, mounted his horse (the only white one in the party) and led the ride to Pontardulais and Hendy.

The group swelled as mounted men rode in from side roads and wayside farms and as others were brought from their beds—some at gunpoint—and forced to disguise, arm, and saddle their horses. But however they came—whether for their half crowns or forced along, or simply because they were true God-fearing, justice-seeking devotees of Rebecca's cause—all were soon infected with the thrill of the march as horns blew, rockets streaked into the sky and men talked excitedly of past exploits. And spirits *were* high because they had become used to riding without serious challenge, except, as some laughingly recalled, by the Lion of Porthyrhyd on being roused by his sixtieth lash!

Collision

It was a clear night, brightly illuminated by a full moon, and

[3] *Carmarthen Journal*, 18 August, 1843.

Chambers, Scott and the soldiers of the 76th, walking in single file behind the roadside hedgerows towards Hendy, had their first intimation that Rebecca was out when they saw the trail and starburst of a rocket above the hills towards Llanon. As they drew near to Hendy Bridge the sounds of horns drifted over the night air, and assuming that the Rebeccaites were riding straight for Hendy, Chambers split his force, leaving Payne and six soldiers to block the Llanelli road and taking Captain Scott and fourteen other soldiers on to the bridge, where they lay in the hedgerow, guns loaded and primed, and waited.

On the far side of the river, Captain Napier, his seven policemen and the three magistrates, were nearing the end of a wearying ten or eleven mile, two and a half hour trek, walking their horses across the fields from Penllergaer, during which they had seen the rockets and heard distant gunfire over in Carmarthenshire. It was about ten minutes to one when they arrived in the field four or five hundred yards on the Swansea side of the toll gate, from which Napier planned to launch his attack, and it was there that they heard voices and the sound of many horses' hooves. The police and magistrates could only guess what was happening, but what they were hearing were the sounds of a hundred and fifty men, nearly all on horseback, riding past the Red Lion Inn, the home of Griffith Vaughan still on bail for gun-running for the Bolgoed rioters, and crossing the Loughor Bridge.

Suddenly Rebecca shouted 'Come, come, come' and there was a great fusillade of shots as her daughters buried their felling axes in the spars of the gate and applied their crowbars, hatchets, pickaxes and sledgehammers to the toll house. Napier ordered his men to secure their mounts in the field and waited for a few minutes until he judged that the Rebeccaites were fully occupied with their work of destruction. And then he led his party on foot from the field, and, giving the order 'Fall in', placed them in line abreast across the road.

So preoccupied were the Rebeccaites (some of whom were also on the Swansea side of the gate) that they did not know the policemen were there until Captain Napier cried 'Stop!' At once, three of the mounted men who seemed to be the leaders wheeled their horses and galloped full tilt at the police. One, whose white horse distinguished him from the crowd, aimed his

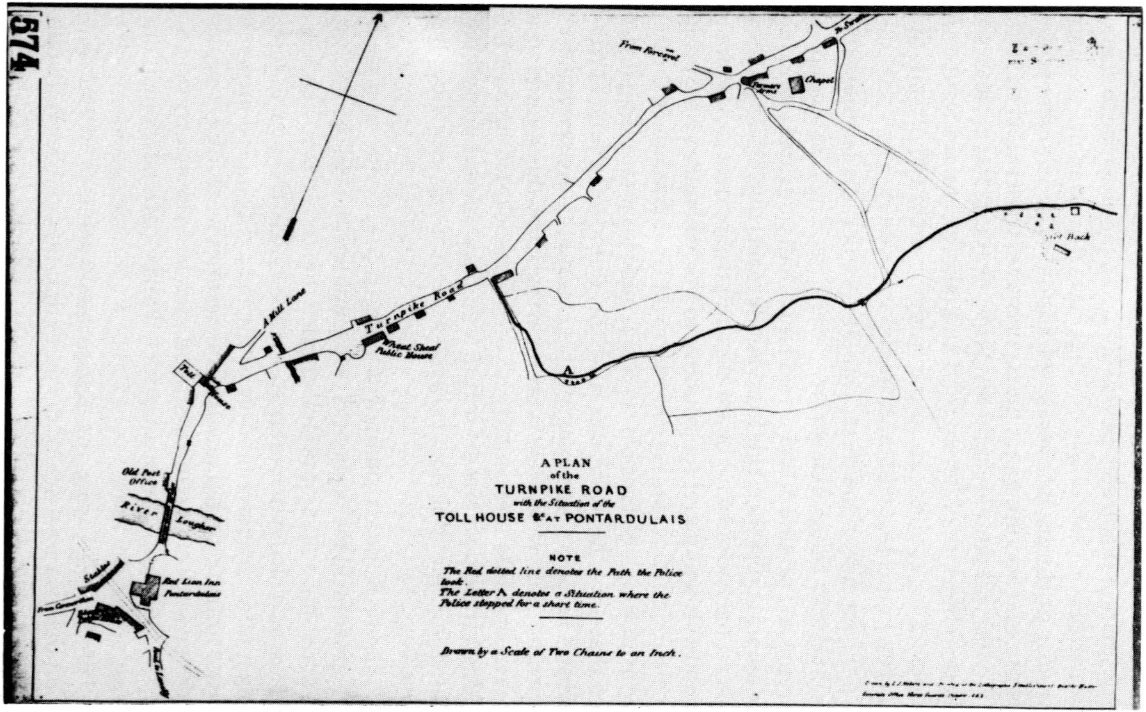

Plan of Pontardulais, drawn for the War Office, Oct. 1843 *(University College of Swansea)*

pistol at Napier and fired. He missed, and Napier, pointing to him and calling to his men 'Mark that man', shot his horse and at the same time shouted 'Fire!' The shot horse reared up, spun around three or four times and threw its rider, while the line of police and magistrates, firing as one, sent a volley of shot whistling across the gate and into the crowd. The Rebeccaites fired a massive volley in return—but immediately broke in panic amid the frightened rearing and neighing of horses flailing about in all directions, the yells of equally frightened men, the ragged crackle of unaimed gunfire and one more crashing volley from the police and magistrates.

But with a hundred and fifty men and nearly as many horses pressing back onto the bridge in total confusion there was panic and chaos for some ten minutes before defeat turned into rout. Captain Napier was still struggling with the dismounted Rebecca leader who had shot at him. He was just gaining the upper hand when he was struck over the head from behind and rendered momentarily unconscious, but Sergeant Jenkins, turning around and seeing his chief fall, fired his pistol at a yard's range and shattered his opponent's arm. The sergeant was too busy disarming another horseman to chase the wounded man as he headed back to the bridge on foot, but Constable John Price saw him running by and seized him. 'Let me go, let me go my good fellow,' he cried, holding his bleeding arm in evident pain. 'You have broken my arm already.' 'Where did you get it broke?' asked the officer. 'Over yonder, at the gate,' said Rebecca. Price arrested him and he gave the officer his name—John Hughes of Tŷ Isha.

Meanwhile, magistrates Lewis Llewellyn Dillwyn and John Dillwyn Llewellyn were fully occupied, the former putting a bullet into the ribs of the horse of one pistol-wielding Rebeccaite and then engaging in a fierce struggle with another (later identified as David Jones) in an attempt to capture him. Even a blow on the head from Constable Williams' cutlass did not completely subdue that one, who struck Williams with an iron bar and fought on until seized by Sergeant Jenkins. Constable Williams had been unable to follow through on the sword cut because he himself was labouring under some disability—through having been stabbed in the thigh by his own cutlass when it fell out of its scabbard as he dismounted some way back on the march to Pontardulais. John Dillwyn Llewellyn also shot a horse, and brought its rider crashing to the ground with a blow to the head from his pistol butt, and he and his fellow magistrates were in the thick of the fight throughout.

Two men had thus been secured, and a third (later identified as John Hugh) was captured by Constable Thomas Jones who saw him fire his shotgun in the volley fired by the massed horsemen when challenged by Captain Napier. The officer saw him throw down his gun, wheel his horse and join in the great press of men and horses heading for the bridge, and he pulled him from his horse and arrested him.

Eventually the jam on the bridge began to clear, and the fugitives galloped and ran back into their native Carmarthenshire, scattering in all directions, heedless of the cries of the wounded and spurred mindlessly on by the homing instinct of the panic-stricken. They galloped and they ran back into those hills until breath could carry them no further.

This was the point at which a properly planned ambush would have brought into play its pursuit element—the cavalry. But the dragoons were late again. Why Captain Frane's Swansea detachment failed to keep its rendezvous at Pontardulais will never be known, but to be fair to those called from Carmarthen, they had nearly twenty miles (or nearly three hours) to ride and they had no precise orders—merely the word that Hendy *or* Pontardulais was expected to be the target. And it was to the former that they went, to link up with William Chambers, Junior, from whom they had received the call. No such co-ordination had been arranged with the eleven men who had taken on the Rebeccaites on the other side of the river, at odds of some fourteen to one, and who now had their hands more than full in securing their three prisoners and sorting out the chaos left behind as the fugitives fled the field.

Within an ace

William Chambers and his infantrymen listened with some apprehension as the sound of volleys and fusillades of gunfire carried clearly over the half mile from Pontardulais for a good ten minutes. Having no idea that there was anyone at Pontardulais to oppose the Rebeccaites and that the gunfire signified a battle, Chambers thought it was merely the sound of an unopposed attack and that when it ceased it would very soon be Hendy's turn. One thing was certain; there were an awful lot of them!

Walking ahead to reconnoitre, Chambers and Captain Scott saw someone walking quickly down the colliery railway line from the Llanon direction. They seized him. Under his straw bonnet the man—farmer Lewis Davies of Ysgubor Uchaf in the parish of Llanon—had his face painted black and red, but the terrified man told them he had been forced to join when a dozen men had surrounded his farmhouse firing guns into the air and threatening to burn it and him in it. He was brought back to the main party on Hendy Bridge and then Chambers saw a group of men walking from the direction of the bridge *towards* Pontardulais. What on earth could be happening? The men changed direction on seeing the magistrate and disappeared into the darkness, but at that moment another figure came through the hedge and ran away, pursued by Private James McCarten of the 76th. McCarten thought he had caught a young girl. Indeed 'she' said 'she' was a girl, but it was a young lad named William Hugh from Talyclew farm in nearby Llangennech, who had his face blackened and was dressed in girl's clothes. He was crying bitterly. Two more were captured when Sergeant Gibbs of the 76th took three of his men into the fields towards the sounds of 'shrieking' and found Thomas Williams, a servant from Llangennech Mill, and Henry Rogers, also a servant, of Penllwyngwyn farm in the same village. Neither armed nor disguised they 'seemed much frightened at the soldiers', which from the outset seemed to bear out their story that they had only followed the sounds of horns and gunfire to watch Becca at work.

All this was only the work of a few minutes and since the main body of the Rebeccaites had still not appeared Chambers gathered his troops and marched them along the road towards Pontardulais in order to intercept them and keep them well away from Hendy gate. It was then that they heard the thunder of hooves. They fixed bayonets, spread out across the road and in the light of the moon they could just distinguish the horsemen only yards away as they reined and formed into line abreast. The foot soldiers' fingers tightened around their musket triggers.

For their part, the mounted men saw a line of figures armed with guns barring the road ahead and, to a smart order, they drew their swords, pointed them to the front and spurred their

The 4th Light Dragoons prepare for action *(Nat. Army Museum)*

The 76th Regiment of Foot: its battle honours under Wellington in India and the Peninsula, so nearly besmirched at Hendy *(Nat. Army Museum)*

horses. But the order 'Charge!' froze on the lips of their leader as he suddenly recognised the line of men facing him as red-coated infantrymen. And in the same instant, William Chambers, Junior recognised his opponents as cavalrymen.

Thus did Her Majesty's 4th Light Dragoons and 76th Regiment of Foot come within an ace of setting a bloody seal on that night of confusion by fighting the first battle between British soldiers on British soil in two hundred years!

Becca caged

When the combined force of cavalry and infantry reached Pontardulais it was all over. They found the gate reduced to matchwood, the tollhouse gutted and partly demolished and Captain Napier and his men in possession of a large collection of tools and weapons and several wounded and abandoned horses. They also had three black-faced, dejected and bloodstained prisoners—Jac Tŷ Isha, David Jones and John Hugh—sitting manacled on the ground by the ruined and shot-peppered toll-house, still wearing their Rebecca disguises.

Jac Tŷ Isha was in considerable pain with a pistol ball lodged in his upper arm, to where it had travelled from his shattered elbow, while David Jones seemed to be in danger of dying from three sword cuts on his head and a number of pistol balls and shot pellets in his back. All three were taken to Swansea by an escort of dragoons and Jac Tŷ Isha and David Jones were put into the prison infirmary. John Hugh's less severe injuries were attended to by the prison doctor before he was put into a cell.

It was at the prison that Jac Tŷ Isha was searched and what was found on him identified him beyond doubt as Rebecca, the leader of the attack. He had powder and ammunition on him of course, but he also had two incriminating pieces of paper bearing handwriting in Welsh. One, a note signed 'Becca', was addressed to Daniel Jones, Brynhir (in Llanon), telling him to 'Come with all to assist to Jac Tŷ Isha Wednesday night next, or you will have no further notice.' The other, addressed to 'Mrs. Becca', was wrapped around five shillings (25p) in coin and, though its message was garbled, later events would show that it contained a threat to the gatekeeper at Hendy. It said, 'I am taking my leave to you, part of Rebecca's children—to William Lewis, Ponthendy [Hendy Bridge] gate—inoffensive wife—was in the Hendy gate, Pontardulais, out of their living, and leaving the people to go half the toll—said he had one as keen that would raise the toll, and he placed Sarah that was formerly in . . . gate—knew was a wife.'

The William Lewis in the note was the man severely whipped by the Rebeccaites at Llandeilo Rwnws (Carmarthen) on 7 July, a well-known and universally hated toll farmer and the lessee of all the Kidwelly Trust gates, including those recently demolished at Sandy Bridge and Furnace, and the gate at Hendy. And 'Sarah' was Sarah Williams, the toll collector at Hendy. She was to die at the hands of the Rebeccaites just two nights later!

Chapter Thirteen

A DEEP AND BROODING SPIRIT

In Llanelli on Thursday morning 7 September, the four captured at Hendy by William Chambers and his soldiers appeared before the magistrates, who decided that they should be charged with taking part in the Pontardulais riot and therefore taken to Swansea to be arraigned with the ring leaders, to whose aid lawyer Hugh Williams had already dashed from Carmarthen.

In both towns vast crowds surrounded the court houses and followed the prisoners whenever they were conveyed through the streets. In both towns, too, the authorities saw all the signs of incipient riot, and strong forces of soldiers were put onto the streets, while the surrounding countryside was in a ferment. No one believed the word of the police and magistrates that the rioters had fired first at Pontardulais. As the stories spread so they became more and more lurid, until the authorities stood accused of something akin to massacre, and many were the families around Llanon and in the Gwendraeth Valley who were left for many days in a state of fear and desperation waiting for news of missing husbands, fathers and sons. They dared not make enquiries about them for fear of attracting the attention of Inspector Tierney and his London policemen, who were now scouring the district searching and questioning everywhere. As ever, Thomas Campbell Foster was on the spot for *The Times* to capture the atmosphere and ugly mood of the people:

> Since the fight at Pontardulais a number of farmers are said to be missing. It is supposed by some that they are wounded, and it is said that the soldiers are gone out for the purpose of capturing some of them.
>
> The miners and colliers near Pontyberem have declared that they will resist the soldiers and that they will undermine and blow up the roads; and they threaten that, as the Glamorgan Police laid in wait for them, they will have an ambush for the Police some day.[1]

[1] *The Times,* 16 September, 1843.

> The attack by the police on the Rebeccaites at the Pontardulais gate and the wounding of some of the parties concerned in that attack have been productive of the most serious consequences. It was fondly hoped and indeed confidently predicted by both the magistrates and the police that it would put an end to Rebeccaism and that such would be the terror felt throughout the country that the Lady Rebecca would be so struck with terror that the outrages would at once be put an end to. The effect has, however, been precisely the reverse.
>
> The Welsh are a peculiar people and they have become completely exasperated in consequence of their countrymen having been shot, as they say, by a villainous body of police.[2]

The prime target for the anger of the Rebeccaites of the Gwendraeth Valley was William Chambers, Junior, the man they had so loudly cheered at the meeting on Mynydd Sylen only two weeks earlier. Despite the fact that Chambers had not reached Pontardulais until long after the last shot had been fired, he was cast as the villain of the piece and was very soon paying the price. His offence was to have been seen kneeling over one of the wounded prisoners by the ruined toll house at Pontardulais. He was giving him water, but by the time the story got back to the Gwendraeth Valley he had personally shot the man and was bending over him to finish him off! More than enough to bring down a storm of fire and gunshot on his property, his employees at his pottery factory in Llanelli and on his farms at Tynywern, Gelligylwnog and Maensant in the Gwendraeth Valley.

For the attack on Tynywern farm, the plan put forward by Evan Jenkins of Gellihir was that Dai'r Cantwr should stand by the door of the farmhouse to prevent Chambers' farm manager, Banning, from getting out, while the gang burned the house down around him. His offence? He owed sixteen shillings (80p) to John the Shoemaker (Jac y Crydd) who lived by the Drovers Arms in Horeb, just along the road from Rebecca's headquarters, the Stag and Pheasant. But there was a row about whether it was really worth killing a man for sixteen shillings, and it was an empty house that went up in flames at Tynywern.

At Gelligylwnog a bizarre ceremony was performed as barns and stables blazed and the farm animals scattered in panic. Thomas Morris brought down a horse with his shotgun and

[2] *The Times*, 20 September, 1843.

called upon one of the others to rip open its stomach with a knife, whereupon he filled his hands with the flowing blood and his comrades dipped their fingers in it 'as a sacrifice instead of Christ.' And there, in the glare of burning Gelligylwnog, the Stag and Pheasant gang received their baptism in blood. They included Shoni 'Sgubor Fawr, Dai'r Cantwr, Thomas Morris, John Daniel and William James of Five Roads, William Walters, landlord of the Stag and Pheasant, Charles Edmunds of Crosnant, Evan Jenkins of Gellihir, David Thomas of Cilferi Uchaf, John the Shoemaker of Horeb and Evan Hugh of Cilferi Isaf.

There was even a conspiracy to murder William Chambers and a price was actually put on his head. Again the plot was hatched in the Stag and Pheasant, and two of the leading lights in it were those who were now assuming the leadership, Shoni 'Sgubor Fawr and Dai'r Cantwr. David Thomas of Cilferi Uchaf put forward the idea after Shoni had said they ought to shoot John Edwards of Gelliwernen, whose courageous daughter Hannah had so thwarted them on the march through Llanon. In a speech lasting about ten minutes, David Thomas (Dai Cilferi) accused Chambers of shooting the men at Pontardulais and called upon his fellow Rebeccaites to 'join all your hearts to get rid of all such people from amongst you.' Not only would God assist them, said he, but 'Anyone who would shoot young Chambers should have Five Pounds.' And twelve men volunteered to do the deed.

Another shillingsworth, that you may be strong

But the vendetta against Chambers was only one aspect of the reign of terror in which Shoni 'Sgubor Fawr and his lieutenant Dai'r Cantwr led the Stag and Pheasant gang on a spree of arson, burglary and armed robbery—frightening people to order, running what amounted to a 'protection racket' by doing the rounds of the farmers and collecting 'contributions' in the name of Rebecca, and attaching themselves to any farm they fancied for as long as it suited them for free food and lodging. No wonder Chambers called Shoni 'Sgubor Fawr 'The most despotic governor they ever had'!

And of course the toll gates continued to receive attention. In fact on the very night after Pontardulais, when the Gwendraeth

Valley Rebeccaites were licking their wounds and many were in hiding, the Stag and Pheasant contingent carried out an attack on the gate at Spudders Bridge, at the southern end of the Gwendraeth Fawr river. As ever, their expedition began with a drinking spree in the Stag and Pheasant, with the Rev. David Jones paying liberally for their beer. Shoni and Dai were there in their gowns and bonnets, as were Tom Morris and John Daniels of Five Roads, Charles Edmunds of Crosnant, and the landlord, William Walters. And they roped in two young farm servants, David Howells of Pantygwenith and David Vaughan of Soho farm, who had called in for a pint.

Well fortified with ale by about ten o'clock, they all rose, picked up their guns, axes and sledgehammers and headed for the door to do Rebecca's work—to hear the Rev. Jones call 'Stop, I'll give you another shilling's worth that you may be strong!' And they drank, and they were strengthened. And after they had gone, the Rev. Jones stayed at the Stag and Pheasant until three o'clock in the morning, leaving word with Mrs. Walters for them to come to breakfast 'on white bread and butter and tea' when their work was done.

The gang headed down from Five Roads towards Trimsaran, calling at Topsail farm along the way to collect Thomas Phillips and his servants, Josuah Thomas and the boys Jonah and Tom, and announcing their arrival at the Spudders Bridge gate by cheering, firing and blowing their horns. Down went the gate in front of the terrified gate keeper and in went the axes to chop it to pieces. When they had done, Shoni gave the gateman two Rebecca letters for delivery to magistrates William Chambers Junior and Mr. Rees of Cilymaenllwyd, giving them notice of an early visit—letters which David Howells believed were written by Dai'r Cantwr when he saw him writing two letters while sitting in a field the day before.

And the next night the Rebeccaites did what the police ambush at Pontardulais had prevented them from doing on the Wednesday night. They attacked the gate at Hendy Bridge. This time the word did not leak out, and there was no ambush waiting for them.

Hendy

Towards one o'clock on Saturday morning, 9 September, Rebecca and her daughters arrived at the two-roomed, thatch roofed toll house at Hendy, in which old Sarah Williams had lived as toll collector for a week. She had been a toll collector for years, at many gates, but Rebecca had a particular interest in her appointment to Hendy, for the note found on Jac Tŷ Isha after Pontardulais told that Sarah Williams was there for the prime purpose of increasing the toll. She had, in fact, received several warnings during that week to get out of Hendy, and now she was to pay dearly for ignoring them.

A hammering at the door brought her from her bed and as she opened the door a number of black-faced and disguised men pushed her aside, dashed into the house and removed all her belongings to the road outside. And as Sarah Williams stood screaming in terror, flaming torches were thrown through the door and put to the roof thatch, and to a rattle of gunfire the tollhouse roared into flame.

Carpenter John Thomas and his wife Margaret, who lived nearby, had gone to bed at about eleven o'clock and were awakened by the gunfire to find their room bathed in a red glow. A glance through the window at the band of bizarrely dressed men dragging furniture out of the tollhouse was enough, and the Thomases stayed fearfully behind their locked doors. Within a few minutes, though, there was a banging at their door and they found Sarah Williams there, screaming hysterically, pleading with them to come and help her save her belongings. John Thomas froze with fear, but his wife ran out of the house and braved the showers of sparks and burning thatch to drag what she could back to her own cottage. She pleaded with the half-crazed toll woman to go with her to the safety of her cottage, but to no avail, so she returned alone. She and her husband remained indoors listening to the gunfire and huddled in the flickering red glare which filled their room for some three quarters of an hour, until the noise began to die away and the flames to subside. Then they heard a sound outside. It was Sarah Williams again, this time crawling on her hands and knees alongside the wall of the house, semi-conscious, her face smoke-blackened, and with blood on her forehead. Hardly had they dragged her inside than she was dead.

If people will not take warning

When day dawned over the smoking shell of Hendy tollhouse the magistrates, police and coroner came, and two Llanelli surgeons, Benjamin Thomas and John Kirkhouse Cooke, performed a post-mortem examination of Sarah Williams' body. They found that gunshot had penetrated her forehead, temple, windpipe, left breast and armpit, and both her arms. There was gunshot in her lungs and a massive amount of blood had collected there, to flood from her mouth as they raised her body to the sitting position. As they declared to Coroner William Bonville, 'There was no cause to which to attribute the effusion of blood but to the shot penetrating the lungs and injuring its vessels.' They were satisfied, they told him, 'that the cause of death was loss of blood and the state of the lungs and pleura arising from the shot found in the lungs.'

'*Destruction of Hendy Gate: Murder of the Toll Collector*' proclaimed the newspaper headlines, their editors evidently as surprised as the authorities at the audacity displayed by the Rebeccaites in returning within three days to the locality in which they had been so soundly thrashed. There was outrage among the magistrates and landowners and every effort was made by the offer of rewards and intensification of police activity to find the killers—a reaction that found scant support among the populace at large. A *Swansea Journal* reporter, travelling on horseback through Pontardulais, Hendy, Llanelli and Llanon, sensed it everywhere he went:

> When we arrived in Llanelli we found the town one scene of excitement and commotion and learned that the cause of this disturbulance to the public mind was a report which had reached the town that the hay and corn upon two farms [Gelligylwnog and Tynywern], the property of Mr. Chambers, had been set on fire during the night by some incendiaries.
>
> Mr. Chambers having gone out with the military to Pontardulais on Thursday morning last has given deep and mortal offence to that portion of the community who sympathise with the Rebeccaites. Expressions of hatred towards that gentleman and a determination to have revenge—'to have blood'—may be heard in every pothouse in the parish.
>
> After a most tedious ride over a road paved with stones of an enormous size which threatened repeatedly to bring our horses—

accustomed to the smooth roads of Glamorganshire—to the ground, we reached the farm at Tynywern. Some idea may be formed of the size of the ricks of hay when we state that they were set on fire at two o'clock in the afternoon and at the time we saw them they were burning furiously and a sufficient quantity remained to continue burning for another twelve hours. There were a great many persons present but they made no attempt to extinguish the fire.

From Tynywern we proceeded in the direction of Pontyberem, Lletymawr and one or two other places, and on our way we heard that the gatekeeper, an aged female, at Hendy gate near Pontardulais had been shot by a party of Rebeccaites on Sunday morning and the gate burned down. Speaking on this subject shortly afterwards to some men we met, one of them said 'Well I am sorry they killed the old woman, but of what service is it to pull down the gates if people continue to exact tolls? The old woman had several warnings and remonstrances upon her obstinacy in persisting to collect tolls. So you see, if people will not take warning what else can you say? You know it is of no earthly use to knock down the gates if people will be so foolish as to persist in collecting tolls.'

At the village of Llanon nothing was talked of but the death of the old woman at the Hendy gate and we are sorry to observe that very few, if any, expressed regret for what had taken place.[3]

But there was more to come, for the people's attitude to the old woman's death was to be given public form at the Coroner's Inquest on Sarah Williams, which was held in the Black Horse at Hendy on 11 September, two days after her death. After hearing all the gory detail of the surgeons' evidence, the jury returned the remarkable verdict that:

The deceased died from the effusion of blood into the chest, which occasioned suffocation, *but from what cause is to this jury unknown.*[4]

Not murder, nor any other class of homicide, but merely suffocation through an effusion of blood into the chest, *through an unknown cause*! Much has changed in the law since 1843, but not the law that made (and still makes) death through gunshot wounds occasioned in the course of a riot anything less than manslaughter. But the verdict did no more than reflect popular feeling and it signalled very clearly to the authorities that they

[3] *Carmarthen Journal,* 15 September, 1843.
[4] *Carmarthen Journal,* 15 September, 1843. (Author's italics).

might be wise to remove the trials of the Pontardulais rioters to a place far away from the evident bias of Carmarthenshire or west Glamorganshire juries. And they took due note.

Chapter Fourteen

PERPETUALLY TO BE CONQUERED?

When *The Thunderer* spoke, Governments listened. And there was no better example of this than the reaction of Home Secretary Sir James Graham when, relaxing for the weekend at his country home, his *Times* was delivered to him on Saturday morning 16 September, 1843.

The army was being pilloried and derided for its manifest inability to come to grips with the Rebeccaites, let alone defeat them in the field. Sir James and the nation had read as much before, but his patience finally gave way as he read the words of Thomas Campbell Foster, penned in his hotel room in Carmarthen only three days before: 'Troops have been marched to Middleton Hall now the mischief is done. Different bodies of Dragoons are going off in various directions and the streets are full of people . . . I may venture safely to say that they will not pass over a single mile of road where two hours previous notice of their approach has not been given.' And further on, beneath an account of the extraordinary proceedings at the inquest on the old woman of Hendy gate, 'I am told that the jury durst give no other verdict; that such a system of terrorism prevails that men dare not render themselves obnoxious by even doing their duty. The necessity of putting the country under Military Law is seriously discussed by many. The miners and colliers near Pontyberem have declared that they will resist the soldiers and that they will undermine and blow up the road.'

In that black week, Sir James Graham had already been told of the battle at Pontardulais in which eight policemen and three magistrates had taken on a hundred and fifty armed Rebeccaites without any help at all from the army, and how the people of the countryside in south east Carmarthenshire were not only crying 'revenge' but actually taking it by gunfire and incendiarism. He had heard of the occupation of Fishguard by the rampaging mob that had destroyed the town gates and shot the local surgeon. He had heard of the attack on the Llanelli harbourmaster and how

Rebecca and her Daughters, as portrayed in the London press
(Nat. Library of Wales)

toll gate after toll gate had been smashed by armed gangs riding, marching and destroying with impunity over the whole of west Wales. And above all he had seen with increasing anger the helplessness of some of Her Majesty's finest troops in the face of what had seemed to him to be a mere peasant uprising.

Coming on top of all this and of *The Times* report only four days earlier that 'Fine bodies of soldiers have been trailed about night after night to no purpose, till the poor fellows are thoroughly sick of it' what the Home Secretary read over his breakfast on that Saturday morning was just about the last straw. And he wrote a private letter to his Prime Minister, Sir Robert Peel. 'My dear Peel,' he wrote:

> That you may be kept informed of what we are doing in South Wales I send you this letter . . . which I have received this evening. I have given positive orders . . . that magistrates who refuse to issue Warrants or to attend the Civil and Military Force if a breach of the Peace is apprehended shall be reported to me.[1]
>
> Colonel Love has under his command a Force of 1,800 men,

[1] See p. 178 for the letter dated 26 September, 1843, from the Home Office to the Vice-Lieutenant for Pembrokeshire.

including a Regiment of Cavalry and a Demi-Brigade of Guns. I am not satisfied with the use which he makes of this Force. It is quite sufficient to conquer the four Counties, which he is asked only to keep quiet in aid of the Civil Power, but it so happens that he keeps the Troops constantly in motion and always arrives too late. If a crime be committed, he instantly sends Soldiers to the place on the *following* day. The troops are thus constantly paraded before the People with apparent impotence and the authorities are brought into contempt.

I am opposed to any further augmentation of the Military Force: if 1,800 men cannot subdue this outbreak 3,000 will not succeed better. I am rather disposed to ask the Duke of Wellington to select a General Officer who will take the chief command; and Colonel Love will resume his former position in command only of his Regiment [the 73rd, or Black Watch] . . . I am always Yours very truly, Jas. Graham.[2]

It is hard to imagine that Sir James Graham had not, like any other professional politician, studied the life and work of the great political philosopher Edmund Burke. But he had either overlooked or failed to understand Burke's view of the application of military force to the problem of civil unrest. And Edmund Burke's words were as true then as they are to-day and as they have ever been:

> The use of force alone is temporary. It may subdue for a moment, but it does not remove the necessity of subduing again; and a nation is not governed which is perpetually to be conquered.[3]

Nor did His Grace the Duke of Wellington heed Edmund Burke. It was not his style anyway. An enemy was an enemy whether he was a Frenchman or a Welsh rustic, and an army properly handled must prevail. So he sent to Wales one of his best generals—Major General Sir George Brown, a veteran, like Colonel Love, of the Peninsular war and the war with the United States of America, but, unlike Love, a man who had spent his last twenty five years or so on the staff of the War Office in London.

It was as if some malign hand of fate was directing Sir George Brown to west Wales to supersede a man whose efforts had been

[2] Letter dated 17 September, 1843, Sir James Graham to Sir Robert Peel: British Library (Peel papers, MS 40449).

[3] Edmund Burke's speech on conciliation with the American Colonies, March 22, 1775.

discredited by *The Times*. For twelve years later Sir George himself would suffer the same fate. As second in command of the army in the Crimea he would watch almost helplessly as that army perished before his eyes of cold, disease and untreated wounds. His chief, Lord Raglan, would die, it would be said, of a broken heart after the disastrous failure of Sir George's assault on the fortress of Sebastopol. Sir George, wounded, ill and broken in spirit, would be recalled in disgrace with the exposure of the generals' appalling mismanagement of the campaign. And the architect of that exposure and his downfall would be another *Times* correspondent—William Howard Russell. Irony indeed.

And it was not as if Sir George Brown fared any better than the man he was supposed to replace. Within five weeks he was back at his desk in the War Office and his only recorded contribution to the affair was to split his force into even smaller detachments spread over even greater distances, to press for the creation of county police forces—as Colonel Love had been doing from the moment he arrived in Carmarthen—and to review a splendid parade and field day of the 4th Light Dragoons in the field known as Parcyvelvet, behind Lammas Street in Carmarthen. There, on a beautiful autumn morning, Major Parlby took his gorgeously dressed troop of dragoons 'through their field exercises and other evolutions much to the satisfaction of the gallant general, who evinced his satisfaction by the expression of his warm approbation.'[4] Up and down and around the field they trotted and galloped, harness flashing and jingling, sabres cutting the air, bugles blowing, and all to the great delight of Colonel Trevor, Colonel Love, many other officers, and a huge crowd of spectators. Not even their attachment to the cause of Rebecca could entirely overcome the pride and thrill of the people in the splendour of their country's cavalry.

But Colonel Love did not seem even to have noticed his supersession by Major General Brown, and the Home Secretary's wish that it should be carried out 'without causing him needless offence or pain' seemed to have been achieved entirely. The gallant Colonel's flow of reports to the Home Office continued unabated. He wanted, for example, to see the London police

[4] *Carmarthen Journal*, 27 October, 1843.

A splendid Parade and Field Day for the 4th Light Dragoons
(Nat. Army Museum)

armed, '. . . particularly as they are about to be employed in the most violent and disturbed part of the country and where the people when they assemble at their nightly meetings are armed with guns, pistols and other weapons; indeed from the hostile feelings against the police I do not think their lives would be safe if they were amongst these lawless people unarmed.'[5] The reply to that was brusque indeed. 'Sir James Graham,' wrote his secretary, 'cannot sanction the use of firearms by the Metropolitan

[5] Letter dated 17 September, 1843, Colonel Love to Home Office: Public Record Office, File HO 45/453.

Police, to which they have not been trained and to which in London they never have recourse.' If nothing else, an interesting comment on the continuing determination of Prime Minister Sir Robert Peel that his brainchild, the Metropolitan Police, should not in even those troubled times be armed except in extreme circumstances. An interesting comment, too, on how things have changed since.

Nor did Colonel Love cease to point out that which he had pointed out when he had first come to Carmarthen, four months before:

> The great cause why the outrages have arisen to such an alarming height may be attributed to the total absence of any Civil Force whatever in the three counties most disturbed, and it is only by creating such a force *backed* by the military that we can hope to put them down. Heretofore the military have been called upon to take the initiative instead of *supporting* the Civil Power, from the obvious reason before stated of there being no civil force to support.[6]

But if the army's role in tackling the Rebecca Riots was of a holding and sometimes preventive nature, and if its attempts to take the initiative continued to fail, there were other influences at work which in due time would prove the truth of Edmund Burke's words on the use of force, and would 'remove the necessity of subduing again.' And that redoubtable investigator Thomas Campbell Foster of *The Times* was, as usual, one of the first to sense it.

A salutory effect

Thomas Campbell Foster, writing from Carmarthen, had not only sensed the widespread lack of sympathy for Sarah Williams of Hendy and the feeling of anger towards the authorities over the affair at Pontardulais, but he had also sensed something else. He had detected a feeling among many of the farmers that things had now gone too far and that Rebecca the Liberator, the campaigner against corruption and oppression, had herself become corrupted by the power that they had so willingly given her:

> It is the opinion of many intelligent gentlemen with whom I have conversed that the shocking murder of the poor old woman at

[6] Letter dated 30 September, 1843, Colonel Love to Home Office: Public Record Office, File HO 45/453. (Author's italics).

Hendy Bridge has produced a salutory effect on the better disposed part of the population and that the farmers who would willingly run the risk of imprisonment for breaking a toll gate shrink with horror from being classed as murderers and giving possible employment to the hangman.

On the other hand, in the neighbourhood of the Pontardulais fight, a deep and brooding spirit of vengeance exists. A very great number of persons engaged in that fight were wounded and escaped. Several farmers in the neighbourhood are dangerously ill of wounds received by them in that encounter. Amongst the friends and acquaintances of these parties the most bitter and rancorous spirit of revenge prevails.

It is said, too, that the better class of farmers are beginning to sicken of Rebecca's proceedings, and with some reason. I am informed that a kind of blackmail is levied upon them. The parties who break gates, etc., are generally paid labourers, led by some few farmers and the Rebecca of the District. They are paid two shillings and sixpence [12½p] a night, out of which they provide their powder and shot. The money is raised by sending round notices to farmers to pay certain sums at certain times and to bring them to meetings of the Rebeccaites. If they refuse, they do it at the peril of having their stacks fired. The Rebecca for the night pays the men from the fund.

This sort of tax on the farmers has caused a great deal of secret information to be given by them to the authorities, and it was from information derived in this way that the police came upon the party attacking Pontardulais Gate.[7]

Shoni 'Sgubor Fawr and Dai'r Cantwr and their comrades of the Stag and Pheasant had brought the proud Lady Rebecca to a pretty pass indeed, for the killer of Sarah Williams was one of them—John the Shoemaker of Horeb. It may well be, as Shoni said, that he had shot her accidentally, but that would not have saved him from being transported for life for manslaughter. And several farmers who had had the temerity to defy Rebecca's call to arms—farmers like Evan Davies of Tyrynys, Llanddarog—had good cause to desire Rebecca's downfall as they surveyed the rubble of their farmhouses pulled down by her hand.

But their time was nigh.

[7] *The Times,* 25 September, 1843.

No Englishman shall manage in Wales

The Gwendraeth Ironworks at Pontyberem and the company's quarries and coalmines gave employment to some two hundred men of the Gwendraeth Valley. More than £100,000 had been invested in their development over the previous four years and the owner, an Englishman named Newman, was more popular with his workmen than were most of his kind among theirs. Which was more than could be said of Slocombe, his over-bearing manager. Not only was he intensely disliked for himself, but he made things worse by incurring the wrath of Rebecca through the diligence with which he had been helping the London police in their so far unsuccessful investigations into a series of robberies committed near Cross Hands. Old John Evans, who lived at Gelliglyd, a cottage on the Cross Hands to Pontardulais road, had had several visits from Shoni, Dai and the Stag and Pheasant gang in which they had stolen his gun and all his money and valuables while threatening to kill him and firing off their shotguns. Slocombe, who tried so hard to help identify his attackers, lived in a house in the Gwendraeth Ironworks, and no one could have doubted that it was only a matter of time before he, too, would receive a visit. Certainly his boss Mr. Newman was very apprehensive; so apprehensive that on Saturday 23 September he wrote to Llanelli magistrate Richard Janion Nevill begging him to get the dragoons to visit his works in the course of their routine patrol, as 'he had great reason' to expect an attack that very night. His request was passed to Captain Lane of the 4th Light Dragoons, who in turn wrote a note timed at 2 a.m. to William Chambers Junior, telling him that 'Newman's application seems founded on somewhat uncertain information and I could not possibly be there before daylight, so I think it is totally absured to attempt the assistance asked for.'

That response to Newman's plea for protection was to prove most unfortunate. At the very time the magistrate was considering Newman's request, David Lewis, a Trimsaran collier, awoke to the sound of a voice calling him to get out of bed. It was Shoni 'Sgubor Fawr, dressed in a gown and bonnet and carrying a single-barrelled shotgun. He had with him a large party of men in female disguise 'who appeared to fill the road', and when Lewis joined them ('out of fear' he was to say later) Shoni led them up towards Five Roads, on the way meeting another party led by Dai'r Cantwr.

At the Stag and Pheasant the Rebeccaites fortified themselves with draughts of William Walters' beer, while Dai'r Cantwr, who had at first been against the idea of visiting Slocombe but was now ready for action, dressed himself in a shawl and bonnet. And off they all marched to Pontyberem and the Gwendraeth Ironworks.

Their arrival at the works was signalled by the flashes and rattle of gunfire and loud shouting and cheering as Shoni began banging on the door and Dai brought on the rest of them to surround the house, where Slocombe's presence was loudly called for. He did not appear, but his wife did. 'Who are you and what do you want with my husband?' she shouted into the darkness from the bedroom window. 'I am Rebecca,' came the reply from Shoni 'Sgubor Fawr, 'and we demand to see him instantly.' Mrs. Slocombe said her husband was not at home and she insisted that was so, in the face of a good deal of abuse, refusing every demand to admit them to the house. Shoni spoke again. 'Mr. Newman has behaved well and we will not hurt him, but if Mr. Slocombe is not out of the country within a week we will make him a head shorter, for no Englishman shall manage in Wales any more.' Mrs. Slocombe had no chance to comment on that threat, for with a blast of shot in her direction the Rebeccaites disappeared into the darkness.

As collier David Lewis laid his weary body on his bed of straw at five or six in the morning in his Trimsaran cottage, he made up his mind. Life was hard enough for a collier without being dragged from his bed in the dead of night to do the bidding of a tyrant like Shoni 'Sgubor Fawr and to be a party to shooting at women, which had been the experience of so many others who went to Slocombe's house that night. He would put an end to it. And three days later he did—by going to the police, who took him to magistrate Richard Nevill in Llanelli to swear his information on oath.

A fragile brotherhood

It was no news to the authorities that Shoni 'Sgubor Fawr and Dai'r Cantwr were the men principally responsible for the reign of terror that gripped that corner of south east Carmarthenshire, but here for the first time was an eye witness prepared to give evidence against them. It was the breakthrough they had long been waiting for. And things could only get better, for it is axiomatic that when violent criminals are put behind bars those who stand to share their fate will immediately begin to look to their own necks. And so it was that when Shoni and Dai were taken it was every man for himself.

Richard Nevill signed two warrants for the arrest of John Jones, alias Shoni 'Sgubor Fawr, and David Davies, alias Dai'r Cantwr, for riot and assault committed at the Gwendraeth works. The warrants were handed to William Francis of the magistrates' clerk's office, whose orders were to co-ordinate the efforts to locate and arrest them, to persuade them to confess and implicate their confederates and then to turn those confederates against them and against each other. He sent some of William Chambers' employees to spy out the land and, without arousing any suspicion in the district, discover the whereabouts of the two men. Inspector Tierney and eighteen of his men spread out through the Gwendraeth Valley during the hours of darkness, with prearranged rendezvous so as to be well placed to act whenever they received the word.

Jonah Davies, one of Chambers' gamekeepers, traced Dai to the Plough and Harrow, just down the road from his Stag and Pheasant headquarters and there he was found, sitting having a pint by the corner of the fire in the back room. He was taken by Francis and two or three policemen without a struggle and conveyed by landlord Thomas Lewis's horse and cart to Llanelli workhouse, there to be interrogated before being taken to the county goal at Carmarthen.

They found Shoni in a pub in Tumble the next day and he, too, was taken off to Carmarthen Gaol and thoroughly questioned. *Both of them named every name they could remember, while at the same time smuggling out messages claiming that their lips were sealed!*

Outside, throughout the district over which they had held such sway, rumours of betrayal were rife and men tumbled over each other to turn Queen's evidence before Shoni and Dai or anyone else should name them first. And as if it had been especially designed and timed to help this process, Queen Victoria's proclamation was issued on 2 October, 'cried' through every

The following Proclamation was agreed to at the Privy Council held by Her Majesty, on Monday, October 2nd, 1843, at Windsor Castle:—

BY THE QUEEN.

A PROCLAMATION.

VICTORIA R.

WHEREAS in certain districts of South Wales, more especially in the Counties of Pembroke, Cardigan, and Carmarthen, tumultuous assemblages of people, disguised, and armed with guns, and other offensive weapons, have taken place by night, and outrages of the most violent description have been committed upon the lives and properties of divers of our subjects; and whereas in contempt of the restraints of law and order, these tumultuous assemblages have pulled down toll-gates, and have violently entered and destroyed toll-houses; and whereas they have also attacked the mansions of individuals, extorting from them sums of money by threats or by violence, and have destroyed by fire the hay, corn, and other property of divers of our subjects; We, therefore, have thought fit, by and with the advice of our Privy Council, to issue this our Royal Proclamation, hereby strictly commanding all Justices of the Peace, Sheriffs, Under Sheriffs, and all other Civil Officers whatsoever, that they do use their utmost endeavours to repress all tumults, riots, outrages, and breaches of the peace; and to discover, apprehend, and bring to justice the persons concerned in the riotous and wicked proceedings aforesaid; and we do strictly enjoin all our Liege Subjects to give prompt and effectual assistance to our Justices of the Peace, Sheriffs, Under Sheriffs, and all Civil Officers, in their endeavours to preserve the public peace; and as a further inducement to discover offenders, we do hereby promise and declare, *that any person or persons who shall discover and apprehend, or cause to be discovered and apprehended, the authors, abettors, and perpetrators of any such incendiary fires as aforesaid, or of any such outrage upon the person of any of our subjects, by which life shall have been sacrificed*, so that they or any of them shall be duly convicted thereof, shall be entitled to the Sum of

FIVE HUNDRED POUNDS

for each and every person who shall be so convicted; and shall receive *our most gracious pardon* for the said offence, in case the person making such discovery as aforesaid shall be liable to be prosecuted for the same, except he be the actual perpetrator of such outrage, or of such incendiary fire, as aforesaid.

And we do also promise and declare, that any person or persons who shall discover and apprehend, or cause to be discovered and apprehended, the authors, abettors, and perpetrators of any such outrages, *other than those last above-mentioned*, in the said Counties, so that they or any of them may be duly convicted thereof, shall be entitled to the sum of

FIFTY POUNDS

for each and every person who shall be so convicted, and shall receive our most gracious pardon for the said offence, in case the person making such discovery as aforesaid shall be liable to be prosecuted for the same.

Given at our Court at Windsor, this 2nd day of October, in the year of our Lord 1843, and in the seventh year of our reign.

"GOD SAVE THE QUEEN."

ISAAC THOMAS, PRINTER, ST. MARY-STREET, CARDIGAN.

(Nat. Library of Wales)

town and village and posted on every public building in the Principality:

BY THE QUEEN. PROCLAMATION VICTORIA R.

> Whereas in certain districts of South Wales, more especially in the Counties of Pembroke, Cardigan and Carmarthen, tumultuous assemblages of people, disguised and armed with guns and other offensive weapons, have taken place by night, and outrages of the most violent description have been committed upon the lives and properties of divers of our subjects; and whereas in contempt of the restraints of law and order these tumultuous assemblages have pulled down toll gates and have violently entered and destroyed toll houses; and whereas they have also attacked the mansions of individuals, extorting from them sums of money by threats or by violence, and have destroyed by fire the hay, corn and other property of divers of our subjects; we therefore have thought fit, by, and with the advice of, our Privy Council, to issue this our Royal Proclamation.

The proclamation went on to command all civil officers 'to use their utmost endeavours to repress all tumults, riots, outrages and Breaches of the Peace' and to arrest the perpetrators, at the same time appealing to all her subjects to assist them. But more to the point, the proclamation offered rewards of from £50 to £500 for information leading to the arrest and conviction of fire-raisers, gate-breakers and other participants in the disturbances. And even more to the point was the offer of the Queen's Pardon for all informers who had been actively engaged themselves, provided that they had not been responsible for taking life or setting fires with their own hands. It was to be a powerful and effective weapon in the hands of the authorities *and some of the first to seize the lifeline—and the cash—were Shoni and Dai's erstwhile comrades-in-arms!*

Over the following weeks there was a veritable avalanche of information and of claimants for the rewards, as the Stag and Pheasant brotherhood, sworn in blood at Gelligylwnog, collapsed like a house of cards.

Indeed virtually every member of the Stag and Pheasant gang, even the pub's landlord William Walters, turned informer for money and the safety of his own skin. A stark contrast indeed to the dignified behaviour of John Hughes of Tŷ Isha. He and his two companions John Hugh and David Jones faced their fates alone and never once betrayed anyone.

In all the confessions—whether made inside or outside Carmarthen Gaol—reference to the fight at Pontardulais and the killing at Hendy was studiously avoided, except for Shoni's claim that one of the Stag and Pheasant fraternity, John the Shoemaker (Jac y Crydd) of Horeb, had shot the old woman accidentally. This is hardly surprising, for the penalties for murder and manslaughter and shooting at the police were very well known. But a close study of the inter-relationship between the various Rebeccaite groups in that area and of the patterns of activity during August and September leaves scant room for doubting the presence of members of the Stag and Pheasant gang at both. It was no coincidence, for example, that on only two occasions—the march through Llanon culminating in the attack on Gelliwernen, and the *débâcle* at Pontardulais—were the participants numbered in hundreds. Thereafter, with the loss of its real leaders by capture and wounds, not to mention the wholely demoralising effect of such a violent clash of arms, the attackers never numbered more than a dozen or twenty—precisely the strength of the Stag and Pheasant contingent of that once large army.

It was no coincidence either that though the temperature would remain high in the area for some time yet, the arrests of Shoni 'Sgubor Fawr and Dai'r Cantwr put an end for good to Rebeccaite violence in south east Carmarthenshire.

Chapter Fifteen

THROUGH THE NET

No one was to know yet that the arrests of Shoni 'Sgubor Fawr and Dai'r Cantwr and the breaking up of the Stag and Pheasant gang would deal the virtual death blow to Rebeccaism in south east Carmarthenshire. Nor could anyone have yet interpreted the pattern by which the riots were spreading from the west towards the north east and leaving only sporadic and relatively minor violence behind them. Not even the military commander —whoever *he* might have been in October, 1843—could have known how much the comparatively peaceful state of the south west of the Principality owed to the presence of his scattered garrisons or how much to the successes of the civil power at Pontardulais and in the Gwendraeth Valley. Or when or where real violence might erupt again.

For one thing there was no shortage of Rebecca letters conveying dire warnings to gate keepers, vicars, magistrates, erring landlords, bailiffs and the fathers of bastard children and, though it was impossible to tell the genuine from the hoax or the mere frightener, they maintained a reign of terror all of their own. Many letters were genuine and the threats they contained were very real, and many of them were now directed at the plight of poverty-stricken tenant farmers dispossessed of their farms, their homes and their belongings through their inability to pay ever-increasing rents and other mounting debts. The bailiff, always the *bête noire* of the poor, became an even more hated symbol of oppression and therefore a target for a special brand of Rebecca's physical violence. On Tuesday 10 October, for instance, two of Carmarthen's most notorious bailiffs fell into Rebecca's hands at a farm just outside the town as they arrived to seize farmer William Phillips' furniture and belongings in payment for his half year rent of £7.10s. (£7.50p).

Bailiffs John Evans and John Lewis had a dreaded reputation in Carmarthen for drunken violence as well as for being particularly oppressive executors of Sheriff's warrants. It was a repu-

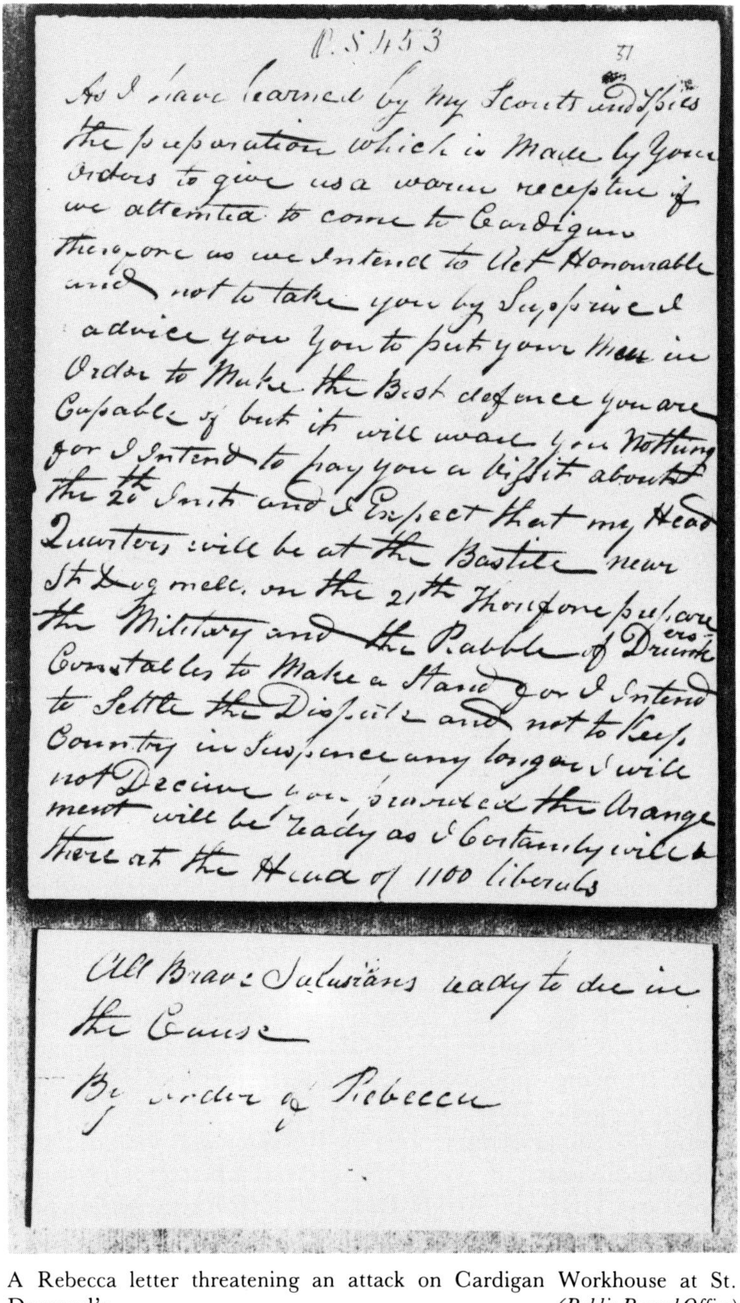
P.5453 31

As I have learned by my Scouts and Spies the preparation which is Made by Your Orders to give us a warm receptive if we attemted to come to Cardigan therefore as we Intend to Act Honourable and not to take you by Surprise I advice you You to put your Men in Order to Make the Best defence you are Capable of but its will avail you Nothing for I Intend to pay you a Visit about the 20th Inst and I Expect that my Head Quarters will be at the Bastile near St Dogmells on the 21th Therefore prepare the Military and the Rabble of Drunkers Constables to Make a Stand for I Intend to Settle the Dispute and not to Keep Country in Suspence any longer I will not Deceive you I warned the Arangement will be ready as I Cortanly will be there at the Head of 1100 liberals

All Brave Saluvians ready to die in the Cause

By order of Rebecca

A Rebecca letter threatening an attack on Cardigan Workhouse at St. Dogmael's *(Public Record Office)*

Cardigan Workhouse *(Pat Molloy)*

tation that went back even beyond their dismissal from the Carmarthen Borough Police Force. John Evans (known as 'Evans the Ball Court') had been one of the leading lights on the 'Blue' (or Whig) side in Carmarthen's Reform election battles of 1831, which had reduced the town to a state of anarchy relieved only by the bayonets of the Argyle and Sutherland Highlanders and the exertions of half a dozen London policemen. As one of the most violent of the rioters, he had served five months solitary confinement in Carmarthen Gaol awaiting trial, and on the coming to power of the 'Blue' party in the Carmarthen Borough Corporation in 1836, Evans the Ball Court was rewarded for his party loyalty by being appointed a constable in the town's five-man 'reformed' police force! After a year's service punctuated by several disciplinary convictions for drunkenness, violence and general indiscipline, he was finally sacked for being found drunk on his beat. His fellow bailiff, Lewis, alias 'John my Maid', had also spent a riotous year with the town's police force, and was thrown out (in 1834) after joining in a traditional Carmarthen

The stone-breaking cells at Cardigan Workhouse in which individual paupers were locked with their daily quota of stones. The broken rocks were passed through the grading grill (fixed horizontally under the protruding block at the side of the door) to fall down the chute to the ground outside *(Pat Molloy)*

election riot—on the wrong side—and using his truncheon on his fellow officers![1]

It was only to be expected that two such bailiffs as Ball Court and John my Maid should attract a more than usual share of Rebecca's wrath, and when they arrived at Tirypound farm, Llangunnor, they found twenty five black-faced, gowned and bonnetted avengers waiting for them. They were thrashed

[1] Their stories are told in *A Shilling for Carmarthen: The Town They Nearly Tamed,* (Gomer Press, 1980).

mercilessly with sticks and horsewhips and Evans was forced to his knees and made to burn the offending distress warrants, take a Bible in his hand and repeat an oath: 'As the Lord liveth and my soul liveth I will never come here to make any distress again.' The bailiffs were then freed and allowed to limp back to town . . . where they went straight to magistrate Daniel Prytherch and swore out a warrant for the man they identified as Rebecca—William Phillips, father of the defaulting tenant of Tirypound. And they would have the last laugh, for father and son Phillips were to go to prison for a year for assaulting them.

Meanwhile, all and sundry were taking on Rebecca's mantle to settle the most mundane disputes by threatening letters, as, for example, did Bridget Williams, a poor old woman of Cenarth, on the River Teifi between Newcastle Emlyn and Cardigan. Seeking to resolve some simple dispute between herself and her neighbour Benjamin Evans, and not being able to read or write herself, she got someone to write a 'Rebecca' letter for her . . . and went to prison for three months for her pains. And she was far from being the only one, for in some cases both the author *and* the writer finished up in the county gaol. In such a confused situation it was not always possible to distinguish the genuine from the hoax, so the victim usually took the safe course and either complied or, as in the case of Joseph Jones of Ffoshelig farm just north of Carmarthen, pleaded for Rebecca's indulgence.

Joseph Jones had been ordered by letter to quit his farm before 30 October or see everything destroyed about him, and he went to the length of printing and publicly displaying a petition addressed to Rebecca '. . . in which he earnestly begged of her not to molest him and stating at the same time that as he had failed to get a farm he begged of Rebecca to inform him whether she would allow him to remain unmolested in his farm until Michaelmas, 1844.' Within three days Rebecca sent her reply:

> Good day to you old friend. It is with the greatest humility and sincerity that I write you these few lines, hoping that they will find you in good health, as they leave me at present through the kindness of Providence.
>
> You received a small note from us and since you have acted in so humble and sensible a manner we cannot fulfil our intentions, entirely because of your humility. Humility is a precious crown and

> it is worth seeking for. Humility can save you from a thousand troubles. Blessed is he who keeps it. Your house is as safe as if it were dressed with humility and bound with brass. Becca cannot injure any humble man. Believe what we say. You can be quite at ease concerning what I wrote to you. Your house will be as safe as the fox's in the rock. You may rely on what we say and entirely in consequence of your humility, *and not for the sake of that old devil Thomas Pantycerrig.* [2]
>
> We cannot injure a man who is so easily handled. May respect and prosperity attend you through life. Joseph, believe us and do not be troubled concerning us. Wisdom will do a great deal and although we are a great number joined together for such purposes you may be at ease until Michaelmas, 1844. Make this known to your neighbours. Now we leave you Joseph. Farewell greatest of friends. I am your kind friend, Becca and her children. [3]

Joseph Jones accordingly remained unmolested at Ffoshelig and, whether by Rebecca's leave or not, there are Joneses there to this day!

At about the same time as Rebecca rewarded Jones Ffoshelig for his humility, she demonstrated yet again her compassion for the poor and her readiness to protect them from their oppressors. And she did it in fine style, at St. Clears, on the night of Thursday 12 October, when she and two or three hundred of her daughters, disguised, armed with guns and making a tremendous clamour with their trumpets and cow horns, surrounded the hovel which housed James Thomas and his family and called them out. Thomas was a pauper and he and his family had been 'on the parish' since he had lost his arm in a farm accident, and this totally unexpected visit from Rebecca filled all of them with terror.

'Be not alarmed,' said Rebecca to Mrs. Thomas as she answered the door. 'We have come as friends and as we think you have long enough suffered from poverty we have provided a better dwelling for you and have come to convey you to it.' Without more ado, and brushing aside all their pleas to leave them in peace, the Rebeccaites loaded the whole Thomas family and all their possessions on to a cart and wheeled them noisily up the Haverfordwest road to the now empty and gateless toll house at Pwll Trap. There they installed them and, bidding them

[2] An ominous reference to the burning of the house and outbuildings at Pantycerrig farm, Brechfa (see p. 163).

[3] *Carmarthen Journal,* 24 November, 1843. (Author's italics).

farewell, marched off with a blare of horns and fusillades of shots to pay a visit to magistrate R. P. Beynon, whose windows they smashed with stones and gunshot. Next morning the magistrate found a note pinned to his front door:

> I beg that Rebecca Gav Posesion to James Thomas of the House that was formerly Belong to Pwlltrap Gate, and if any Person will com and Throw him out, Rebecca will and her Children will remember him in future time. The First that will come there shall be drag between four horses—Rebecca and her Children.[4]

And the Thomas family remained undisturbed in Pwll Trap toll house for many a long day!

On the march

Such a profusion of threatening letters, coupled with continuing though sporadic, far-flung and relatively minor acts of violence, and frequent and widespread meetings, both open and secret, of farmers and Rebeccaites, called for a constant state of vigilance and readiness on the part of the troops, the London policemen and the magistrates, of whom another twenty were sworn in in Carmarthenshire alone in the first week of October.

On Thursday 12 October, Major General Brown's orders began to take effect. Fifty officers of A Division of the Metropolitan Police, under the command of Inspector Martin, and men of the 76th Regiment of Foot marched into Carmarthen, to be deployed in combination throughout that county and Cardiganshire. Lieutenant Lacey, a sergeant and twelve rank and file marched out to Llandysul, Ensign Grant, a sergeant and fifteen men went to Tregaron, Captain Scott, two sergeants and thirty men to Lampeter, and detachments of varying ranks and numbers, each with a couple of police officers, went off to Newcastle Emlyn, Aberystwyth, Llangyndeyrn, Pontargothi, Porthyrhyd, Cynwyl Elfed, Brechfa, Llansawel, Llanfihangel-ar-arth, Llandyfaelog and Kidwelly, while elsewhere in the three counties other units asembled and marched to other towns and villages. Seven officers and a hundred and fifty five men of the Royal Marines garrisoned Pembroke, while two officers and fifty marines went to Haverfordwest, two officers and forty two to Cardigan, two officers and forty to Narberth, and others to

[4] H. Tobit Evans, op. cit.

Fishguard, Newport, Eglwyswrw, Llandisilio, Llawhaden and Robeston Wathen. And the twelve officers and one hundred and sixty troopers of the 4th Light Dragoons were divided for the protection of Carmarthen, Newcastle Emlyn, Llandeilo and Llandovery, while the men of Colonel Love's own regiment, the 73rd of Foot (the Black Watch) provided a strong presence in Carmarthen, Aberaeron, Newcastle Emlyn and Lampeter.

Not only was hardly a village missed in General Brown's network of garrisons, but even tiny hamlets were given their own small detachments of troops so as to afford close support to each other in the event of any of them coming to action. But the action began to move away towards mid Wales that October, as the destruction of gates at Llanwrda, Llanegwad and Llandovery in the north east of Carmarthenshire paved the way for Rebecca's sudden appearance far to the north in Radnorshire and Montgomeryshire. It was, though, a pattern which would be seen only with hindsight and the authorities meanwhile grappled with a bewildering sequence of violent happenings.

At Cwmdŵr near Llanwrda, Rebecca was represented by her 'sister' Charlotte for the first time since the attack in May on the Water Street gate in Carmarthen, and for the only other time in the history of the disturbances. And a violent affair it was as, fresh from their destruction of the Cwmdŵr gate, the Rebeccaites went for the local Vicar:

> The firing of a volley of guns disturbed Mr. Jones and his family from their peaceful slumbers, which was followed by incessant striking at the doors and a demand for Mr. Jones' appearance to speak to Miss Charlotte, as she had a particular message to convey to him from her sister Becca. When Mr. Jones came forward she gave him the alternative of removing his furniture out of the Vicarage within ten minutes, that the house might be set on fire, or that he should pledge his word that he would not take into his possession a few fields which he had purchased and which adjoin the Vicarage, as it was contrary to Becca's law that he as a clergyman should hold land.
>
> Backed as Rebecca's Vice Regent was by some hundreds of well-armed attendants ready to perform her commands, Mr. Jones was compelled as a matter of personal safety, not wishing to have his house burned over the heads of himself his wife and family, to comply with Becca's demands and to engage that the tenant who

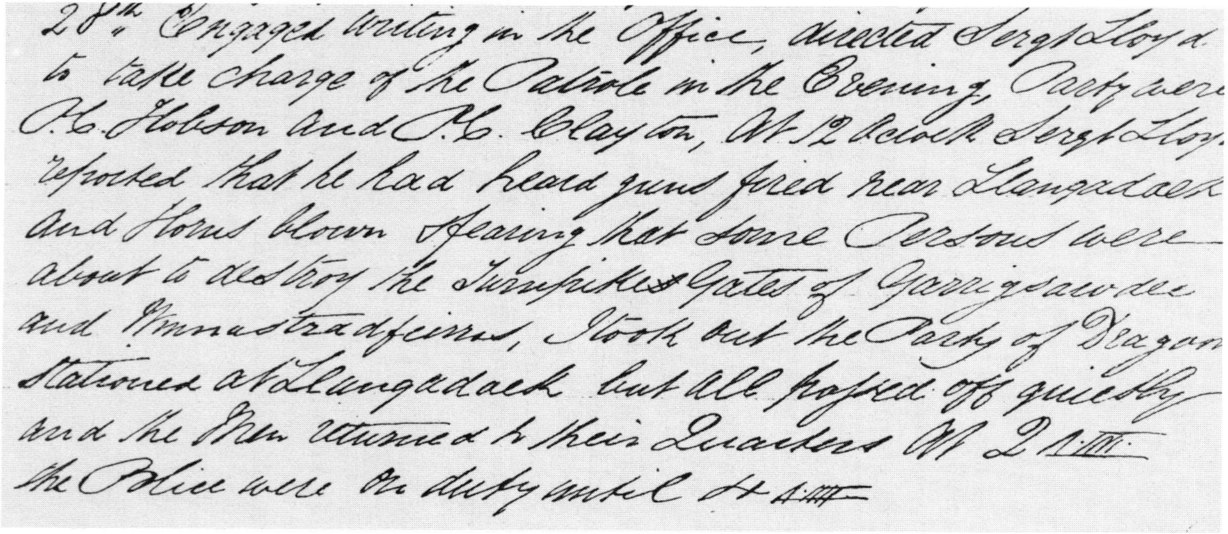
28th Engaged writing in the Office, directed Sergt Lloyd
to take charge of the Patrole in the Evening, Party were
P.C. Hobson and P.C. Clayton, At 12 oclock Sergt Lloyd
reported that he had heard guns fired near Llangadock
and Horns blown Hearing that some Persons were
about to destroy the Turnpike Gates of Gwynysawdee
and Ynnastradfeiris, I took out the Party of Dragoons
stationed at Llangadock but all passed off quietly
and the Men returned to their Quarters At 2 A.M.
the Police were on duty until 4 A.M.

A false alarm: Police Supt. Bidwell's entry in the Llangadog Station Diary recording the turning out of the Dragoons on 28th Oct. 1843
(Dyfed-Powys Police Museum)

had occupied the fields should be allowed to retain possession at a reduced rent, the amount of which was then stipulated.

The Rev. Mr. Jones of Llansadwrn after his visitation by Rebecca's party wisely determined to quit the Vicarage and to retire with his family to Llandovery.[5]

And four nights later, nine miles away, up beyond Llandovery on the Builth road, it was the turn of Dolauhirion gate to be destroyed yet again, by the same band of Rebeccaites. Two of them were recognised and arrested later, but in the meantime this particular band of Rebeccaites also settled a few scores among local landowners who were pressing on their tenants through high rents or foreclosure. They threatened the owner of Caecrin Mill 'in the most awful manner with Becca's extreme vengeance unless he relinquished some law proceedings against a late tenant' and they burned the entire house and outbuildings of Nantyrwhale farm near Cilycwm so that a new tenant could not take possession. And while Thomas Morgan and Thomas Lewis were being committed for trial for destroying Dolauhirion gate and terrorising the Vicar of Llansadwrn, Rebecca and her daughters made a surprise ascent into the mountains high above Llandovery and the steep valley leading to the source of the Towy. There they invaded Lord Cawdor's Rhandirmwyn lead mines and terrorised his imported Cornish miners, whom the Carmarthenshire men saw as job-stealing interlopers. There were, it seems, no bounds to Rebecca's search for justice, rough though that justice might often be.

Further north, just over the Carmarthenshire-Breconshire border on the road to Builth, the gate at Cefn Llanddewi was destroyed and a guard of two parish constables from Brecon was brought in to protect it after its immediate re-erection. But they were not sharp enough to beat Rebecca for they:

> . . . found their avocation rather dry and insipid and accordingly on Monday night [9 October] retired to a house a short distance off to have a drop of something wet and comfortable. The ever-watchful Becca then immediately seized the opportunity of their temporary absence to set fire to the house, and the whole building was consumed before the policemen or any others could render any assistance towards extinguishing the flames.[6]

[5] *Carmarthen Journal,* 6 October, 1843.
[6] *Carmarthen Journal,* 13 October, 1843.

A Brecknockshire toll gate *(Nat. Library of Wales)*

The gate at Llangurig, twenty three miles north east of Aberystwyth on the London mail coach road, was the next to go, followed by the three gates at nearby Rhayader two nights later, in an attack 'attended by all the paraphernalia of Rebeccaism, her ladyship being dressed in full costume, attended with upwards of two hundred well-mounted followers, with a due proportion of blowing of horns and firing of guns.'[7] And even at the very moment that Llangurig gate was being chopped to pieces:

> . . . a number of persons made an attack upon the Corton turnpike house and gate near Presteigne [thirty eight miles south east of Llangurig], battering the windows, doors and gates with stones, to the great terror of the keeper, a large athletic man, who took refuge under his bed and only recovered from his fright through his assailants having been alarmed by the approach of a carriage and departing.
>
> The miscreants then proceeded to the gate close to the town and having commenced their attack there, the keeper, a female, gallantly sallied forth mop stick in hand, knocked down one of the party and secured him, whereupon the rest made a hasty and cowardly retreat. We are happy to say that five of them were recognised by the

[7] *Carmarthen Journal,* 13 October, 1843.

Rhayader, a town surrounded by six toll gates *(Rhayader Museum)*

heroine and have been committed to Presteigne gaol. They proved to be, as no doubt the rest were, inhabitants of Presteigne.[8]

But the incident that brought Major General Brown himself hurrying from Carmarthen to mid Wales was the spectacular military-style entry of about two hundred Rebeccaites into Rhayader, where the three gates had been destroyed and re-erected only three weeks earlier.

It was about two in the morning of Friday 3 November when John Francis, the keeper of Rhayader's north gate, about a quarter of a mile out on the Llanidloes road, was awakened by a gentle tap on his window and a soft voice that made his hair stand on end. 'Lie still, or death will be your doom,' said the voice. It was an injunction the gate keeper and his wife were only too happy to obey, as axes crashed into the spars of their gate to cries of 'Work away little wenches!' and the crash of gunfire. And then a silence, broken only by that soft voice again, warning John Francis not to take toll again if he wished his house to remain in one piece.

Alerted by the sounds of gunfire, Sergeant Shew of the Metro-

[8] *Carmarthen Journal,* 13 October, 1843.

politan Police and his six special constables—the sole representatives of law and order in the town—came running along the road from town, to find only a heap of broken timbers where the gate had been, but no sign of the gate-breakers, who had evidently taken to the fields. No sooner had the sergeant persuaded John Francis and his family to answer the door than there was a sudden eruption of gunfire from the other side of town, and off ran the sergeant and his six breathless special constables to save the town's east gate on the Penybont road. Once again the cry of 'Work away my little wenches!' sent axes and sledgehammers crashing into the gate and cross-saws rasping away at their stout oaken posts. And old Sarah Rees and her daughter took due note of Rebecca's parting caution that '. . . if a gate should again be put up in this place we will take the house down level with the turnpike road!' They piled more furniture against the door of their toll house as a fusillade of shots underlined the message.

Gasping for breath came the sergeant and his special constables, who paused only to glance at the wreckage and then ran on to try and intercept the Rebeccaites on their way to the third gate, on the Wye Bridge. They caught up with them by the Bear public house in North Street and an astonishing sight it was.

The east gate at Rhayader, later in the century
(Mr. Jack Cadwallader, Rhayader)

The Wye Bridge at Rhayader, with the toll house on the far side
(Dyfed Archive Services, Carmarthen)

Two hundred men, their faces blackened, wearing petticoats, shawls, bonnets and straw hats, marching in step 'with a slow and measured pace' in the standard four-abreast military formation, the front and rear files with shouldered muskets and those in the centre carrying swords, hatchets, sledgehammers, saws and more guns. Words of command rang out and were instantly obeyed as the silent column struck down with the butts of their muskets those special constables who ventured near.

Desperately, Sergeant Shew placed his unarmed men across North Street to oppose the two hundred marchers, and shouted to them: 'My men, I hope you will not fire.' But without a word they wheeled around the Lion and Castle and to the roar of nearly a hundred blank cartridges which they fired towards the police officers, disappeared into the darkness on the Aberystwyth road.

The police pursuit understandably faltered here and though the sergeant afterwards claimed that 'through not being close enough to them and owing to the darkness of the night he lost sight of them', they at least let go an opportunity to catch them up as they halted for a while at Jones Harvey's mill. Harvey's offence to Rebecca had been to supply a new gate to replace one smashed by her daughters, so she took the opportunity to fire a few shots in his direction and tell him that they would 'pull his castle down to the ground' if he should do it again. And if further evidence were needed that the police pursuit had run out of steam it was provided by the length of time spent by the Rebeccaites in pulling down the stone-built Wye Bridge toll house. The gate keeper and his family had fled, but their furniture was buried beneath the large heap of stones which had lately been their home. And after holding Rhayader with virtually no challenge for about two and a half hours, the disciplined column marched with perfect military bearing into the early morning fog which had now begun to wrap itself around the deserted streets of a thoroughly frightened town.

Too late, again

The dragoons arrived late again, which was hardly surprising in view of the fact that Captain Arkwright and his troopers had to cover nearly forty miles from Carmarthenshire. It was more than twenty four hours before they presented themselves in the town, to be followed a further twenty four hours later by a detachment of men of the 7th Regiment of Fusiliers. By the time Major General Brown arrived in a fast carriage from Carmarthen, more London policemen had been brought from other parts of mid Wales to patrol the streets of Rhayader. But the authorities had nothing to show from that night of Rebeccaite bravado but two arrests and a desultory examination of the prisoners by the magistrates, the result of which was that they were released without any charge being brought against them.

Rebecca's sudden appearance in Radnorshire and Montgomeryshire, so far beyond the Carmarthenshire border, had shaken General Brown and sent him scurrying northwards to see for himself what could be done. He had thought his net of troops and police had been thrown wide enough to contain all his troubles, but here he was, taken by surprise and encountering precisely the problem which had so dogged Colonel Love and brought about his replacement. Irony indeed that within only five weeks of his arrival in Wales to infuse new energy and ideas into the army's campaign against Rebecca, General Brown himself should have to learn the bitter lesson enunciated by Edmund Burke. Within a few days more he would be off back to his War Office desk, leaving Colonel Love to cope as best he could with those pestilential Welsh rustics.

And how curious it was that what seemed to be something like Rebecca's final fling at the business of toll gate breaking should occur so far (over a hundred miles) from her first foray at Efail-wen; in mid Wales, in the broad and peaceful Severn Valley where this story began, with the Chartist riots that first brought Carmarthen lawyer Hugh Williams to notice as a champion of rioters, a reputation which would make him a prime suspect in the search for Rebecca.

I take credit to myself

Hugh Williams had come a long way since the Chartist trials at Welshpool Assizes four years previously. He had acquired quite a reputation through his defence at magistrates' courts of farmers charged with refusing to pay toll, through presiding over farmers' meetings and drawing up petitions for them and, more lately, through his appearance at the gates of Swansea and Carmarthen gaols to take up the cases of the Pontardulais rioters and the Stag and Pheasant gang. And he had begun to relish his reputation and even to court it. At dinner on the night before Mynydd Sylen he had confided to his friend Linton his intention that Rebeccaism in the shape of the 'toll gate movement' should be 'a preparation for farther political action.' And on that mountain top, in the sunshine of that hot August day and with the waters of Carmarthen Bay sparkling in the distance behind him, he had warmed to the cheers of eight thousand Carmarthenshire countrypeople and stood forth as their champion—not exactly espousing the cause of Rebecca, but not exactly condemning it either.

At the great outdoor meeting on the hill of Llynllechowen, between Llanon and Llandeilo, on 13 September, he followed the same tack, which was more than could be said of some of his fellow speakers, especially an unnamed Dissenting Minister. According to Colonel Love's report to the Home Secretary:

> His voice and gestures were violent in the extreme and a farmer who stood by my informant said his speech [in Welsh] was directed at both the government and the church. The meeting broke up

quietly and there were drunken people about the roads all night, which were patrolled by the cavalry until this morning.[9]

Again according to Colonel Love, the meeting on the hill of Allt Cunedda just north of Kidwelly, on 27 September, 'turned out a complete failure, not more than fifty people having attended.'[10] Perhaps Hugh Williams felt a little more secure here for he went rather further in his public stance on Rebeccaism and told his small audience that:

> . . . he took credit to himself for having been one of the first who had taken public notice of the multiplicity of toll bars which infested that part of the Principality. He had written a pamphlet on the subject in 1838. In consequence of the agitation in the country the attention of England had been attracted to it. He was very glad that this agitation, commencing in the demolition of the gates, however unlawful it might be, had had one good effect; it had attracted the notice of the press, and from its having done so he was induced to think it would ere long attract the notice of the Government. They (the representatives of the press) had observed a great many attempts made by different gentlemen from the most laudable motives to endeavour to correct the abuses respecting the turnpike trusts and to relieve the country from their taxation. They had closely observed the [peaceful] attempts to reduce the tolls and had pronounced them futile.[11]

Having got as close as he had ever done—in public—to condoning the destruction of toll gates, Hugh Williams then stepped back again and '. . . strongly deprecated the violence which had taken place in the country; he felt it must weaken the effect of their petitions. He strongly deprecated acts of private revenge which lead to universal terrorism.'[12]

Thus far and no farther then. For the moment. But the time was approaching when he would go farther, provoked by the trials of Jac Tŷ Isha and the others of the Pontardulais battle at a special Assizes, commissioned by the Queen to open at Cardiff on 26 October. All eyes in west Wales would be on that first major Rebecca trial, whose conduct and outcome would be a major factor in dictating the immediate course of events there.

[9] Letter dated 15 September, 1843, Col. Love to Home Office: Public Record Office, File HO 45/453.

[10] Same, dated 29 September, 1843.

[11] *The Times,* 30 September, 1843.

[12] *The Times,* 30 September, 1843.

Chapter Sixteen

DRAW NEAR AND GIVE YOUR ATTENDANCE

At Windsor Castle on Monday 2 October, 1843, the Prime Minister Sir Robert Peel, the Home Secretary Sir James Graham, and others of Her Majesty's Privy Council, bowed out of the royal presence, taking with them two documents which were to be of crucial importance to the government's fight against Rebecca. The young Queen had signed a proclamation promising huge rewards and royal pardons for informers, a document which would strike a loud chord in south west Wales, particularly among the erstwhile supporters of Shoni 'Sgubor Fawr and Dai'r Cantwr (arrested a week earlier) and those they had held in thrall in and around the Gwendraeth Valley. She had also signed a 'Special Commission'[1] to her judges, The Baron Gurney and Sir Cresswell Cresswell, to open an Assize in Cardiff for the trials of those held for the Bolgoed and Pontardulais riots; trials that would present the first real opportunity to test the will of the Rebeccaites against the power of the law. It would be a crucial test, and it was therefore necessary that the trials should be seen by all to be fair and free of the political or other establishment pressure which—to any thoughtful observer of the behaviour of some west Wales magistrates—had so discredited the law in the eyes of the people of that part of the world.

As to the proclamation, Foster of *The Times* had serious misgivings about its timing. Writing from Carmarthen on Saturday 7 October, he reported on a meeting of three thousand farmers held at Crugybalog, near Newcastle Emlyn, four days earlier, at which he had detected a distinct change of mood among the people. It was a change which, he felt, owed much to the signs brought into the district by Hall and Ellis that the government was prepared to listen to the people's grievances, and to the

[1] Known as the 'Commission of Oyer, Terminer and General Gaol Delivery', the Queen's Commission was the authority for holding County Assizes, which were held four times a year to coincide with the four seasons. 'Special' Commissions were sometimes issued to cope with the aftermath of serious riots.

beneficial influence of a 'gentry' jolted by the violent events of the past months into a somewhat belated recognition of their responsibilities in the matter. 'It is quite true that still a few gates here and there continue to be broken down,' he wrote:

> . . . but the general feeling of the people no longer countenances these outrages. Confession has done much to molify animosity, and if this wise course be pursued there can be no doubt that the disturbances which have distracted South Wales will gradually subside.[2]

And there was evidence all around of the desire of the farmers to shake off the cloak of violence which they had so willingly worn before things had begun to get out of hand. In Llanelli, for example, only a week before Foster wrote his report on the Crug-ybalog meeting, the Tirfran gate on the road to Felinfoel was found to have been removed from its hinges in the night and thrown into a coalpit. As soon as the word got around, about forty local farmers retrieved the gate and replaced it. Times were indeed changing!

Foster clearly had this changing atmosphere in mind when he expressed his concern about the possible harm the proclamation might do at what seemed to him to be a most delicate juncture: 'I cannot but think,' he wrote:

> . . . that the Proclamation recently issued by the Queen with the advice of her Government is ill-timed and injudicious. It is calculated to keep alive animosity which had better be suffered to die away, and it can only serve to set servant against master and to create ill-blood, suspicion and acts of revenge. For every man who is made a witness against his neighbours there will be added one more faggot to the flame of private revenge and intense animosity. Let the Government then, instead of endeavouring to rip up old sores, seek to do justice to the people, listen to their well-founded and not unreasonable complaints, and this once orderly and peaceful population will settle down, satisfied, into its former quietitude.[3]

Foster saw, too, signs that the west Wales agricultural economy, whose backward state lay at the root of much of the troubles, was ripe for improvement and that some improvement was already underway in Carmarthenshire, where the County's Agricultural Society held its annual general meeting on Thursday 5 October. 'The Society,' he wrote:

[2] *The Times,* 9 October, 1843.

[3] Ibid.

> . . . however little good may be effected by such associations in England, is, from the peculiar circumstances of the country, calculated to produce the most beneficial results among the farmers here. Already many of them are beginning to see, by comparison with better and improved modes of cultivation and with better breeds of stock, how ruinous are their own closely hugged and antiquated systems. Their prejudices are giving way to the evident profit of improvements.[4]

And a week later he was even more optimistic:

> There appears to be a general and prevailing belief that South Wales is gradually becoming more settled. In those districts where the cause of discontent has been removed and where the gentry have foresaken their sulky exclusiveness and come forward and met the people, the most satisfying results have followed. For instance, the Parish of Penbryn in Cardiganshire was in a state of great excitement against tithes. The praiseworthy manner in which Mr. E. Lloyd Williams came forward and reasoned with the people with some concessions on the part of the Lay Improprietors has restored peace and tranquility to the Parish.
>
> The inhabitants of the neighbourhood of Cardigan and the whole of the district through which the River Teifi runs, up to Newcastle Emlyn, centred their chief animosity against the Llechryd Weir. The fair and open manner in which the proprietor and leaseholder of that weir [Mr. Gower of Castell Malgwyn] met the people at Llechryd the other day and the willingness he expressed to abolish the weir at a low rate of compensation, coupled with the manner in which some of the gentry then came forward to subscribe towards that compensation, was immediately followed by expressions of satisfaction and contentment by the people.

He went on to say that Mr. Gower had been told by the people that 'Becca there is now dead and they will protect both him and his mansion, and he may dismiss both soldiers and police whenever he pleases as totally unnecessary.'[5]

But Foster's world of optimism was, for the moment at least, merely an oasis in a desert of desperate military measures as troops and police—now numbering nearly 2,000 of the one and 150 of the other—took up their new dispositions under Major General Brown's plan of campaign, and as Rebecca smashed gates in Radnorshire and Montgomeryshire with all the panache

[4] *The Times,* 9 October, 1843.
[5] *The Times,* 14 October, 1843.

and numbers she had displayed earlier in the south west. And while the Queen's Proclamation began to fill Carmarthen Gaol with prisoners, at fifty to five hundred pounds a time—a dozen being added between 15 and 20 October alone.

By 24 October, Foster was in Cardiff for the opening of the Special Commission and his first dispatch from that town, now full of excited anticipation and packed with witnesses, jurors, sightseers, soldiers and policemen, displayed a certain world weariness. It was a weariness born of months of riding miles every day over difficult country, of spending nights in inns and hotels of wildly differing quality and degrees of discomfort, and of writing late into the night under the eye-straining light of candle and oil lamp. Of the ordinary Welsh people he had met and of whose hardships and patient endurance he had written with such sympathetic understanding, he had nothing but admiration: 'There is no peasantry that I know of more faithful than the Welsh or more attached to their masters or their landlords,' he had written in Carmarthen on 27 September. 'They will obey you faithfully and labour for you cheerfully; you may lead them with a silken thread, but you cannot drive them. And depend upon it, neither the bayonet nor the bullet will coerce them.'[6] But for one class of Welshman Foster harboured quite different sentiments. And they came to the boil when he found how that class was cashing in on the shortage of accommodation and everything else caused by the great influx into Cardiff for the Rebecca trials:

> The chief thing which strikes a stranger looking out for a quiet lodging is the extraordinary rapacity of the Welsh genus of lodging house keepers. A Welshman's conscience in overreaching is not over-particular. 'Taffy was a Welshman, Taffy was a thief' is a common nursery rhyme, and the shopkeepers here, like the tradesmen I have met with wherever else I have been in my now long sojourn in Wales, will consider for a long time from your appearance what amount of extortion you will bear, and then modestly ask you six or eight times as much as would in England be thought a fair remuneration. However, I am getting used to this sort of thing in Wales and as I cannot help it have made up my mind to 'grin and bear it' and get out of it as soon as I can.
>
> It is the national failing. You see it in the landlords in the letting of

[6] *The Times,* 30 September, 1843.

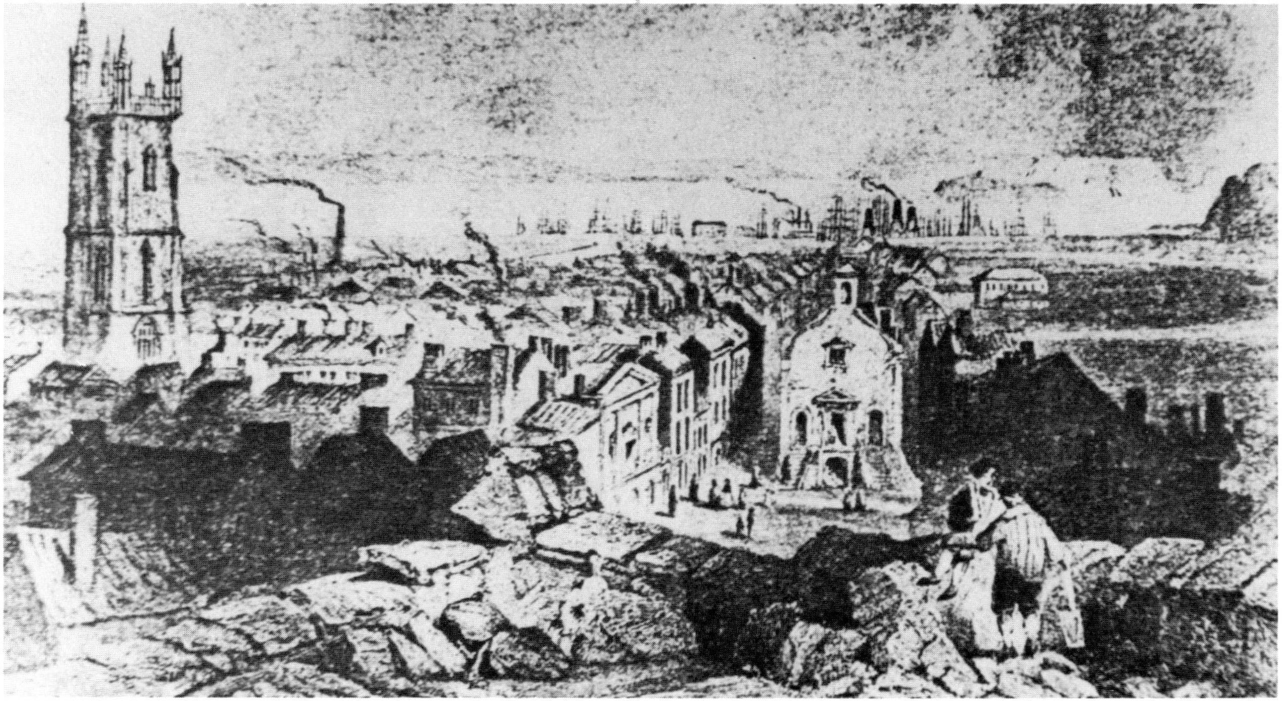

Cardiff (*Carmarthen Library*)

their farms by auction or tender; you see it in the farmers in their sub-lettings at double rent; you see it in the innkeepers—but by this class I have been too much victimised to trust myself in expressing what I think about them.[7]

But he 'grinned and bore it' and paid up whatever exorbitant price was asked for whatever kind of food and lodging he was able to find. And late into the nights, in the guttering light of candle or oil lamp, he wrote up each day's proceedings of those historic trials.

How say you, John Hughes?

The scene before the court house in Cardiff on that October Friday morning was a spectacular feast of colour and sound as the judge's procession arrived in the midst of a vast crowd. Several carriages bearing bewigged and gorgeously dressed footmen, escorted by javelin men on foot and surrounded by mounted dragoons, drew to a halt at the steps, to a fanfare from the judges' trumpeters and a present arms by the redcoats of the 73rd Regiment. Footmen hurried to open carriage doors and lower their steps, and out came the two judges, their long wigs and trailing scarlet robes embodying all the majesty of the law. And all the dread, too, for the more observant among the crowd noted the folded black cap carried in the hand of Baron Gurney, as he and Sir Cresswell Cresswell were accompanied into the building by Sir John Homfray, the High Sheriff of Glamorgan. Splendidly attired himself, in his white frills and black silver-buttoned velvet tailcoat, the High Sheriff held his hand to the hilt of his sword, as a reminder of his nonceremonial duty of protecting Her Majesty's Judges while in his domain.

And well he might, for all kinds of dark rumours were circulating. The Chartists in Merthyr were still very much a cause for concern as word continued to come out of their clandestine meetings of arms distributions, of preparations for insurrection and of contacts with the Carmarthenshire Rebeccaites. Suspicion of threats to jurors raised by several requests to the High Sheriff for excusal from jury service through fear of retaliation was hardened by a number of outright refusals to be sworn, for which fines were imposed and cheerfully paid. So great was

[7] *The Times,* 26 October, 1843.

the tension that when on the day after the opening of the trials the High Sheriff's coach was overturned by his drunken coachman coming out of Bute Castle and he suffered a broken arm which kept him away from the rest of the proceedings, wild rumours of an armed attack upon him swept the whole of south Wales.[8] The strong guard of honour of infantry and cavalry outside the court house clearly had more than ceremonial drill in mind as they presented their bayonetted muskets and raised their sabres in salute to Her Majesty's Judges and the High Sheriff of Glamorgan.

Inside the court house all was frantic activity as attorneys ran to and from clusters of barristers taking last minute instructions and dealing with last minute crises. Hugh Williams was there, in deep conversation with barrister Edward Crompton Lloyd Hall and Queen's Counsel Mathew Davenport Hill, relaying the final messages from their clients Jac Tŷ Isha, John Hugh and David Jones, who were waiting nervously and manacled in their cells below the dock steps. And suddenly a hush descended on the crowded court. The door behind the bench opened and the judges and the High Sheriff entered and stood beneath the Royal Coat of Arms while the clerk called for silence.

'Oyez, Oyez' cried the clerk. 'All persons having any business before my Lords the Queen's Justices draw near and give your attendance.' Then came the long recital of the Queen's Special Commission from its parchment, at the end of which judges, High Sheriff, barristers and attorneys bowed gravely to each other and sat down, that the business of the court might commence.

Baron Gurney then addressed the Grand Jury on the charges and the prisoners awaiting trial, and outlined the evidence contained in the depositions, on which they would have to decide whether or not to find 'true bills of indictment' fit to go for trial before a petty jury. A true bill was found against all the defendants.[9]

'Put up John Hughes' called the clerk, and 'a hale, powerful and goodlooking farmer',[10] his arm (now permanently disabled) still in a sling seven weeks after being shattered by a pistol ball,

[8] *Carmarthen Journal*, 3 November, 1843.
[9] The Grand Jury system was abolished in 1933.
[10] *The Times*, 28 October, 1843.

emerged from the depths of the dock and stood pale faced to hear the charges against him. 'John Hughes, you are charged in this indictment, on the first count that you on the 7th day of September, in the County of Glamorgan, did unlawfully, riotously and tumultuously assemble together with divers others, to the disturbance of the peace. How say you, John Hughes? Are you guilty or not guilty?' Jac Tŷ Isha stiffened, looked straight at Baron Gurney and spoke loudly and clearly. 'Not guilty, my lord.' 'And on the second count,' continued the clerk, 'you are charged for that you on that day and in that place did feloniously, unlawfully and with force begin to demolish and pull down the dwelling house of one William Lewis. How say you? Are you guilty or not guilty?' 'Not guilty.' 'And on the third count you are charged for that you on that day and in that place did shoot at one Charles Frederick Napier with intent feloniously and with malice aforethought to kill and murder him. How say you? Are you guilty or not guilty?' 'Not guilty.' 'You may sit,' said Baron Gurney.

Then began the business of empanelling a trial jury, which proved to be a long and difficult one as defence counsel Mathew Davenport Hill rose to challenge the whole basis of the jury selection by saying that the Sheriff had not chosen the panel 'indifferently and impartially.' A bold and serious challenge. 'Do you tender any evidence, Mr. Hill?' asked Judge Gurney. 'I could draw your Lordship's attention to a case where your Lordship—as counsel—tendered such a challenge,' replied the Q.C. For all his seventy five years his lordship's memory seemed sharp enough, and he took up the point immediately. 'As you have that case in your memory,' he said, 'do you remember the specific ground of the challenge? That the sheriff himself was a member of a society to which the prosecutor [the chief witness] belonged?' Mr. Hill did not, and found after a long argument that a sweeping and unsupported challenge just would not do. True, as Mr. Hill was complaining, the jury in waiting did not include farmers from the west of Glamorgan (where Pontardulais and Bolgoed lay), but the court heard that this merely followed the common practice that jurors were chosen from people living within a reasonable radius of the trial venue. Furthermore, though no farmers appeared among the jury in waiting—as Mr. Hill also complained—enough of them had claimed exemption or paid fines rather than be sworn to show that there had been no deliberate exclusion of farmers either. So the jury was sworn from the panel of gentlemen and tradesmen of Cardiff and Merthyr randomly selected by the sheriff.

From the fog of battle

The Attorney General, Sir Frederick Pollock, opened the prosecution and called a stream of witnesses to try to recreate in the calm and cool atmosphere of that oak-panelled chamber the wild and confused ten minutes of gunfire, rearing frightened horses and mass panic of that moonlit night at Pontardulais. The key prosecution witness was, of course, Captain Charles Frederick Napier, the Chief Constable of Glamorgan, whose dramatic evidence was listened to with rapt attention. He described the moment when he fell in his men across the road and when, on the call of 'Stop!', the leading rioter—one of three horsemen who appeared to be in command—wheeled his horse and fired at him. And so on, right through the frantic melée to the final identification of his pinnioned, wounded, white-robed and black-faced attacker as John Hughes, the prisoner.

Mr. Hill rose to cross-examine, and it soon became apparent that his interest lay mainly in how the police came to be armed in the first place; how they had come to fire at all and what orders on that point had been given to them by Captain Napier—before or during the action. Pressed on this, the Captain replied that he did not recollect that he had given any other directions to his men than to 'mark' the man who had shot at him. The rioters had already fired a volley and cheered as they passed the Red Lion, after which he and his party 'had been all the time under a continuous dropping fire', and, though he had shot the horse of the man who had fired at him, he felt sure the Rebeccaite was actually unhorsed by a shot from his own party. As to why the police had fired—on what orders—the Captain explained that he 'had not given them instructions to fire, nor any instructions save general orders for the occasion.'

The position in law then was as it is now, that they could only fire their weapons if it was necessary to do so to protect their own lives or the lives of others. And whether or not that was so on that moonlit night at Pontardulais, when eleven armed men faced more than a hundred and fifty, would be a question for the jury to ponder.

Mr. Hill's questions were also designed to shake the identification by the Captain and his men of John Hughes as the one who had wheeled his horse and shot at him, and to show that the rioters in general and the prisoner in particular were not carrying their guns with any intention of shooting anyone. Furthermore, he tried his utmost to show that his client could not be proved to have had anything to do with any of the damage done that night, and (in the classic 'each way bet') even if he *had* begun to demolish and pull down the toll house, as was alleged, he could not be guilty as charged if the demolition had not been *completed.* Mr. Mathew Davenport Hill, Q.C., was doing his level best with that most difficult of all defences—the defence of a man who had been caught red-handed.

Captain Napier was followed into the witness box by the two magistrates, John Dillwyn Llewellyn and Lewis Llewellyn Dillwyn, the former of whom *did* remember the Captain giving the order to fire after the three horsemen had ridden at them and shots had been fired. Both magistrates described a fierce encounter at very close quarters enveloped in what has often been called the 'fog of battle', in which the best that could be expected of any witness, on either side, was an account of the action on his own small piece of the battleground. And cross examination of the magistrates—as indeed of the rest of the prosecution witnesses—failed to penetrate that fog in the sense of producing a coherent view of the whole field of action. Several police officers spoke of hearing Captain Napier give the order to fire as he went for the horseman who had fired at him. But the common thread running through the whole of the prosecution evidence—the thread that Mr. Hill found it impossible to break—was that great volley fired by the hundred and fifty Rebeccaites as they passed the Red Lion, the continuous firing which followed it as the gate was smashed and the toll house gutted, and the charge of the three horsemen at the police line on Captain Napier's challenge to them to desist. And there were other potent, if silent, witnesses for the prosecution: the sledge hammers, pick axes, crowbars, axes, guns, powder horns, shot bags, bugles, cow horns, wigs, bonnets and gowns recovered by Superintendent Peake after the battle, together of course with those damning 'Rebecca' notes found on the prisoner when he was searched at Swansea Gaol.

The one prosecution witness who found himself in trouble under Mr. Hill's cross examination was Constable John Price. He had, he said in evidence, heard someone in the crowd call 'Fight to the death!', which words were followed by the firing of 'a great many guns.' 'When did you first recollect that you had heard the expression "Fight to the death"?' asked Mr. Hill. 'I cannot recollect,' replied the officer. 'It was not in your deposition before the examining magistrates,' persisted the defence counsel. 'No' agreed the officer. 'I did not state it then because I was in a hurry.' He paused uncomfortably. 'I was not in a hurry to-day,' said the constable weakly. 'Oh!' said Mr. Hill, eyeing him for a moment, before throwing a knowing glance at the jury and sitting down with a great swirl of his black gown.

The prosecution case had closed.

Rising to present the case for the defence, Mr. Hill began by attacking the wording of the indictment; claiming that it was defective and that the prisoner was thereby entitled to an acquittal. It was a highly technical argument, very much a play on words. The ownership of the house had not been properly established, he said, and 'an indictment of which the averment is so general and speaks of trustees without specifying their names cannot be sustained.' The two leading counsel for the prosecution put their case and the two judges ruled against Mr. Hill, who thereupon introduced the evidence for the defence.

It was a defence, though, in which the prisoner himself could play no part at all, for the great difference between criminal trials in 1843 and those held to-day is that the prisoner had no right to be heard in his own defence. That right, so taken for granted to-day, was not conceded until 1898, so Jac Tŷ Isha's defence could consist only in an impassioned speech by his counsel (itself a right conceded by law only seven years earlier) and the calling of witnesses either to the facts or to his character. And since the only witnesses to the facts would themselves have been participants in the riot, there would only be witnesses to the prisoner's character—several farmers and an innkeeper from Tumble and Llanon. But the speech for the defence was a *tour de force*—punching home the points on which his cross examination had been based, but playing even more heavily on the emotions of the jury and on the fact that the effect on the prisoner of a guilty verdict 'might be to send him into exile and to inflict on him a punishment more severe' than the death penalty which had been only recently withdrawn from the crime with which he was charged. As he sat down he received a whispered compliment on his performance from his adversary, the Attorney General.

And then the final speech for the prosecution: 'You have heard,' exclaimed junior counsel for the Crown, 'a very eloquent and powerful address, and I must certainly rejoice that in a case which has excited so much public interest and which is of so much importance to the prisoner at the bar, the prisoner has had all the advantage of all the professional talent and eloquence he could obtain.' Having said that, the Solicitor General went through the points which the prosecution were required to prove by the Act of Parliament under which John Hughes was charged, and pointed out to the jury how the prosecution witnesses had proved them all.

Commenting on the defence criticism of the police and magistrates in going armed and opening fire, counsel said:

> I am not here to vindicate the police, but before we pass censure on them, it is very easy for us in this court—not surrounded by danger and not mixed up in an affray—to censure persons for their conduct who were engaged in one; but I ask you before you join in the censure to put yourselves in the position of these policemen [and magistrates], eleven in number, attacking a crowd of two hundred and fifty armed men, who apparently fired at them. It is under these circumstances that the police fired again as quickly as they could load, without looking to see if any of the crowd were running away.

Judgement

It was now time for Baron Gurney to direct the jury on the law, to sum up the evidence and to remind them of their duty. But before doing so he addressed them on the reason for holding the trial at Cardiff. 'It is no small consolation,' he said, 'that you have been called on to fulfil the duties you are assembled to perform in a place far removed from the scenes where the recent offences were committed, and where the minds of persons are naturally excited by those transactions. You are thus enabled coolly and dispassionately to consider all the facts that are laid before you.'

That the prisoner 'formed a part' of what happened that night in Pontardulais the jury could surely have no doubt, said the judge, who then went through the evidence on which they would have to decide just what that part was and how it fitted—if it did fit—the charges against him.

'The *facts* of the case are what you have maturely to weigh and consider. Should you believe the prisoner, after that solemn consideration of the evidence laid before you, to be innocent of the crime with which he is charged, you will acquit him of that charge. But if, on the other hand, you believe him to be guilty, you will find a verdict accordingly.'

The jury retired, and half an hour later they tapped on the jury room door and were led by the usher back to their benches. 'Have you elected a foreman to speak for you?' asked the clerk. The foreman stood. 'Just answer yes or no. Are you agreed upon a verdict on the charges against the prisoner at the bar?' 'Yes.' 'How say you on the charge against John Hughes of riot? Do you find John Hughes guilty or not guilty?' 'Guilty,' replied the foreman across the deathly hush of the courtroom. 'And do you find John Hughes guilty or not guilty of beginning to demolish and pull down the dwelling house of William Lewis?' 'Guilty.' 'And do you find John Hughes guilty or not guilty of shooting at Charles Frederick Napier with intent to murder him?' 'Guilty.' 'And that is the verdict of you all?' asked the clerk. 'It is,' said the foreman. 'But we recommend the prisoner to mercy on account of his previous good character.'

'Take him below,' said Baron Gurney. And the court adjourned, to pass sentence on the morrow.

Jac Tŷ Isha spent a sleepless yet dream-wracked night, but he had still to wait next morning while his two companions, David Jones and John Hugh, were put up and charged with their three counts of riot, demolishing the toll house and aiding and abetting him in the crime of shooting at Captain Napier with intent to murder him. They, too, had had a sleepless night, their particular torment being the apparent hopelessness of a plea of not guilty in the light of their leader's failure in his. Hugh Williams conveyed to them in their cells their counsel's view that their cause was indeed hopeless and that a guilty plea might attract a degree of leniency. And they took the advice. Their counsel, Mr. Mathew Davenport Hill, Q.C., rose to address the court on behalf of the three convicts, now standing together in the dock:

> When prisoners think it right to submit themselves to the law without trial [by pleading guilty] perhaps it will not be considered presumptuous in me in venturing to call your Lordships' attention to this fact as showing their contrite spirit and doing all that lies in their power to atone for the offence of which they have been guilty. Perhaps your Lordships will think that this example of guilty and fallen men will not be without its use in showing that they no longer stand up in defiance of the law, but, waiving their right, submit themselves to the punishment which must be inflicted on them.
>
> They all belong to respectable families. A few months ago they might have held up their heads with the proudest in the land, because they were innocent; because they were men acting according to what was right, and walking within the bounds of the law. From that state your Lordships see into what an abyss they have fallen. They are now felons; they are stigmatised by that name which is the most reproachful known to the law; their property is forfeit [to the Crown].

After pointing out that two of his clients had already received some punishment in the form of disabling gunshot wounds, Mr. Hill made reference to the Commission of Inquiry, now beginning its work in Carmarthen, which he saw as complementing the work of the court in trying to bring peace to the Principality. 'I learned with great satisfaction,' he said:

> that while your Lordships were sitting under this commission, in a neighbouring county a commission of a different character has been opened. I have read with infinite pleasure the address of the right honourable gentleman who opened that commission. These two great measures, taken together in conjoined and co-ordinate operation, I feel will be the very best means of putting an end to these fatal disturbances. If that commission proceeds under the same spirit—if it shows that wise forebearance which characterised the proceedings of the Attorney General in the exercise of his high function—I am sure that the happiest effects must be produced.

With that strong expression of contrition and moving pleas for mercy—throwing in for good measure the conciliatory example set by the Commission of Inquiry at Carmarthen—Mr. Mathew Davenport Hill, Queen's Counsel, ended his defence of the Pontardulais rioters.

The presiding judge, Baron Gurney, thanked Mr. Hill, and not a sound could be heard as he leaned forward to address Jac Tŷ Isha, David Jones and John Hugh:

> John Hughes, David Jones and John Hugh. You stand convicted of a felony, and a felony of a very aggravated description. You banded and associated yourselves with others; you assembled in large numbers at the dead hour of night; you armed yourselves with deadly weapons, and you proved that you were not indisposed to use them. Thus prepared, you proceeded to the demolition of a turnpike gate and then of a turnpike house. You associated yourselves in such numbers as to overwhelm all resistance on the part of the owner of the house or even his neighbours.
>
> You were interrupted in your purpose by magistrates and peace officers, and then you made use of firearms with which you had equipped yourselves—thus setting the law at defiance and disturbing the peace of the country. All these circumstances were a very great aggravation. Until of late such crimes were of very, very unfrequent occurrence in this country. The interruption you received will, perhaps, prevent the repetition of the crime in *this* county, but it is impossible for the court to be ignorant that in neighbouring counties the perpetration of such crimes continues to this day. It is absolutely necessary that the law should be enforced, that the peace of the country should be preserved and that good order should be restored.
>
> The jury, after a long and patient hearing, have found you John Hughes guilty; and you David Jones and John Hugh have pleaded guilty to an indictment of a similar description, and your learned counsel in his address to this court has very properly impressed upon us the contrition which you both have manifested.
>
> This circumstance is not forgotten, but still an example is necessary. You, from the respectability which you formerly maintained and the rank in life which you occupied, are persons of whom it is particularly necessary that an example shall be made, to deter others from a repetition of your crime. You are all liable to be transported beyond the seas for the term of your lives, but considering all that has been stated with respect to you, David Jones and John Hugh, the court is of opinion that it is impossible to pass a less sentence than that which I am about to pronounce, *which is that each of you shall be transported for the term of seven years.*

And then, turning to Jac Tŷ Isha, Baron Gurney continued the court's judgement:

> With respect to you, John Hughes, the court cannot entertain the

same view of your case. You appear to be one in a station of society far above the rest—one not likely to be misled by others—and yet, upon the evidence, proved to be a leader, if not *the* leader, of this lawless multitude.

Your conduct at the time, as well as the papers found in your pocket, demonstrated that you were a leader—that you were active in collecting adherents and associates, and that something like threats had issued from you against those who were not forward in joining your illegal course.

You have been recommended by the jury to the mercy of the court. The court finds extreme difficulty in any degree lessening the punishment which the law awards to your offence. The law says you are liable to transportation for life, and, giving all consideration to the recommendation of the jury [to mercy] and to all the circumstances which have been so ably stated by your learned counsel, *the court is of opinion that you be transported beyond the seas for a term of twenty years.*

As to any further extension of mercy, you must recommend yourselves to the grace and mercy of the Crown; but that mercy cannot be expected if offences of this kind are repeated and the peace of the country is not fully restored.

I have now discharged a most painful duty, and I trust that the mercy of the Crown, as well as the punishments inflicted by the court, will have the effect of deterring all who might be disposed to associate themselves together for the purpose of committing offences against the law.

To assist your Lordships

The three Pontardulais rioters were taken below, in the deathly silence of a courtroom heavy with the atmosphere of retribution and stern punishment, and the trials of the other six prisoners commenced. But then, as the hands of the great courtroom clock slowly marked the passage of that fateful day, the atmosphere gradually lightened with the realisation that something unusual was happening.

Lewis Davies, the Llanon farmer captured by William Chambers, Junior and his soldiers as he fled from Pontardulais, pleaded guilty to helping to destroy the gate with Jac Tŷ Isha's band of Rebeccaites. The Attorney General said that having 'given his best attention to the case' he 'did not feel it necessary to press for the judgement of the court.' He was content, he said, to receive the prisoner's promise of good behaviour. And an unbelieving Lewis Davies was freed.

Then came the trial everyone in west Glamorgan had been waiting for—that of the Morgan family of Cwmcille Fach for their Sunday morning battle with Captain Napier—that 'great battle of kettle and gridiron notoriety'[11] when the Captain had gone to bring in Henry Morgan. And the five of them pleaded guilty to 'cutting and wounding' the officer or to assisting in the assault—all crimes carrying long sentences of transportation

Old Morgan Morgan and Esther Morgan's promises to be of good behaviour were accepted by the Attorney General in view of 'their advanced age and other circumstances of the case' and the judges gave them their freedom.

The felony charges of aiding and assisting in the assault against sons and daughter, Rees, John and Margaret Morgan, were dropped at the request of the Attorney General and the lesser ('misdemeanour') charge was substituted, upon which the Attorney General caused consternation in the court by observing that '. . . having ascertained the circumstances under which this aggravated assault took place, I do believe that they were under a mistake with respect to the right to resist [referring to their belief that it was illegal to execute an arrest warrant on the Sabbath]. Under those circumstances I am not disposed to press for a severe punishment in this case. But, as the law has been resisted, the offence must, at the same time, be marked by some sentence which will manifest the severe displeasure of the court.'

Mr. Hill, their defending counsel, merely pointed out—to assist their Lordships in deciding how to deal with the case—that John Morgan had been shot and wounded in the affray. And then Baron Gurney delivered the court's judgement:

> You have been convicted, on your own confession, of having assaulted a constable in the execution of his duty. It is most important that officers in the execution of their duty should receive the protection of the court; and the resistance of them and assault upon them under such circumstances is a very grave offence.
>
> In this case it appears that in the resistance which was offered the life of the officer was in danger, and I have no doubt that if he had not, in his own defence, discharged a pistol, his life would have been sacrificed and that all of you would have had to answer for the

[11] *The Times* (Editorial), 1 November, 1843.

charge of murder and have ended your days by an ignominious death.

I observe that the Attorney General has forborne to press against you any indictment charging you with the higher and felonious offence. I feel, however, that notwithstanding the forebearance of the Attorney General, an example must be made, particularly when resistance to a peace officer has been offered, and in the manner in which that resistance was given.

You, Margaret Morgan, will go to prison for six months, and you Rees Morgan and John Morgan will go to prison for twelve months. The court has received information respecting the goodness of your characters, and that is the only reason why we have not considered it necessary to sentence you to hard labour also. Take them down!

It should then have been the turn of the men charged with destroying Bolgoed gate—Daniel Lewis, Matthew Morgan, William Morgan and Henry Morgan (whom the trouble at Cwmcille Fach had been all about)—to be tried, along with Griffith Vaughan, landlord of the Red Lion at Pontardulais, who was also charged with acquiring guns and ammunition for the rioters. But there had been a hitch of the kind not uncommon when the prosecution's evidence against Rebeccaites depended on one solitary informer. The infamous John Jones of Cwm Scer, Llangyfelach, whose rivalry for the affections of Elizabeth Williams had driven him to denounce Daniel Lewis, was 'not available' to give evidence. So the case was adjourned to the following Spring Assizes—by which time members of the informer's own family had denounced him as a liar and he had solved the problem by a hurried emigration to the New World, leaving the Crown without any case at all.

Daniel Lewis and his fellow prisoners returned in triumph to a wildly enthusiastic reception from the cheering crowds of Pontardulais. And Daniel and Elizabeth lived happily ever after![12]

The rogues who found them guilty

For Hugh Williams, by now renowned as the defender of the Rebecca Rioters, the outcome of the trials of the Pontardulais three was a bitter blow. For once his lawyer's capacity for cool

[12] For this reconstruction of the Cardiff trials the author has drawn on the very detailed accounts in *The Times* and the depositions contained in the Assize records in the Public Record Office.

judgement suddenly deserted him, and what he did in that moment of anger came to light in the most sinister circumstances so far as the authorities were concerned.

On the evening of Sunday 5 November, in a dimly lit, smoke-filled room at the Three Horseshoes inn at Merthyr Tydfil, the Chartists held one of their clandestine meetings, and one of Captain Napier's informers was sitting among the audience of three hundred. He heard David Thomas describe his visit to the Cardiff trials and his meeting with a number of Carmarthenshire farmers to whom he was introduced by Hugh Williams. And then the chairman, butcher Evan Williams, called upon Francis August, the Market Street shoemaker, who produced a letter which had been addressed to him by Hugh Williams. He read it to the meeting and Captain Napier's man made a careful note:

> I am obliged for the letter sent to me by David Thomas [who had attended the trials] and according to instructions in that letter I did all that I could for the persons who were tried then, but for all that, it was a packed jury. I do not say that Sir John Guest [the Dowlais ironmaster] or Lord James Stuart had anything to do with it, but I have no doubt they had, but if I was to say so I could not prove it.
>
> I need not mention who the rogues were who found them guilty. No doubt the liberty-loving men of Merthyr know them [the jury] very well *and I do hope they will do their best for them.*
>
> And you may well know who were in the witness box. It was the police, or the 'Blue Devils' as we may call them, and they would swear anything, for it could not be proved that they [the rioters] were on the intent of pulling down the toll house.
>
> I hope you will prepare for the election as it is likely there will be one in a short time, and I will stand for one, to oppose Sir John Guest to the utmost of my power. I am ready to stand in the cause of liberty at any time or any place, but I do not pretend to be a leader, only a follower. I will not advance before the crowd.
>
> I shall not enter further on the subject until I hear from Merthyr again. Please remember me to all my friends about Merthyr, and especially to David Thomas.[13]

Whether he did 'hear further on the subject' from the Merthyr Chartists is not recorded and his expression of his intention to stand for election was probably something else said in the heat of

[13] Reports from Capt. Napier to Col. Love; Public Record Office, File HO 45/453. (Author's italics).

the moment. But his outburst in that letter would serve to convince many people who already suspected him that he was indeed 'the instigator and undiscovered leader of the Rebecca Movement.'[14]

Of high courage

And what of the leader of the 'Blue Devils' who 'would swear anything' against the Rebeccas?

Whatever anyone might say about him, there can be no doubt that Captain Charles Frederick Napier had shown himself a man of high courage at Cwmcille Fach in fighting off the murderous attack on him with hammers, hatchets, reaping hooks and a saucepan of boiling water, at odds of five to one; and then at Pontardulais in leading his small band of ten men into a rampaging mob of a hundred and fifty or more. He had been shot at and knocked unconscious (to add to the severe cuts and bruises suffered at Cwmcille Fach), but in the face of a storm of gunshot he had seen the three leaders secured and had driven the rest in panic from the bridge.

And yet he was the subject of 'considerable ridicule' for 'his fight with the old woman with the frying pan',[15] while his exploits at Pontardulais were protrayed in a savagely different light by at least one radical newspaper. Certain people, said *The Welshman,* were:

> . . . lost in admiration at the shedding of simple men's blood and bepraised the cool and determined courage (!!!) displayed by Captain Napier's force aided by a gallant band of gentlemen and justices of the peace. Some of the latter went out armed, waited for their prey behind hedges and gunned down poor farmers' sons as they would have done game if they had been boar hunting, while others—or the same for aught we know—performed similar prodigies of valour and amongst others went up to a farmer's horse and coolly discharged the contents of the barrel into the body of the poor animal, whose entrails soon protruded to attest the humane and glorious deed.[16]

But all this was something the 'New police' of the day had to take in their stride, for they were reviled and ill-used by people of

[14] W. J. Linton, op. cit.
[15] David Williams, op. cit., quoting *The Atlas,* a London newspaper.
[16] *The Welshman,* 5 January, 1844.

all classes all over the country. Regular police forces were looked upon even by the 'upper classes' with the gravest suspicion as potential instruments of central government, and the 'lower orders' had never had any respect for policemen of any kind. It was not an easy time to be a chief constable.

Nevertheless, Captain Napier's performance at Pontardulais won him a reward of £500 under the terms of the Queen's Proclamation (which applied to police officers as much as to anyone else), added to which Parliament passed a vote of thanks for the service he and his men had performed in capturing the Rebeccas.

He was to serve as Chief Constable of Glamorganshire for twenty three years more, during which time he earned a high reputation for the discipline and efficiency of his force. In 1850, for example, Swansea's *Cambrian* newspaper, in fiercely attacking the way in which the town's police force was being managed, said:

> If we compare the appearance, intelligence and activity of our police force with the force under the command of Captain Napier, what a contrast is visible.[17]

And while moves to have the two forces amalgamated came to nothing, Captain Napier was brought in to help reorganise that in Swansea, one outcome of which was the appointment of the first detectives in the force.

He was immensely popular, not only with his own men for his leadership and the memory of his courage in the Rebecca years, but also with the people of Glamorganshire, who respected his preference for persuasion over confrontation in policing industrial disputes. His soldier-like bearing and sense of discipline and duty never left him.

Standing on the platform of Cardiff railway station on a cold and windy January day in 1867, Captain Napier caught a cold, from which arose complications that caused his death two months later, at the age of sixty three. The Glamorganshire Constabulary, always noted for recruiting only the tallest and fittest of men for the difficult job of policing the tough industrial areas of the county, provided an impressive guard of honour to

[17] *The Cambrian,* 18 October, 1850.

escort its Chief Constable to his last resting place, before a crowd of many hundreds of mourners.

The Glamorganshire Constabulary had come a long way under Captain Charles Frederick Napier in the twenty three years since their brush with Rebecca.

Chapter Seventeen

THE THREADS ARE DRAWN

On Tuesday 24 October, 1843, three distinguished gentlemen met in Carmarthen by command of the highest authority in the land:

COMMISSION
VICTORIA R

> VICTORIA, by the Grace of God, of the United Kindom of Great Britain and Ireland, Queen, Defender of the Faith. To our Right and Trusty and Well-beloved Counsellor, *Thomas Frankland Lewis,* and our Trusty and Well-beloved *Robert Henry Clive* and *William Cripps* Esquires—greeting: Whereas We have thought it expedient that a Commission should forthwith issue for the purpose of making a full and diligent inquiry into the present state of the Laws, as administered in South Wales, which regulate the maintenance and repair of Turnpike-roads, Highways and Bridges; and also into the circumstances which have led to recent acts of violence and outrage in certain districts of that Country:
>
> Now know ye that We, reposing great trust and confidence in your zeal and ability, have authorised and appointed, and do by these Presents authorise and appoint you, the said *Thomas Frankland Lewis, Robert Henry Clive* and *William Cripps,* to be Our Commissioners for the purposes aforesaid.

The Royal Commission went on to set out the sweeping powers conferred on them for the performance of this difficult task and concluded with her command to 'Our Justices of the Peace, Sheriffs, Mayors, Bailiffs, Constables, Officers, Ministers, and all other Our loving subjects whatsoever, that they may be assistant to you and each of you, in the execution of these Presents.'

It was a mighty task indeed; to travel around this remote and hitherto neglected corner of the Kingdom and convince a suspicious and often sullenly hostile population of the genuineness of their mission. For it to succeed in the face of the deep-seated distrust of the ordinary people for their local institutions of administration and justice whose intransigence and insensitivity had so enraged them, it must attract evidence from every shade of opinion and every level of society. It must get to work quickly, and be the means of producing some early and positive action. Nothing less would do now, after what the people had learned from their recent experience—that direct action seemed to attract rather more attention than humble petitions.

So Thomas Frankland Lewis, the Chairman of the Commission, a much admired and experienced public servant and native of Wales, Robert Henry Clive, grandson of the renowned Clive of India, scion of the noble house of Powys and devotee of modern agricultural science, and William Cripps, noted barrister and Member of Parliament, got to work immediately. On the day after their arrival they held their first meeting and put in hand the printing of large numbers of handbills and the publication of newspaper advertisements announcing the dates and venues of their public hearings and explaining exactly what they were about. And over the next two months, in Carmarthen, Haverfordwest, Narberth, Newcastle Emlyn, Cardigan, Aberystwyth, Rhayader, Presteigne, Brecon, Llandeilo, Llanelli, Swansea, Bridgend, Cardiff and Merthyr Tydfil, they took oral and written submissions from around three hundred witnesses, whose evidence was to run to four hundred and forty pages of print. They interviewed everyone from the landowning gentry to humble tenant farmers, from turnpike trustees to cart drivers, from hated 'toll farmers' to men on bail for gate-breaking, from Dissenting Ministers to tithe-troubled Vicars, and from Lords Lieutenant to small town magistrates.

The list of witnesses is full of names indelibly linked with the history of Rebeccaism. John Harries of Talog Mill was there to describe the grievances which lay behind his presence in the Talog ambush and the Carmarthen workhouse riot, for which he was now on bail awaiting trial, and Thomas Thomas, the Talog shopkeeper, gave their side of the Talog riot: (Question from the Chairman) 'Did the sheriff's officers coming over to seize [from John Harries] make a disturbance there?' (Reply) 'Yes.' (Question) 'State what took place.' (Reply) 'Half of them were tipsy.' (Question) 'Who were tipsy?' (Reply) 'The policemen; and they went a way that was not leading to John Harries' house and kicked up a row.'

Francis McKiernan and George Laing, also on bail on charges

of gate-breaking (at Llanelli) came to complain about the tight ring of gates which hampered their coaching and haulage interests, while avoiding any mention of the charges hanging over them.

Barrister Edward Crompton Lloyd Hall, self-styled 'Pacificator' and would-be Daniel O'Connell of Wales, now heavily committed to the defence of such offenders, was there to put on record his conviction that west Wales would never prosper until '. . . the Welsh language is got rid of as a coloquial tongue.' The people, he said, '. . . are so conscious of the fact that the acquisition of the English language is necessary for their advancement in life that they desire very strongly to obtain it.'

Thomas Bullin, the most notorious of the 'toll farmers', poured out his hard-luck stories of lost investments, inadequately protected toll gates and of the folly of surrendering to mob violence.

William Chambers, Junior, who on any view had put up with more than his share of aggravation in the past year, struck a slightly jaundiced note when asked about the new-found willingness of farmers to enrol as special constables: Asked by Thomas Frankland Lewis if he thought that 'the readiness of being sworn in as special constables arises from a hope of getting off those sentenced' he replied 'Yes, that is the real reason. It is not from their great love of country, but they feel the inconvenience of these disturbances inasmuch as a great number of the farmers upon whom blackmail has been levied do not like paying, especially in these distressed times, and I am sure that many of them in the Parish of Llanon are exceedingly glad that those men have been transported.'

Chambers' superior in matters of law and order, the Vice-Lieutenant of Carmarthenshire, Lieutenant Colonel George Rice Trevor, son of Lord Dynevor, dealt with the question of possible political motivation in the disturbances:

> At the time of the Newport Riots [four years previously] there were certainly a great number of Chartist emissaries endeavouring to make the best use they could of their lecturing and so on in this county, and we had the satisfaction of believing at that time that they had made very few proselytes. We believed that they had made a very little way in those parts of the county where you might have expected they would have made most, namely among the colliers. A

> good many of those hireling orators came from Merthyr and they made very little progress indeed, and I remember hearing it stated that some of those colliers threatened to put those fellows down the pit if they did not leave that part of the county.

But the Vice-Lieutenant had a stern and lofty rebuke for *Times* reporter Thomas Campbell Foster when asked if '. . . the discontent having once become excited by the unwillingness to submit to payment of toll' had 'gradually extended itself to other objects?' 'Yes,' replied the Vice-Lieutenant, 'and my belief is that a great deal of the dissatisfaction that has been prevalent in this country has been fostered by the efforts of certain newspapers. I think the articles published in *The Times* newspapers have done the greatest possible injury and have fomented discord and discontent to a very considerable degree in this county.'

And did the Rebeccaites really want *all* toll gates removed? The answer to this came from the 'horse's mouth', so to speak; from one of the leading (and undetected) Gwendraeth Valley Rebeccas, Stephen Evans of Cilcarw Uchaf: 'We do not wish to have the *gates* done away with, but only to have the [side] bars done away with. The bars were put there rather from spite. They leased the gates there to one person and we were obliged to pay the utmost farthing in every direction. The trustees have erected bars in every place to catch us.'

Lady Charlotte's tears

By the time the Commissioners arrived in Swansea in the closing stages of their three hundred and forty miles journey in search of constitutional solutions, three men who had chosen an altogether different path began a far longer journey; one that to all intents and purposes was a journey into oblivion. The time had come for Jac Tŷ Isha, David Jones and John Hugh to leave Cardiff Gaol for the long, long voyage to the other side of the world—to the penal settlements of Tasmania thirteen thousand miles away—a voyage from which they could expect never to return, whatever the time limit to their sentences. Their wretchedness and hopelessness is impossible to imagine.

Back in their home county of Carmarthenshire, strenuous efforts had been made to obtain some mitigation of their sentences, and sympathy for their plight extended over the whole breadth of the south west. Public meetings and petitions called for mercy, and one deputation of three hundred farmers from the parish of Llanon accompanied Morgan Hughes, father of Jac Tŷ Isha, to Llanelli magistrate William Chmbers, Junior to tell him that:

> . . . the farmers in that neighbourhood were desirous for the restoration of tranquility and for that end had sent them to signify to him their willingness to be sworn in as special constables. Mr. Chambers promised to attend at Llanon for that purpose. They solicited Mr. Chambers to exert himself to obtain a commutation of the sentence passed on John Hughes, but that he has declined to do while the person who shot the woman at Hendy gate remains undiscovered.[1]

And the convicts themselves, by now clearly desperate, put their marks to a document designed to use their own plight to persuade others to abandon the path of violence that had brought them to it. And also, no doubt, to attract that mercy which their trial judge had advised them to seek from the Crown. The message—in the form of a handbill—was displayed far and wide in the Principality.

But came the day—7 December, 1843—when, manacled and dressed in rough canvas and arrow-head marked suits, they boarded a paddle steamer at Cardiff docks for Bristol, from where the Great Western Railway would take them to London to await the assembly of a shipload of transportees for Tasmania. They were, of course, the objects of a great deal of attention by the other passengers as their vessel steamed across the Bristol Channel, and two of them—ironmaster Sir John Guest of Dowlais and his Lady Charlotte—actually spoke to John Hughes and felt a certain sympathy for him. Or rather for his predicament, for which the incurably romantic Lady Charlotte said she 'shed a tear.' It is unlikely, though, that they whose view of the dreadful predicament of their own underpaid, ill-fed and poorly housed ironworkers was that it was an inevitable and incurable consequence of economic hard times, would have felt that Jac Tŷ Isha's twenty year sentence was a year too long. And why should they, all those years ago, in a world so vastly different from ours? Sir John Guest had, of course, been a member of the Grand Jury which had found 'True bills' of indictment against the three men.

[1] *Carmarthen Journal,* 10 November, 1843.

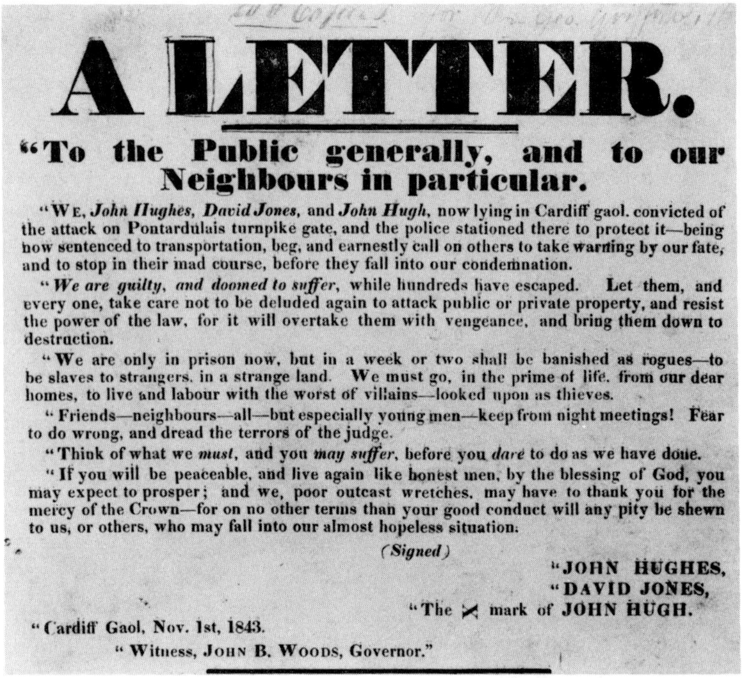

A LETTER.

"To the Public generally, and to our Neighbours in particular.

"WE, *John Hughes, David Jones,* and *John Hugh,* now lying in Cardiff gaol, convicted of the attack on Pontardulais turnpike gate, and the police stationed there to protect it—being now sentenced to transportation, beg, and earnestly call on others to take warning by our fate, and to stop in their mad course, before they fall into our condemnation.

"*We are guilty, and doomed to suffer,* while hundreds have escaped. Let them, and every one, take care not to be deluded again to attack public or private property, and resist the power of the law, for it will overtake them with vengeance, and bring them down to destruction.

"We are only in prison now, but in a week or two shall be banished as rogues—to be slaves to strangers, in a strange land. We must go, in the prime of life, from our dear homes, to live and labour with the worst of villains—looked upon as thieves.

"Friends—neighbours—all—but especially young men—keep from night meetings! Fear to do wrong, and dread the terrors of the judge.

"Think of what we *must*, and you *may suffer*, before you *dare* to do as we have done.

"If you will be peaceable, and live again like honest men, by the blessing of God, you may expect to prosper; and we, poor outcast wretches, may have to thank you for the mercy of the Crown—for on no other terms than your good conduct will any pity be shewn to us, or others, who may fall into our almost hopeless situation.

(Signed)

"JOHN HUGHES,
"DAVID JONES,
"The ✕ mark of JOHN HUGH.

"Cardiff Gaol, Nov. 1st, 1843.

"Witness, JOHN B. WOODS, Governor."

A letter from Cardiff Gaol: the Pontardulais rioters use their plight as a warning to others *(Nat. Library of Wales)*

What most impressed Sir John, Lady Charlotte and others who came into contact with the convicts was the wide-eyed and even child-like amazement they displayed at everything they saw—these men who had never travelled further than a day's ride to market, who had never seen either ship, train or city, and who might just as well be on their way to the moon for all that their past way of life had prepared them for such a journey.

But it was the conditions under which they were to be kept in London while waiting for the departure of the convict ship (as conveyed to its readers by the *Carmarthen Journal*), that were calculated to bring home to the people of Wales the dreadful consequences of the kind of lawlessness in which they had engaged:

> On their arrival at Millbank [Penitentiary] the dreariness and solitude of which clearly affected them, they were observed to weep.

On being conducted into the cells the little spirits they had left entirely foresook them. The discipline of the place is harrowing, the solitude is frightful. The silent system is rigidly observed and even noises of a purely mechanical nature are excluded for the purpose of rendering the solitude more appalling. The officers of the prison are not allowed the exchange of a single word with the wretched inmates. When the poor wretch speaks there is no reply. The officer looks coldly and sternly at him and imposes silence, and with the motion of the head or a close 'hush', deposits his food and glides noiselessly away.

During the brief phase allotted for exercise, the convict is no better off. He is conducted into a solitary court of small dimensions, where, alone, he is cut off from the little pleasures which even a community of suffering affords. He sees nothing but high dark walls and as much of the face of Heaven as is visible between their tops. After a brief stay there, at a signal from the officer, the convict retires to the solitude of his cell, peopled only with his own sad and desolate thoughts, which eat away into his heart and which he would fain wreak upon some expressions of remonstrance or complaint. But even this little consolation is refused him, and the perpetual silence which is imposed upon him is a part of the discipline of the establishment, which resembles not a little the solitude of the Trappist Monks without the resignation of that ascetic community.

Millbank Penitentiary, London: halfway house to the convict ships
(BBC Hulton Picture Library)

> Even in this preparatory school, this half-way house to some penal settlement beyond the seas, there is a refinement in the punishment. The dress which the convict is obliged to put on upon entering the prison is of a nature to make him lose what little self-respect he may have left. It is a kind of harlequin attire, one side yellow the other blue, one leg white the other green, the lower garment patched up with motley pieces which renders him an object of loathing and contempt unto himself and derision to others.
>
> Fortunately for the wretched convicts they do not long abide here. Whenever circumstances require that their stay should be protracted, the effect of this discipline soon becomes apparent in reigning madness or confirmed and incurable idiocy. And this is the place to which for the present the unfortunate men who left the Cardiff Gaol last week are confined, a salutory but terrible warning for those who imagine that the laws are to be broken with impunity.
>
> If the preliminary sufferings of the convicts are so great as not infrequently to drive them mad, what must be the terrible reality of the convict's life on his arrival in the penal settlement in Van Dieman's Land.[2]

And this 'salutory but terrible warning for those who imagine that the laws are to be broken with impunity' was to be reinforced a week later by the reports on the trials of those other prominent Rebeccaites, Shoni 'Sgubor Fawr and Dai'r Cantwr.

Queen's Evidence

It was before the normal Carmarthenshire Winter Assizes that the Stag and Pheasant gang were brought to account, at nine o'clock on the morning of Wednesday 27 December. And yet again it was the familiar partnership of Hugh Williams and Edward Crompton Lloyd Hall who shuffled the papers from which the defence would be presented.

But first, Shoni stood alone in the dock to face the charge of shooting at Walter Rees with intent to murder him, during that drunken spree which followed the great Mynydd Sylen meeting at which Shoni had so vociferously joined the rest of the eight thousand in foreswearing violence. He pleaded not guilty, and five witnesses gave evidence against him, evidence that his barrister failed to dent in the slightest by his determined cross-examination.

[2] *Carmarthen Journal,* 22 December, 1843.

The Guildhall, Carmarthen, the setting for the trials of Shoni, Dai and thirty-six other Rebeccaites, Dec. 1843

Shoni not being allowed (as the law then stood) to speak for himself, the only evidence for the defence was presented by Mr. Hall in a lengthy speech to the jury. And that defence consisted of yet another classic example of the lawyer's 'each-way bet.' Shoni was never there. His identity had not been fully made out. But even if he *had* been there and if he *had* fired the gun, said Mr. Hall sensing the weakness of his submission, he could *still* not be guilty. Because Walter Rees could not have been standing behind the door when the gun was fired, as Rees had testified. *If he had, he would have been killed.*

The jury's view of that curious line of defence was expressed in only half an hour. Guilty!

And then it was time to assemble the leaders of the Stag and Pheasant gang together in the dock of Carmarthen's fine Guildhall. But there were only four of them. *The others were waiting outside, ready to give evidence against them should they plead not guilty.* It was only Shoni, Dai, William Walters (landlord of the Stag and Pheasant) and Thomas Morris (described by magistrate William Chambers, Junior as one of 'the worst men in the Beccas'[3] who stood in the dock to face the consequences of the crimes in which so many others had cheerfully joined them.

And the benefits flowing from Her Majesty's Proclamation to those turning Queen's Evidence were immediately made manifest.

The Attorney General, Sir Frederick Pollock, rose and told the court that he entered a *Nolle Prosequi* (a withdrawal of the prosecution) against William Walters on the one charge against him—of demolishing Spudder's Bridge toll house in company with Shoni, Dai, Thomas Morris 'and divers others.' So Walters walked free . . . to collect the cash that represented the other half of his reward for helping to break up the gang that had spent so much time under his roof quaffing his ale and arming and disguising themselves for the fray!

And then it was the turn of Thomas Morris. The charge of demolishing Spudder's Bridge toll house was put to him. 'Guilty' he replied. And up stood the Attorney General again. This time it was to say that the Crown did not press the court to pronounce any judgement; he would be satisfied if Morris would

[3] *The Carmarthen Antiquary,* Vol. I (Chambers papers).

enter into his own recognisance for good behaviour in the sum of £50. And Thomas Morris, the man who had shot the horse from which had flowed the blood in which the brotherhood had sworn their oath at Gelligylwnog, left the dock as free as a bird—to collect *his* share of the Queen's reward money.

John Jones (alias Shoni 'Sgubor Fawr) and David Davies (alias Dai'r Cantwr) were now quite alone. And now utterly resigned to their fate, for they both pleaded guilty—Shoni to rioting at the Gwendraeth Ironworks, shooting at Mrs. Slocombe with intent to murder her, shooting at James Banning (William Chambers' steward) with the same intent, burgling John Evans' house at Gelliglyd and stealing his gun, demolishing the toll house at Spudder's Bridge, and demolishing two farmhouses at Llanddarog belonging to farmers who had disobeyed his orders. A mere sample of what could have been laid against him.

Despite his confession to several other crimes (he had been involved in at least eight) and in exchange for valuable information, Dai faced only two charges—rioting at the Gwendraeth Ironworks and helping to demolish the Spudder's Bridge toll house.

They pleaded guilty to everything, and Edward Crompton Lloyd Hall had little left to do but to address the judge in a plea for mercy for his clients, in which he 'expressed their contrition at having broken the laws of the country, and prayed for mitigation of punishment.'[4] And then Mr. Justice Cresswell addressed the two convicted men:

> John Jones, you have been convicted of shooting at fellow subjects; you have also pleaded guilty to a charge of riotously and tumultuously demolishing a house. I have but too much reason to suppose that you are implicated in other offences of the same character. You David Davies have pleaded guilty to a charge of demolishing a toll house, with others, and I know from your own statement that you have been guilty of many similar outrages. Whatever may have been the motives that actuated you, you appear to have been willing agents and have not been seduced into a breach of the law. As for you, John Jones, you may feel grateful that the shot you fired did not take a fatal effect, as if it had, instead of my passing on you a sentence of banishment from your country, I

[4] *Carmarthen Journal,* 29 December, 1843.

should have been obliged to pass the dreadful sentence of a violent death, but after the proofs you have given of the disregard you entertained for the safety of your fellow subjects and the rights of property in this country, it will be utterly impossible for you ever to return to it. You David Davies will not be banished for so long a term, but still for a very long period of time. Probably the greater portion of your life will be spent in a foreign land, and how different will be your position then to what it was here. You will be compelled to work but will receive no payment for your labour except such food as will serve to support your strength in order that you may work again. You will be, not in name but in reality, slaves. To that I must sentence you. The sentence of the court is that you John Jones will be transported beyond the seas for the term of your natural life, and that you David Davies be transported for twenty years.[5]

For a few seconds there was utter silence in the court as Shoni and Dai, shackled together with wrist and leg irons, took in their sentence. And suddenly they burst out laughing and turned to descend the dock steps, while the whole court sat in dumb amazement, listening to the laughter as it died away into the depths of the Guildhall. A mere gesture of defiance, for no sooner were they back in their cells in Carmarthen Gaol, than Shoni was sobbing bitterly and Dai began work on a 'farewell song' that echoed his preaching days and displayed the talent for lyricism that had once held out a promise for better things:

Oh sad is my fate; I am an object of pity to all who know me; I have lost the good name that I once possessed; heavy is my sorrow; it has overtaken me and stricken me down; in my youth misfortune came; instead of freedom, a long bondage is my lot, a dreary journey is before me, and as a convict shall I shiver to the end of it; I am to be sent from my dear native country; I must bid a long, a last farewell to my father's house where I received so much kindness in my infancy; I shall in future dwell among the swarthy race beyond the sea, far, far from my native country; Oh such troubles overcome me and oppress me severely; transported to a foreign land for twenty years; Oh pity my hard fate; farewell to my native land; its rugged mountains and its pleasant valleys which delighted my view must be hid from me; farewell to Gwalia, its fertile fields, spacious harbours and fine plantations; farewell to Great Britain, the garden of the universe; to the sons of Gomer I bid adieu![6]

[5] *The Welshman,* 5 January, 1844.

[6] An extract from a translation from the Welsh printed in *The Welshman,* 16 February, 1844.

for not once in over two hundred and fifty incidents had the army, for all its marching, counter-marching and morale-sapping night watching, had one opportunity for a clash of arms with its opponents. With the spectacular exception, it must be said, of the charge of Major Parlby's troop of the 4th Light Dragoons at the storming of Carmarthen's 'Bastille' six months before. And the few musket shots fired uselessly into the darkness by a sentry of the 73rd Regiment made nervous by the shadows and rustlings of the trees around Gelliwernen.

Accommodation problems leading to the billeting of troops on alehouse keepers were not the least of Colonel Love's problems. What nonsense, he told the Home Secretary, that his men should be 'distributed in small, detached public houses, *the resort of the people whose irregularities they were sent to suppress.*'[2]

The drunkenness this encouraged among the soldiers led to some very nasty incidents and several Courts Martial, one such incident involving the near-murder of a publican in the Pembrokeshire village of Cilgerran, three miles from Cardigan, when a number of drunken Marines went on the rampage after becoming involved in a fight with some of the locals:

> The Marines, fearing that their opponents would prove too powerful for them, loaded their rifles and also went to a public house called the White Hart, kept by one John Bowen, for the purpose of procuring the assistance of one of their comrades. But the landlord, Bowen, informed the men from a window upstairs that he was not at home, whereupon they beat the door. Bowen then proceeded downstairs to expostulate with them and to beg of them to leave, when one of the Marines named Hornet, by the request of Sergeant Lord, shot him.
>
> This dreadful occurrence has occasioned the greatest excitement in the neighbourhood.[3]

For Sergeant Major George Ellis, the hard-bitten disciplinarian of Major Parlby's Troop of the 4th Light Dragoons, the drink problem took a rather different turn, highlighting the problems posed in those days by the army's practice of taking all its women and children everywhere it went. The time was approaching for the dragoons to march out of Carmarthen, and

[2] Letter dated 27 December, 1843, Col. Love to Home Office: Public Record Office, File HO 45/453.

[3] *Carmarthen Journal,* 29 December, 1843.

Sergeant Major Ellis began to get his things together. What he found (or rather did not find) sent him straight to Chief Constable Henry Westlake and on to the Guildhall to start proceedings against a number of the town's publicans and shopkeepers. The Sergeant Major's wife, left for much of her time with her children in one tiny room of a Carmarthen inn, had developed 'a sad propensity in indulging in alcoholic drinks and it had gained so fast on her that rather than go without her favourite beverage, gin, the clothing of both mother, father and children were made a sacrifice to gratify this grievous evil.' The Chief Constable discovered that '. . . the greater part of the missing things were pawned for drink and other articles sold or pledged to different other persons with a view to procuring the same articles', and in ordering the offenders to return the goods 'His Worship at the same time intimated that where cases of the same kind were encouraged by publicans the magistrates had determined to withold their future licences.'[4]

And though the use of workhouses helped a little in the way of providing barrack-like accommodation and getting the men and their families out of the pubs—at the standard weekly billeting rates of 10s.6d. (52½p) for a Major, 8s.0d. (40p) for a Captain, 6s.0d. (30p) for a Lieutenant, sixpence (2½p) for a Sergeant and threepence (1¼p) for the rank and file—the fact that the troops were linked with such a hated institution could hardly be expected to endear them to the populace.

Farewell young warriors

There were, of course, happier experiences. Many of the soldiers married local girls, and their descendants—as Welsh as any around them in their west Wales villages—carry English, Scots and Irish names as one more legacy of those eventful years. And when the dragoons did leave town they left many broken hearts behind them. In their first days in the town, while being looked on with suspicion by the 'lower orders', they had received fulsome tributes from the 'respectable' inhabitants for their *élan* in the charge up Waterloo Terrace on that scorching June day, but since then:

[4] *Carmarthen Journal,* 22 December, 1843.

> . . . the excellent conduct of the men whilst on duty here has gained the esteem and approbation of the whole town.
>
> A number of the young warriors were invited to a parting ball given at the Red Lion, Priory Street,[5] on Tuesday evening [19th December], which was kept up with great spirit until *seven o'clock* the following morning.[6]

The bugle calls were already sounding across the roofs of old Carmarthen town as the dashing, blue-uniformed 'young warriors' of Her Majesty's 4th Light Dragoons emerged from the long and heavy night of leave-taking in the Red Lion into a dark and cold Priory Street, to disperse to their billets, gather up their baggage and horses and form up in Guildhall Square for their departure before a large and admiring crowd. Handshakes were exchanged by the officers and town worthies, and kisses between the troopers and their girls, and the Troop was called to attention. 'Prepare to mount,' ordered Major Parlby. 'Mount!' Sword salutes and then a bugle call. And to the order 'Threes to the right. Walk march', to the clink of harness, the thud of hooves on the earthen surface of the square, and amid the cheers of the townspeople, the troopers left Carmarthen town.

In a small but revealing footnote, the *Carmarthen Journal* reporter added the human touch. 'Many a tear was shed by our lovely lasses on the morning of their departure . . . and the effects of the night's entertainment [at the Red Lion, until seven in the morning] were plainly visible on several of the men as they mounted their horses for their departure.'

As well as taking with them the hearts of the 'lovely lasses' of the town as they rode out beyond Abergwili on the Brecon road that morning, the dragoons had riding with them some of its young men, lured by the cavalry's dash and finery and by the blandishments of the regiment's recruiting sergeants. Young David Thomas was one. He had taken the Queen's Shilling in the workhouse, the Troop's headquarters. He had learned his horsemanship under the Troop's riding master in the workhouse yard and on Parcyvelvet Field behind Lammas Street, and now, under the admiring gaze of his fellow townspeople, he proudly rode away. Fate had many things in store for Trooper Thomas and the 4th Light Dragoons, including a part in one of the most

[5] Still open for business.
[6] *Carmarthen Journal,* 22 December, 1843. (Author's italics).

famous cavalry actions in British history—the Charge of the Light Brigade at Balaclava—in which this large and powerful Carmarthen man distinguished himself as a hero among heroes. Not only did he reach and cut his way through the Russian guns at the end of that 'valley of death', but he picked up one of his severely wounded officers and carried him back through a storm of crossfire to the British lines—to earn himself the Distinguished Conduct Medal and a place in the Regimental history of the 4th Light Dragoons.[7]

The most obnoxious burthens

It was six weeks into 1844 before another Welsh toll gate was touched. This time at Llangurig, in the centre of the Principality, where two hundred armed and disguised Rebeccaites made clear their feeling that only two of the four gates around the town on the Aberystwyth road were really needed by the turnpike trust. They destroyed the other two. And then, a fortnight later, back south in Carmarthenshire, forty men destroyed Llanybydder's Plasbach gate in true Rebecca style, and still later (on 27 March) it was a gate on the edge of Cardigan town that fell to Rebecca's axes, under the noses, so to speak, of the Royal Marines and London policemen who were supposed to be protecting it.

In the meantime, on 6 March, only five months after signing her Commission before her Privy Council, Queen Victoria—and her government—received a weighty volume containing her Commissioners' thirty seven page report, four hundred and forty pages of verbatim evidence, and a mass of statistical and background information on the causes of the Rebecca Riots.

And what a vindication of the people's demands for justice it proved to be.

Where there were not straightforward breaches of the law and maladministration by those in positions of trust and authority, there were insensitivity and failures in communication; where there were misunderstandings leading to inflamed feelings among the ordinary people there were apathy and lofty disdain among those whose duty it was to allay them; and where the law

[7] His story is told in the author's book *Four Cheers for Carmarthen.*

should have secured justice between the poor and their betters, the price of justice had been set too high.

The law could not, and did not, countenance riot, destruction and physical violence as a means of obtaining redress for the wrongs so manifestly done to the people. But it cannot be doubted that what had been so obvious to Colonel Love and Thomas Campbell Foster from the moment they set foot in west Wales, what had been confirmed by Hall and Ellis on their brief visit there, and what was now so abundantly proved by the report of the Commission of Inquiry, carried considerable weight in the way the law-breakers were being dealt with. On virtually every matter coming under their scrutiny the Commissioners found for the people, and made recommendations for reforms.

The Commissioners' report was a complete vindication of the people's discontent with what it called their 'most obnoxious burthens.' The government studied it urgently and got down at once to work on the new legislation and policy changes necessary to remove those causes which it was within its power to remove. Other causes—the gulf between Disraeli's 'two nations', the poverty and distress arising from economic and agricultural depression and the geographical remoteness of west Wales—the causes which the Commissioners had put beyond the power of legislation to remove—would be removed only by the passage of time and the effect of the beneficial changes that would come with it: in social conditions, communications, agricultural methods, and education. And there was still a long, hard struggle to come for the common people.

A final judgement

It was Spring. Time again for the County Assizes. And there were still fifty seven west Wales men waiting to see what the law had in store for them for the parts they had played in disturbances stretching back almost a year—back to the Talog ambush and Rebecca's march on Carmarthen.

First came the Pembrokeshire Assizes, which opened in Haverfordwest on Tuesday 12 March, 1844, before Mr. Justice Maule, and the first into the dock were William Walters and David Vaughan of Little Newcastle, charged with riotous assembly at Prendergast gate on 25 August, 1843. They pleaded guilty and were each sentenced to twelve months imprisonment.

And then the police and soldiers pressed twenty eight men into and around the dock to face charges relating to Rebecca's audacious occupation of Fishguard town, the incident which had so exposed the timorousness of the Pembrokeshire magistracy. But their lone accuser, Thomas Williams, had already decamped under threat of Rebecca's vengeance—and at the expense of the Home Office, who were not keen to have a murder on their hands!

Mr. Vaughan Williams, Q.C., rose and entered on behalf of the Crown a withdrawal of the charges. The Pembrokeshire Assizes were over.

The Carmarthenshire Assizes opened in the county town's Guildhall the following week with twenty seven prisoners for trial on charges arising from the Rebecca disturbances, and the first into the dock were those involved in the Talog ambush and the attack on the Carmarthen workhouse. John Harries, the Talog miller, stood charged with riot (the ambush of the police and army pensioners) at Talog, with writing a Rebecca letter (the one threatening the invasion of Carmarthen) and with riot at the workhouse. On the charge of riot at Talog he was joined with John Jones, Jonathan Jones, Howell Lewis, Jonathan Lewis, David Davies and David Lewis—all Talog men. And on the third charge (of rioting at the workhouse) Harries stood with Job Evans, a forty eight year old farmer, David Thomas, a twenty three year old farmer (the member of Rebecca's 'Band of Music' who had beaten Chief Constable John Pugh over the head with his bassoon) and three of the 'idlers of the town' who had gone out to join the march on Carmarthen—Isaac Charles, a nineteen year old tailor, David Williams, a twenty seven year old weaver, and John Lewis, forty year old Dan y Banc coracleman.

All were found guilty and heard a remarkably restrained Attorney General tell the jury that 'Conscience makes cowards of us all. A Welshman would never show such cowardice were he not conscious of being engaged in a bad cause'[8]—a reference to the Rebeccaites' flight from the dragoons. It was a speech followed by an almost embarrassing series of tributes to the good

[8] *The Cambrian,* 15 March, 1844.

character of the prisoners, not only from prosecution witnesses but even from some county magistrates!

There can rarely have been such sighs of relief in Carmarthen's Assize court dock when their sentences were handed down, on charges for which transportation had been staring them in the face: twelve months hard labour for John Harries, who was obviously one of the ringleaders of the whole affair, and eight months imprisonment for each of the rest of them. For charges on which any one of them could have been transported for twenty years.

Thomas Lewis and Thomas Morgan came up next, for destroying the gate and toll house at Dolauhirion near Llandovery. 'Guilty of being present but not of destroying the gate and toll house' announced the foreman of the jury, upon which the judge immediately discharged the prisoners.

Three others—John Jones, Thomas Hughes and Benjamin Jones—were found guilty of destroying the gate and toll house at Pontarllechau, Llangadog. They were released on their promises to be of good behaviour. And then James Thomas and Thomas Thomas of Llwynypiod, Pontyberem, were found not guilty of being with Shoni and Dai in the riot at Porthyrhyd when they shot at the wife of the 'Lion', the much-abused and much-ridiculed parish constable.

Nineteen down and eight to go, and not one sentence of transportation among them. But then the blow fell, as eight men stood in the dock to face charges arising from Rebecca's visit to Daniel Harries at Llanfihangel-ar-arth to 'persuade' him to be generous to the other claimant in the disputed will. They all pleaded guilty. And then came the sentences: for David Thomas (the Rebecca for the occasion), twenty years transportation, and for each of the rest, ten years transportation. There was uproar in the court as:

> . . . the relatives of the convicts thronged about the prisoners' dock and gave vent to their grief by loudly lamenting the loss of their friends. Crowds of wives, sisters and daughters gathered about the prisoners as they were being removed, and filled the air with wailings and lamentations truly heartrending to hear. The prisoners, closely guarded by the Sheriff's men and a party of constables were then removed to the County Gaol.[9]

[9] *The Welshman,* 29 March, 1844.

A week later, chained in twos and threes by wrist and leg irons, the eight were loaded into a wagon and, escorted by cavalry with drawn swords, taken down the Llanstephan road to Black Pool, where they were rowed out to the *Phoenix* paddle steamer for Bristol, on the first stage of their long journey to Tasmania.

The making of a myth

The long sentences of transportation handed down to some of the Rebecca Rioters have over the years invested the Rebecca trials with something of the character of 'political' trials and the fate of the transportees with an aura of martyrdom. But it is worth examining the evidence.

The sentencing of David Thomas and the other seven men to transportation for beating up Daniel Harries at Llanfihangel-ar-arth may at first sight seem to have been in stern contrast to the leniency with which most of the gate-breakers were treated. And so it was. But what has to be taken into account is that they had also robbed the old man, of a gold sovereign. They had beaten him, had held him and threatened him, and had ransacked his house. Of a gold sovereign. Little enough, it might be thought, to justify such heavy sentences, but it is noteworthy that out of the ninety three defendants sentenced at Cardiff, Carmarthen and Haverfordwest (leaving aside for a moment Shoni, Dai and the Pontardulais rioters), only those eight had stolen anything. And only those eight were transported, for, unlike riot, assault and gate-breaking, robbery carried a life sentence—and in any case it hardly accorded with Rebecca's image as an honest and honourable seeker after justice.

The sentences handed down to the more prominent Rebeccaites of the Gwendraeth Valley also need to be seen in the context of the penal policy of the day and not through that fickle telescope called Hindsight. Shoni and Dai had such a catalogue of crime against them—of burglary, arson, destruction, theft and shooting at people—that under the penal system of the time they could expect no less than they received. And they had nothing in the way of the grievances of the true Rebeccaites to redeem them.

As to Jac Tŷ Isha and his comrades, they were found guilty of going in such numbers and so equipped with firearms and other weapons as to overwhelm any or all opposition. But, above all, they were the only Rebeccaites ever to fire at the police or soldiers and the only archetypal Rebecca leaders ever caught *in flagrante delicto*. The whole country would be watching their trials and if any of the Rebeccaites were going to be held up as examples, it would be those three.

The age of the presiding judge, Baron Gurney, and his response to the jury's recommendation to mercy for Jac Tŷ Isha may also have been factors in the spread of the belief that there was something out of the ordinary in the conduct of the trials.

Seventy five year old Baron Gurney's age was in no way exceptional, either then or now, and there is not the slightest indication in all the accounts of the trials that his mental agility was in the least impaired. As to his response to the jury's recommendation to mercy, a comparison of the sentences he passed on the three Gwendraeth Valley men (and those of transportation passed later at Carmarthen) with others for 'ordinary' crime might help to put them in their proper perspective in relation to contemporary penal policy.

They could all have been transported for life—meaning the whole of their natural lives, without any remission that would allow them to return. On completion of the sentences they actually received, Jac Tŷ Isha would have been forty four years of age, David Jones twenty eight and John Hugh thirty two.

In the five years after the Rebecca trials, the following sentences of transportation were included among many others recorded in the 'Felons' book of Carmarthen Gaol:[10] ten years for stealing in a dwelling house (a married man of twenty eight with three children); twenty years for highway robbery (a married man of thirty six with two children); fifteen years for stealing a horse (a married man of thirty one with one child); ten years for stealing sheep (a married man of thirty five with *seven* children); ten years for burglary; seven years for perjury; seven years for burglary; ten years for housebreaking and stealing clothes; ten years for theft; ten years for stealing clothes from a clothes line; seven years for stealing a pocket watch.

The reaction of *The Times* to the trials and sentences is particularly interesting. Its editorial of 1 November, 1843, had this to say about what it saw as the leniency of the courts towards

[10] Dyfed Archive Services, Carmarthen: Acc. 4916.

the majority of the Rebeccaites. The court's leniency, said the editorial:

> . . . is as wise and equitable as it is merciful. It is equitable because, as our readers too well know, there is much to palliate—though, of course, not enough in law to excuse—the violence of the Carmarthenshire peasantry. The grievances which provoked their crimes—though not pleadable, even in extenuation, in a court of justice—cannot fail to have their weight with all those who soberly balance the punishment against the moral guilt which has drawn it forth. And because it is equitable it is also wise. Public opinion, which gives weight to the blow of the law, refuses to ratify a sentence which, however legally sound, is yet at variance with a common sense appreciation of the crime as it stands. [11]

But of the sentence passed on Jac Tŷ Isha, the otherwise sympathetic *Times* had this to say:

> This case, indeed, appeared to be of that kind which most precisely justifies the severity of the law, and the criminal is accordingly sentenced to transportation for twenty years—a condemnation subject, of course, to such mitigation as is often earned by subsequent good conduct—which will hardly be thought too severe for a leader of such outrageous and systematic violations of the public peace. [12]

That far distant land

But whether deserved or not, the sentences were not interfered with by the Home Secretary despite all the many representations to him on the prisoners' behalf, and as Rebecca herself began to pass into history, so did the convict ships *London* and *Blundell* set sail from the River Thames into the mists of the English Channel for the long, long voyage to the far side of the world. Confined in tiny quarters with the scum of the country's gaols, fed on a subsistence diet, buffetted by storms, and sweating under the heat of a tropical sun, the thirteen Welshmen spent the next five months at sea, not knowing what lay in store for them nor if they would ever see their homeland again.

Certainly the five Gwendraeth Valley Rebeccaites did not, while the fate of the eight transported for beating and robbing the old man at Llanfihangel-ar-arth is unknown.

[11] *The Times,* 1 November, 1843.
[12] Ibid.

Transportation beyond the seas: below decks on a convict ship
(BBC Hulton Picture Library)

Manacles and muskets aboard a convict ship *(BBC Hulton Picture Library)*

Shoni 'Sgubor Fawr, the first of them to arrive in Tasmania (aboard the *Blundell*) disappeared from the records in 1858, after a fourteen year catalogue of theft, drunkenness, assault and general misconduct, during which some twenty different employers grappled with the impossible.

Dai'r Cantwr, Jac Tŷ Isha, David Jones and John Hugh were landed a few days later from the *London,* but within a week twenty one year old David Jones was dead. He had nearly died at Pontardulais after receiving three sword cuts on the head and several pistol balls and shot pellets in the back, from which he never really recovered, and the rigours of the harsh regime in Millbank Prison and the long voyage to Tasmania had broken him physically and emotionally. The feeling of utter loneliness and hopelessness that engulfed him at the end of it all must have been the last straw. He was buried in a convict's grave.

John Hugh served his seven years sentence without blemish —saving a minor offence of drunkenness—and after marrying a woman who had also found her way to Tasmania as a convict, he seems to have settled down to spend the rest of his life there.

Dai'r Cantwr came to a particularly sad end, at the age of sixty one, after more than thirty years of drifting in and out of jobs and sliding further and further into a hopeless and twilight world of drunkenness, magistrates' courts and prison cells. His lonely end came one night in an outbuilding on a bed of hay, when, settling down to sleep off the drink, he lit his pipe and in doing so set fire to the hay around him. His burned body was found on the blackened hay where the smoke had suffocated him. A far cry from the romantic aura that had surrounded him during and after his trial—an aura that had glowed and spread in his absence into a flood of spurious 'Dai'r Cantwr' ballads, equally false rumours that he had returned to his beloved Welsh valleys and even some impersonators begging alms on the strength of his reputation as a romantic victim of oppression and working class martyr.

In the kind of juxtaposition that only capricious fate can contrive, Hugh Williams died at about the same time, but in rather different circumstances. The Carmarthen lawyer, described as 'a man of large business till he lost favour by his defence of poor men'[13]—poor men like Dai'r Cantwr—died at the age of

[13] W. J. Linton, op. cit.

seventy eight at his villa in Ferryside overlooking Carmarthen Bay, whose distant waters had sparkled in the sunlight behind him as he savoured his moment of triumph on Mynydd Sylen. And he died a wealthy man, surrounded by his family, still basking in his reputation as the 'instigator and undiscovered leader of the Rebecca Movement'[14] . . . a reputation that owed not a little to his involvement in the trial of the man who had died lonely and unmourned in that far distant land.

Of all the transportees, only Jac Tŷ Isha can speak to us now down all those years, through the last remaining fragment of a letter he wrote to his parents at Tŷ Isha in Tumble in 1864; the parents he had not seen for twenty years:

> . . . Dear Parents, if I ever arrive in the land that gave me birth I am aware I shall not be able to work, by experience of others that followed the same track but unable to meet the severity of the climate compelled to retreat back to this country again. But if it is God's will for me to come home, as my intention is firm as ever, I do not intend to return here again, for I think I'll suffer the storm (tho' I am afraid) as to be buried amongst my relations and friends.
>
> Pardon me for my writing the last time—being rather out of trim at my first hearing of your going to lawyers about my pardon, I would, if I could, have stopped you in your proceedings, but the distance between us was too great. At the time I wrote I was rather agitated with grog—tho' you have no occasion to regret over my drinking for it is but little. That time I met a countryman. Him being a jovial man we enjoyed a few glasses together amusing ourselves with homeward conversation and our mother tongue in which he is perfect.
>
> I am very happy in reading part of your letter of your good health. May the Lord keep us the same until we meet again on earth, [which] you may depend is my prayer, tho' I cannot give rash promises as yet. Give my kindest love to my brothers and sisters and all my relations. May God bless them and their little ones. Also my warmest emotion to all my neighbours and friends. Dear friends, forget me in all but your applications to God. Farewell. Your banished but obedient son,
>
> John Hughes.[15]

John Hughes' dream of returning to Wales remained a

[14] W. J. Linton, op. cit.

[15] I am indebted for a loan of this letter (of which this is an edited extract) to Mrs. Lettie Richards of Tŷ Isha Road, Tumble, a descendant of John Hughes.

Jac Tŷ Isha living out his life in Tasmania *(Mrs. Lettie Richards, Tumble)*

dream. He lived in Tasmania to the ripe old age of eight two, a dignified, white bearded old man who had never breathed a word about those who escaped after the encounter in which he was captured, and who took his exile stoically. He married and brought up a family, whose own descendants still correspond with the descendants in Tumble of the parents he never saw again after mounting his horse for that ride to Pontardulais, a hundred and forty years ago.

But all this was in the future and we have not yet finished with 1844, for though the trials were over and the convict ships had sailed, the curtain was not quite down on that Welsh drama. The dubious honour of being the last to receive Rebecca and her daughters in the old style was about to be accorded to a gate keeper in the hills of north Carmarthenshire.

Maintaining to the last every bit of Rebecca's traditional panache, some fifty black-faced, white-gowned and bonnetted riders smashed the gate and toll house at Plasbach, between Llanybydder and Lampeter, in the night of 21 April, in a blaze of gunfire and to a fanfare of bugles and cowhorns. And as they rode off noisily into the night, with the hills around the Teifi Valley softening and then swallowing up the harsh notes of their horns, they carried with them a tale to tell their children and their grandchildren of one of the most remarkable periods of Welsh history, a tale that would be told for as long as there remained a Welshman with a taste for justice.

Chapter Nineteen

TO NOBLE ENDS

On a drab Monday morning in September, 1846, the great doors of Carmarthen gaol swung open, and out walked a farmer who had not seen his native Carmarthenshire hills nor smelled the sweet air of the green and winding Towy Valley for two whole summers. Henry Evans was already known as 'The last of the Rebeccas'[1]—the last of the Rebeccaites to be arrested, for the last Rebecca riot,[2] and the last of them to come out of prison. 'When he entered the gaol,' proclaimed the *Carmarthen Journal*:

> . . . he was not able to speak a word of English, nor did he know his alphabet, but when he was discharged he was able to speak English fluently and was able to read the Bible and repeat it to the Chaplain, who expressed great satisfaction at his progress. This speaks well for the discipline of the prison, and great credit is due to the Chaplain and the Governor for the pains they have taken to make this man a good and useful member of the community.[3]

As Henry Evans stepped out towards his farm at Llanegwad, along Spilman Street, through Priory Street, to the east of the town, his knotted kerchief slung over his shoulder holding his few possessions, he probably reflected on this transformation. But as he passed through the toll gate at Glangwili and walked by the tiny earthen floored stone cabins whose turf roofs and low doorways seeped the grey smoke of unhearthed wood fires; and as he spoke to blacksmith and cart driver, cottager and drover, on his seven mile walk back to his little holding and the family that had not seen him since his arrest two years before, he soon saw that nothing had changed. And he found no use either for his newly-acquired language among the people he met on his walk back to a way of life and its struggle to make ends meet that had not changed one jot.

[1] *Carmarthen Journal,* 18 September, 1846.

[2] With three others (who were found not guilty), breaking into the farmhouse Craigyrafar, Llanegwad, and putting John Davies 'in bodily fear', in August, 1844.

[3] *Carmarthen Journal,* 18 September, 1846.

Little did it matter to him that a new turnpike roads act, speedily passed on the recommendation of the Commission of Inquiry, had swept away most of the iniquities of the old and paved the way for even more radical changes in other laws that had so inflamed popular feelings. Nor would it occur to him that the philosophy behind the efforts made in prison to teach him English and to read the Bible to the prison chaplain in that tongue (so as to make him 'a good and useful member of the community') might soon find much more substantial form. Already the government had been stirred to action by the Commission's view that '. . . the ignorance of the English language which pervades so large a portion of the country' was 'a serious impediment to the removal of those evils which most require correction.'

The exhaustive and controversial reports on the enquiry the government set up to look into the state of education in Wales (which became known as the 'Blue Books') would make the inculcation of the English language a high priority for what was intended to be the release of the people of rural Wales from their 'peasant' mentality, which seemed to imprison them more than any man-made law could do. But, though many warning voices were raised, that objective would be pursued with such single-mindedness and such insensitivity as to leave a legacy of bitterness that could only blunt the good intentions that lay behind it and create problems of a different kind for future generations. Exactly in line, of course, with the equally well-intentioned efforts then being made by Christian missionaries all over the world (Welshmen among them) to convert whole populations in total disregard of the customs and cultures that had sustained them so well before the modern world caught up with them. But, once again, things look so different through that unreliable telescope called Hindsight.

Much of the credit for the survival of the Welsh language and culture in the face of such a heavy-handed approach belongs to the Dissenting Churches (so roughly handled by Thomas Campbell Foster for the inflamatory tone of their writings and preachings) which went from strength to strength, encouraging radical political thought and giving their people a sense of purpose, independence and pride. An island in a sea of change and disorientation.

There is a power at work

All of this was, of course, way above the heads of such as Henry Evans, 'the last of the Rebeccas.' Their only problem after all the upheavals of the past three years remained as it had always been: how to feed their families and keep a roof over their heads. And it showed no sign at their level of getting any easier. Nor would it get much easier for their children or their grandchildren—or such of them as might hold back from the fast growing tide of emigration to the New World and to the mines and furnaces of the south eastern valleys. No. A long and hard road would have to be travelled before real relief came to the ordinary people of rural Wales. It was a road which would wind through the ups and downs of agricultural depression and revival, depopulation and the easing of pressure on land, the gradual breaking down of the 'peasant mentality' that was 'suspicious of innovation and change, believing the old tried methods to be the best,'[4] and the breaking of the stranglehold of arrogant non-resident squires and gentry over their tenants—a stranglehold in which even the exercise of such voting rights as they had was dictated for them, and their 'peasant mentality' thereby sustained. That long hard road would wend its way through enlightened legislation and changing social attitudes; through the extension of democracy, and the advent of free universal education, improved agricultural techniques and new systems of local government. All well into the future, and all beyond the immediate comprehension of most of those who had fought under Rebecca's banner.

So what achievements *could* Henry Evans contemplate as he walked that dusty road along the banks of the River Towy after paying the price for riding with Rebecca? What *had* he and the rest of Rebecca's daughters gained in that long and costly struggle? Had it really been worthwhile?

It had. And its achievement was not to be measured by the numbers of toll gates that were removed, nor in the amounts by which the tolls had been reduced, nor in the easing of the oppressive Poor Law or the other measures passed by a government suddenly awakened to a new reality.

The real and lasting achievement had already been recog-

[4] *Land and People in 19th century Wales* (David Howell), op. cit.

nised by Edward Crompton Lloyd Hall as the Rebecca Riots had approached their climax. '*The people*,' he had written, '*have discovered their immense power, without knowing how to use it constitutionally*'[5]—a power which had already challenged and (albeit unknowingly) put the final nail into the coffin of the old and decrepit institutions of law and order and paved the way for the new. And what a revelation that feeling of power was to a people so inured to hardship and the indifference of their betters that they accepted every additional imposition or inequity as part of life's natural and inevitable burden on the poor; the burden that the Almighty in His wisdom had placed on them when He had ordained their station in life.

The Rev. Caleb Morris, a Welsh minister practising in London, saw just what was happening in his native country when he visited it early in 1843 and described the enormous significance of it in his journal:

> The mental and moral activity of the Welsh people is in advance of their material condition. Their spiritual happiness is greater than their temporal comforts. Beccaism, bad though it be, is an expression of inward development. It is a sign that the reign of immobility is passing away. Numbness and inactivity in civil matters are gone. Beccaism has made people of all classes think of their individual social interest and a new era has begun. There is a power at work. May it be wisely guided and decided to noble ends. There is great need for reform. Let us work and pray for our Fatherland.[6]

If this awakening was a revelation to the common people, it was a sharp lesson to those who had hitherto taken their passivity so much for granted. And though frustration would reach boiling point again in Wales later in the century, in what became known as the 'Tithe war', governments and those responsible for local administration would in future be rather more responsive to the needs and feelings of the people than in the days before Rebecca took to the road.

Their separate ways

And what became of the journalist and the soldier who had been sent to west Wales as those troubles had reached their

[5] Letter to Home Office, loc. cit. (Author's italics).

[6] *The Life and Ministry of the Rev. Caleb Morris* (by Evan T. Tyssil, 1902)—quoted in *Carmarthenshire Antiquary*, Vol. 1.

climax; the two men whose very different errands had focussed so completely on the one basic objective, of finding Rebecca?

After the close of the Cardiff trials, Thomas Campbell Foster of *The Times* had taken up his last assignment of all in the Principality and added a few hundred miles more to his already prodigious travels. He had followed the Commissioners into all the main towns of mid, south and west Wales, listening to the witnesses who came before them—and drawing a quiet satisfaction from having heard it all before and having already brought much of it to the attention of the nation. And he had good reason to be satisfied. He had gained the confidence of a people who had lost confidence in just about everything but the justice of their cause; he had opened up a new field of journalism—the sustained, wide-ranging, searching and fearless form of enquiry known to-day as 'investigative journalism'—and he had maintained his newspaper's reputation for stinging governments into action.

Foster was verbally abused and publicly insulted by magistrates whose arrogance and contempt for the lower classes he had so effectively exposed, and yet he was presented with a token of appreciation—a silver goblet and tray—by a group of leading Welsh citizens which included a Member of Parliament, a newspaper editor, a wealthy landowner and the lawyers most prominent in the rioters' defence.

So pleased were his employers at *The Times* with his work in Wales that within a few months they sent him to Norfolk to investigate rural unrest there. A year later came the beginnings of that most disastrous period of Irish history, the famine years, which left nearly a million dead of starvation and drove a million more to brave the coffin ships of transatlantic emigration, leaving Ireland's population reduced from eight to six million and harbouring a bitterness whose depths have not been plumbed to this day. And Foster's brilliant and devastating analysis of the appalling conditions he found there caused a sensation.[7]

But journalism was not to be his whole life. He entered the law, was called to the Bar and became an eminent Queen's Counsel and Recorder of Warwick, earning fame as the prose-

[7] *Letters on the condition of the People of Ireland*—a series of dispatches to *The Times* reprinted in one volume in 1846.

cutor of the nineteenth century's most notorious criminal, Charlie Peace, who was condemned to death at Leeds Assizes in 1878 and executed.

Thomas Campbell Foster died in July, 1882, at the age of seventy, and was accorded an obituary in the newspaper that had sent him by train and fast stage coach to Wales nearly forty years before. But that obituary contained not one word about it.[8] *The Times* had forgotten. Nor did that leading authority on the lives and works of the eminent, the *Dictionary of National Biography*, mention Foster's Welsh experiences in its brief entry on him, though it did remember those of the man alongside whom Foster rode on that dramatic night's cavalry patrol through the head of the Gwendraeth Valley. The *Dictionary of National Biography* in its four hundred word entry on Sir James Frederick Love, K.H., summed up *his* exploits in Wales in twelve: 'Was in command in South Wales during the Rebecca and Chartist riots.'

Colonel Love supervised the withdrawal of the bulk of his substantial military force in the spring and summer of 1844, reducing the Welsh garrison to its normal peacetime strength. And it was in June that year that a movement of considerable—almost symbolic—significance took place. On Tuesday 18 June the Colonel took the salute of the men of the 76th Regiment of Foot as they paraded on Carmarthen Quay and boarded the *Phoenix* paddle steamer bound for Bristol and a troop train of the Great Western Railway. He bade them farewell with his thanks for the 'zeal and alacrity' with which his orders had been carried out in their 'peculiarly trying and arduous duties' and he stood proudly with his staff officers as the crowds cheered the departing steamer, whose whistle could be heard long after the wooded hills along the winding River Towy had hidden the vessel from sight.

It was a ten hour voyage to Bristol, and somewhere in the Severn Estuary that June evening the *Phoenix* passed her sister ship the *County of Pembroke,* thrashing her way down channel to Swansea. The rails of both ships were crowded with red-coated soldiers cheering and exchanging soldiers' banter, as the steamers sounded their own salutes—for the *County of Pembroke* was heading west with another Regiment, one whose presence in

[8] *The Times,* 3 July, 1882.

west Wales would have been unthinkable not so long ago. It was a Regiment of Welshmen, the 41st (Welch), fresh from their triumph in Afghanistan under Carmarthen's own hero, General Sir William Nott.[9] One of the company officers was a Carmarthen man, Captain Vaughan, who, like his fellow officers, had many other men of the town and county of Carmarthen under his command. And their home county was their destination. There could not have been a plainer statement of the government's faith that peace had been restored to west Wales.

Colonel Love would remain for several years yet, for part of the time retaining his appointment as Colonel Commanding South Wales, and for the rest as a 'half pay' officer on the army reserve, enjoying the delights of a now peaceful and ever beautiful corner of the Kingdom and of being a leading and popular figure on the west Wales social scene. That tall, erect, side-whiskered figure in scarlet and gold braid, the covetted Waterloo Medal gleaming among the array of other decorations on his breast, was in great demand by the ladies at many a glittering county or hunt or regimental ball during his happy sojourn in west Wales with his wife Mary, in the years after the shadow of Rebecca was lifted from his thoughts.

In 1852, at the age of sixty three, Sir James Frederick Love was appointed by Queen Victoria to be her Lieutenant Governor in Jersey, with the rank of Major General. But the old war horse was not done yet, and not one to regard any job he undertook as a sinecure. He made his mark in Jersey by expelling none other than the great writer Victor Hugo, whose offence had been to criticise the Queen and to meet her arch enemy the Emperor Napoleon the Third in Paris. More significantly, in the context of this story, the Lieutenant Governor came into conflict with the Crown over a subject dear to his heart after his Welsh experience—the establishment of a new system of civil police. And he won. He was not one to forget a hard-learned lesson.

Life completed its full circle for Major General Love, when he returned to the place where, in 1804, he had begun his soldiering, as a fifteen year old Ensign in the 52nd Light Infantry, and

[9]Major General Sir William Nott, GCB (1782-1844), whose statue (cast from the bronze of cannon captured at Maharajpur and donated for the purpose by the Honourable East India Company) stands in Nott Square, Carmarthen. His story is told briefly in the author's book *Four Cheers for Carmarthen.*

had learned the trade of the light infantryman under the master himself, the great Sir John Moore. In 1856 he became commandant at the birth-place and nursery of the British light infantry, Shorncliffe Camp in Kent, and for the last five years of his fifty-eight year army life he occupied the pinnacle of the fighting soldier's profession, as Inspector General of Infantry. And in 1866, at the age of seventy seven, he died peacefully.

Undiscovered leader?

But who was the lady who had wrought such havoc in Wales all those years before, and the mystery of whose identity had so occupied the thoughts of Love and Foster? Who was that troublesome female who had so stirred a part of the Kingdom that seldom entered the thoughts of its rulers; that female whose name had been spoken in the highest circles in the land? *Who was Rebecca*?

Let us look again at the questions asked at the very beginning of this story. Was she an all-powerful and ubiquitous leader? Of what class of society had she come? What were her motives? Did she and her daughters want political power for themselves, or was Rebecca really a shadowy figure in the background, manipulating the poor people and exploiting their hardships for her own political ends? Or was 'Rebecca' a name adopted by many leaders, over a wide area, and if so were their activities co-ordinated or did they spread spontaneously?

And where better to start looking for the answers than by looking at the man whose reputation as 'the instigator and undiscovered leader of the Rebecca Movement' still comes to the fore in any discussion on the Rebecca Riots, despite the reservations expressed about it by the leading authority on the subject:[10] Hugh Williams, solicitor, Chartist, Carmarthen's delegate to the National Convention of the Workingmen's Association, and renowned defender of rioters.

To have preserved his anonymity through such a long period of what (if he had indeed been the instigator and leader) would have been intense activity for him would have called for the kind of security precautions employed by to-day's professional terrorists. To have avoided being touched by the avalanche of inform-

[10] David Williams, op. cit.

ing that followed the Queen's Proclamation and the decimation of the east Carmarthenshire Rebecca band would also have called for the most amazing good fortune. What a price Hugh Williams' head would have commanded in a climate where men were being betrayed for as little as £7, where even a magistrate's *life* would have been taken for £5, and where as much as £500 could have been earned for delivering up a 'mastermind' such as this. £500: more than thirty years rent for a modest farm holding, fifty years pay for the highest paid farm servant, and twenty one years' wages for a collier!

Furthermore, for one man to have been able to exert even the most delegated of control over such a wide operational area would have called for staff work of a very high order. And how then would Hugh Williams have escaped the eagle eye of that able investigator Thomas Campbell Foster, who had obviously never heard of him until he met him in the farmers' meeting in the Blue Bell in Cynwyl Elfed on 16 August—after two whole months of questioning people all over west Wales, including his highly privileged admission to the secret Rebecca night meeting in the hills around Llangadog. The breadth and thoroughness of Foster's investigation, his ability to gain the confidence of the ordinary people and his determination to identify not only the causes but also the motive power behind the disturbances would surely have led to more than the occasional inoccuous mention he gives Hugh Williams had there been the least substance in the claim.

And Foster was not the only one anxious to identify whoever might be masterminding the disturbances. For all that Colonel Love's disguised policemen and informers dug and delved among the countrypeople; for all that the Postmaster General secretly scrutinised Hugh Williams' mail, and for all that magistrates, policemen and gaol warders pressed Rebecca prisoners to earn light sentences or the dropping of charges against them, not one word was ever said to suggest that Hugh Williams had advised, guided or even spoken to an active Rebeccaite, let alone that he had directed or led them. And nowhere in the voluminous Home Office papers of the period is there a scrap of evidence in support of the contention that he was in any way involved.

His so-called 'treasonable' speech at the Chartist torchlight meeting, so often cited, but so rarely quoted, as evidence of his disaffection,[11] contained not one word advocating any but constitutional action to achieve the aims of the Charter. Even the archaic and criticism-stifling law of sedition that existed at the time could not be stretched far enough to embrace that speech. His promise to the London Convention that 'the radicals of South Wales were prepared to assert their rights at any time and in any manner they might be called upon by the London Committee'—a typically ambiguous Chartist declaration—is also quoted against him. But always out of context. What needs to be added is that he said it in support of a resolution he was seconding at the Convention: 'That this meeting recommend the people of the United Kingdom to hold meetings and to appoint deputations to request their representatives [their members of parliament] to support and vote for the "People's Charter", and to support the prayer of the national petition.'[12] A rather different approach than is hinted at in the part of the record most usually quoted.

In fact none of Hugh Williams' recorded speeches contained one word tending to condone or encourage violence. On the contrary he specifically condemned it in every speech, even including the one at Allt Cunedda, where he made his first, hesitant, claim to have aroused public feeling over the turnpike laws in the first place and to approve of simple 'gate-levelling.'

A classical trap

All that seems to be left is Hugh Williams' reputation for defending some of the Chartist and Rebecca rioters, but even that has been misunderstood. It fails to take into account the fundamental difference between the roles of solicitor and barrister in the criminal courts. A solicitor could not practise in the Assize Court in 1843 any more than he would be able to practise in its equivalent (the Crown Court) to-day. What this means is that Hugh Williams never *defended* a rioter in his life. He defended and secured the acquittal of many a farmer charged at the magistrates' courts with the minor offence of refusing to pay toll, but even in that class of case he did not become involved until early July, 1843—four years after Efail-wen and eight months after the resumption of the disturbances, towards the

[11] The speech can be read in *The Silurian* of 19 January, 1839.
[12] *Carmarthen Journal,* 21 September, 1838.

end of 1842. But they were very able defences all the same, backed by a thorough knowledge of the intricacies of the turnpike laws and of the limitations of the powers of the trustees. Then as now it could pay a solicitor to make a special study of a particular problem of the day and thereby secure a reputation as the best defender available in that class of case.[13] But rioters on trial at the Assizes he did *not* defend.

Then as now the role of the solicitor was to *prepare* the defence and secure the services of the best available barristers. And it has always been the case that some barristers become specialists in particular classes of criminal case. The fact that Edward Crompton Lloyd Hall gravitated towards the defence of the Rebecca Rioters is hardly surprising either, given the all-consuming interest in the matter shown by his postal bombardment of the Home Office. The self-styled 'Pacificator'—a man unwaveringly opposed to Rebeccaism—simply saw a role for himself as a mediator in a situation where the bridges between the 'two nations' seemed to be burning. And there was never a shred of evidence to the contrary.

As to the conduct of the rioters' defences and the trials themselves, there was nothing in any of the proceedings to distinguish them from any criminal trial taking place to-day. The barristers were not solely *defenders,* but, as has always been the case, they were employed as prosecutors too, often in consecutive cases, in the same court, before the same judge, and they conducted their defences entirely within the bounds of their professional ethics and courtesies. *In not one case did the defence put forward any justification for the acts alleged, and nothing remotely political intruded into the barristers' speeches.* In short, all the defences were based on perfectly normal propositions: that the prosecution witnesses were mistaken or lying; that the accused was elsewhere at the time; that even if he did the act alleged it did not amount to the crime charged; or that the charge itself was incorrectly worded and the accused was entitled to automatic acquittal.

Of course the solicitor preparing the barrister's brief had a great deal of hard work to do, and the fact that Hugh Williams did most if not all of it for the Chartists and the Rebeccaites without charge is greatly to his credit. And it was absolutely in character, for he was a sincere advocate of the rights of the

[13] In these days it might be the drinking and driving or the drugs laws.

labouring classes and a tireless worker for the Chartist and other radical causes. He was also active in civic affairs over many years, holding office at various times in the corporations of Carmarthen and St. Clears and always working for the betterment of his constituents and for the removal of what he saw as corruption in local administration.

He was a public benefactor too. As Portreeve (Mayor) of St. Clears, while living at Gardde, the property of his wealthy wife, he paid for the erection of a new market hall and established a prosperous cattle mart on Gardde land. And through it all he never compromised his radical beliefs. As a member of the Carmarthen Board of Guardians, for example, responsible for the administration of the Poor Law, he lost no opportunity to attack its more inhumane provisions and thereby added to the suspicion which already attached to him as a Chartist. Just as in September, 1844, when he was alleged to have 'encouraged the attempt to inflict the punishment of the *Ceffyl Pren* at the time of the Saint Clears Fair . . . on a person who had given information against the Rebeccaites.'[14] What might have been added was the fact that he had been consulted by the organisers of the affair, who had themselves been spoken to by Police Superintendent Wood of the Carmarthenshire Constabulary. Hugh Williams had advised that 'there was no law against it, provided no breach of the peace occurred', a view supported by a local magistrate, who added that '. . . as long as the people conduct themselves in a peaceable manner I do not know what authority we have to interfere with them, any more than with a procession of Oddfellows or Ivorites.' Quite right, said Home Secretary Sir James Graham, who had himself advised the county authorities to adopt a policy of persuasion rather than prosecution in such cases.[15]

There remains, of course, Hugh Williams' outburst against the jurors who convicted Jac Tŷ Isha. But even that was not what it seemed. The Chartists knew very well what Hugh Williams meant when he hoped they would 'do their best' for the Merthyr shopkeepers who had convicted Jac Tŷ Isha. And they set about it . . . by passing a resolution that they would 'not buy any article [from the shopkeepers] for twenty years, which was the length of

[14] David Williams, op. cit.

[15] Dyfed Archives, Carmarthen: Acc. 4282.A.

time they had transported John Hughes, the Rebecca.'[16] Had the word 'Boycott' been invented then, no doubt it would have been used in the Chartist's resolution to describe their intention to subject the Merthyr jurors to stern, but non-violent, social ostracism.[17]

All the same, Hugh Williams' outburst was an unpardonable action for a solicitor, but perhaps the most revealing of all, for it exposes his great weakness. One need look no further for the originator of the story that he was 'the instigator and undiscovered leader of the Rebecca Movement' than Hugh Williams himself. He was vain. He became intoxicated with the applause of the crowd. At dinner on the night before Mynydd Sylen, feeling sure that tomorrow would be his day, he could not resist boasting to his friend Linton. And in the August sunshine on that mountain summit he basked in the warmth of the applause of eight thousand people who saw him as their spokesman—for which he earned a rebuke from magistrate William Chambers, Junior, who chaired the meeting. Chambers wrote to him in regard to his clash at the meeting with a fellow magistrate, and told him that 'a heedless rabble would eagerly applaud anything that appeared to hit at those in authority' and that he had 'thought him too old a soldier to be tickled by idle cheers.'[18]

At Allt Cunedda, Hugh Williams got closer than he had ever done to condoning the Rebecca Riots, and then, when the jury at Cardiff convicted Jac Tŷ Isha, he could contain himself no longer. Having teetered on the edge for so long he finally fell into the classical trap of the politically ambitious who court popularity—the trap that ensnares so many in our own times: his mind espoused the cause, while his heart abhored its excesses. Yet to weaken his stance on that cause by condemning its excesses unequivocally and with all the authority he possessed would be to see those cheering and adoring crowds melt away into the summer haze, to leave him standing alone on his mountain top.

[16] Capt. Napier's report on a Chartist meeting at the Three Horseshoes, Merthyr, 5 Nov. 1843: Public Record Office, Ref. HO 45/453.

[17] In 1880, Capt. Charles Cunningham Boycott, the agent of an absentee landlord in Co. Mayo, Ireland, was completely ostracised by the people of the district and prevented from making even the smallest purchase; but he added a new word to the English language.

[18] *Carmarthenshire Antiquary,* Vol. 1 (Chambers papers).

A most potent force

No. The Rebecca Rioters were neither instigated nor led by Hugh Williams, or anyone else. Not even by the Dissenting Ministers whose inflamatory writings and preachings, so roundly condemned by Thomas Campbell Foster, undoubtedly exacerbated matters through the literal meaning put on them by their unsophisticated congregations. Nor were the disturbances politically inspired or motivated by disaffection to the Crown, as was abundantly proved, time after time, to the satisfaction of Foster, who was very much the man on the spot. Even Captain Napier's informant in the clandestine Chartist meetings in Merthyr found nothing but confirmation of this in the inability of the Chartists to make any effective contacts with the Rebeccaites. And when the so-called Rebeccaite emissaries from Carmarthenshire attended a Merthyr meeting they did not even know the aims of the Charter movement.[19] So much for the impression made by the orations of the Chartist emissaries to west Wales.

The chief elements in the Rebeccaites' operations which have always argued for a mastermind or a guiding hand were the style of their execution and the manner in which they spread over such a large part of Wales. There was certainly much about the almost martial style of many of the attacks and the bearing of the participants to suggest military planning and training, but this is easy enough to explain. As in the arming and drilling of the Chartists at Llanidloes and in the hills above Newport, there was no shortage of ex-soldiers and trained militia men to bring that kind of order to Rebecca's bands. Not only did the population contain time-expired regular soldiers, but under the Militia Act every man between eighteen and forty five was compulsorily entered for the ballot from which 30,000 men were drawn for annual training as an army reserve for home defence. In fact, so conscious was the government of the existence of this reservoir of trained or partly-trained soldiers in what seemed to be a most disaffected part of the country that the Home Secretary ordered that all 'Chelsea Out-pensioners' in west Wales should come under the command of Colonel Love, thus putting them back under military law so as to detach them from their neighbours.

[19] Capt. Napier's report on a Chartist meeting at the Three Horseshoes, Merthyr, 2 July, 1843: Public Record Office, File HO 45/453.

As to the spread of the rioting and the suspicion that it was co-ordinated in some way, if the same thing had happened in England that would have had to be the case. But England was not Wales. In Wales there was a circumstance—a phenomenon—which made all this possible without the need for central leadership, planning or co-ordination. That circumstance was a combination of three factors: widespread family connections, the facility for communication afforded by the network of markets and fairs, and the familiarity to all the people of the *modus operandi* of Rebeccaism—the *Ceffyl Pren*—as a way of correcting injustice and social misbehaviour.

The fairs and markets were to the people of the area they served what the chapel was to its congregation—a meeting place, a social centre for the exchange of news and gossip, a place for grumbling and sharing ideas about how different things could be and what could be done about it; a place for meeting and deciding to marry; a place for cementing friendships. And according to one authority a fair would attract people from as far as thirty miles away.[20] The facility this afforded for linking people over even greater distances can be imagined, and Thomas Campbell Foster could add the extraordinary example of the transmission of the news of an arson attack to a distance of thirty seven miles from the scene, overnight, in hill country with no stage coach link. And when the magic of the name Rebecca was added to the message and the message became invested with the authority of the Scriptures and the chapel preachers, a most potent force came into being; a force that developed an almost irresistible momentum. A force that became personified in a Rebecca who was as real as if she were made from flesh and blood.

In her true spirit, Rebecca made an irresistible appeal to the Godfearing, law-abiding, hard-pressed countrypeople of Wales. The occasional perversion of that spirit by evil influences of greed and private revenge and the attempts by some to divert it to their own political ends, was merely the fate of any movement which employs violence in pursuit of social or political change, as more recent history continues to remind us.

[20] David W. Howell, op. cit.

A champion waiting

The remarkable thing is not the spontaneous and unco-ordinated spread of the Rebecca Riots, but their beginning—under the faint light of guttering candles in a barn at the foot of the Presely hills, across the bog from Twm Carnabwth's stone-built, turf-roofed cabin. As remote a spot as could be imagined. Yet the most likely place for all. For this provides the *real* answer to the question 'Who was Rebecca?'

Rebecca was a champion waiting to be called upon. A paradox; a product of a biblically dictated way of life calculated to produce conformity and obedience, which yet produced a stimulus to law-breaking. Or did it?

To the handful of people huddled around the candlelight in Glynsaithmaen's barn there was a higher law than man's. It was not man's law but God's that placed them and kept them in such a lowly station and buffetted them with wet summers, bad harvests, poverty and hunger. This they understood, and they prayed and drew comfort from Scriptural explanations for their plight, and they bore it without complaint.

In their remote and unsophisticated world there was little enough reason for man's law to intrude, but when it did it was obeyed, provided that it accorded with the people's simple notion of natural justice. But when it failed or oppressed them; when it so far diverged from God's law as to imprison the poor in its workhouses, support rapacious landlords, impose on poor chapel goers the burden of supporting an alien church; when it allowed such money-grabbers as Thomas Bullin to erect a toll gate where there had been none before and to hit them when they were at their lowest, they looked for justice. And when man's law refused them justice, or set too high a price on it, they knew instinctively where to turn.

They turned to their own time-hallowed form of natural justice, reaching far back into their own unwritten history and traditions where lay the old familiar remedy, knowing in their hearts that they were right to invoke it. Then they looked to their Bibles for a sign, without which right would not be on their side nor success attend their endeavours. They found it. *And they blessed Rebecca.*

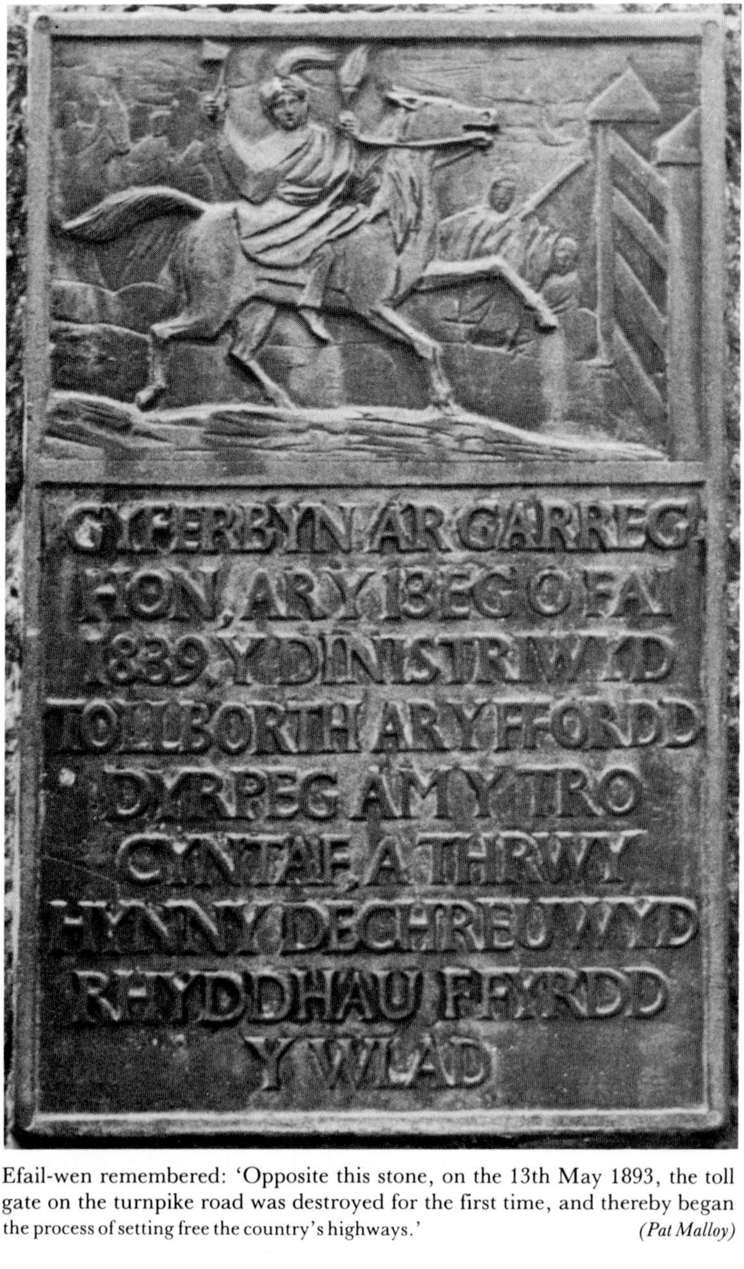

Efail-wen remembered: 'Opposite this stone, on the 13th May 1893, the toll gate on the turnpike road was destroyed for the first time, and thereby began the process of setting free the country's highways.' *(Pat Malloy)*

Rebecca's descendants re-enact Efail-wen 125 years on, in 1964. The man in the centre striking the gate is Mr. Lloyd Davies, a descendant of Davies of Glynsaithmaen *(Ken Davies (Photos) Carmarthen)*

INDEX

Persons not distinguished by rank, title or position are identified with their home farms, villages or towns, as appropriate.